Truth of Voice

Henrietta

My Autobiography

Ferguson Publishing House

2013

Truth of Voice
My Autobiography

First Published in Great Britain in 2013 by
Ferguson Publishing House

Picture credit: Craigmillar Archives Trust.
http://craigmillararchivestrust.webplus.net/index.html

ISBN: 978-0-9928082-3-5

Ferguson Publishing House
17 Promenade
Edinburgh
EH15 1HH

Find out more about the author online at www.henriettas.org

Henrietta

Henrietta is a naturally gifted clairvoyant, spiritual healer and teacher based in Edinburgh, Scotland.

She was born with the gift of clairvoyance, passed down through the female line on her mother and father's side of the family. As she has walked through her life since birth her gift has matured and developed until in 1997, she started giving the address on platforms at Spiritualist churches.

In the years that followed she travelled the width and breadth of the country, giving the address at numerous venues around Scotland and private readings to those who travelled to see her.

Now she has premises in Edinburgh, and continues to see people who come from all over the country, and the world, to see her.

To date she has given readings that number into the thousands.

Henrietta is a very well known and respected clairvoyant throughout Scotland. She continues to be outspoken, and holds a high reputation and regard in her field.

Find out more about the author online at www.henriettas.org

To my precious & beautiful daughters,

who shone like my beacon of hope

My Autobiography

1953 - 1999

"Every situation in life has a solution"

My Grandfather

Craigmillar Castle Terrace

One quick shag up a tenement's back close, conceived out of wedlock, and months later I was at the wedding, but not in the photos!
My parents were two people now in a situation of marriage that neither was happy with.
Their first home was a back room in my father's Great Grandma's house, not a good start.
Due to her having a difficult time during my birth, my Mother became bitter, twisted and forever angry, while my Dad was as proud as a peacock. I was the first daughter to be born into his family in 150 years. My Dad threw himself into work and kept out of her way as much as possible.
The move into the Terrace was closer to her parents; our tenement was number One, a stair of four families, my Grandparents lived at number four in a stair of six.
Craigmillar, a large housing estate in the east side of Edinburgh was a great place to grow up as a kid. Everyone knew everyone else and helped each other when in need.
My Gran, Jessie Rennox was a 'Ma Broon' type figure; soft and gentle with a fearsome no nonsense approach.

Whenever someone was in need, Jessie Rennox was there. Giving birth, dying, man jailed, no wages from a drunken husband, whatever the reason she was always capable of helping. I would be sent many a time to someone's house with a pot of soup or stew to feed a family. The most notorious jailbird would always be respectful to her she was a wonderful individual.

As I grew up, she was to be my Saviour. One day I shall write about her. My mother's temper always flared up without warning, and most of the time I was in her path. I became brilliant at racing down our long lobby, out into the stairwell, jumping down two flights of stairs as though I had wings and flying across the road into Gran's care. After a few days when "Ellen's temper had calmed down" I'd go home.

However one day I didn't make it. My gran walked in as she was bashing me over my back with my scooter. My gran's raised voice made her stop. Another day it was very heavy rain outside and I asked a couple of times to go out to play. She grabbed me and dressed me in a summer dress, knickers and me sandals and threw me outside. Very quickly I became soaked to the skin but she wouldn't let me back in the house. I remained outside becoming wetter and colder. My gran was returning from an errand when she came across me still standing outside. I was promptly taken to her house but I was ill for several days. To this day if I become too cold, get damp or wet I am floored with a chest infection.

My childhood days with my friends were great, we would play around Craigmillar Castle trying to catch a glimpse of the elusive Green Lady ghost.

Long days exploring the nearby burn catching tiddlers and anything that moved, in my Gran's home-made fishing nets, usually out of old nylon stockings and always making sure all our catch was emptied back into the burn before we headed home.

Long walks down to Portobello a nearby beach resort with sandwiches, bottles of homemade lemonade and a silver sixpence. Long summer days on the beach, playing on the sand, at the swing-park and trying to dam up the stream that ran into the sea! Great days. The sixpence was for our bus fares home. However nine times out of ten we all bought chips and a buttered roll each and walked home. No one had a watch, but we always knew when to head home.

Sundays were usually spent exploring the museum at Chamber Street, up the city centre. Although we had fun playing hide and seek in the various parts of the expansive building we always learnt something fascinating so it was never a wasted pastime.

Also playing Cowboys and Indians in our nearby woods. I

was always an Indian because I couldn't make the firing noise of a gun with my mouth but I could shout "thump" the noise of an arrow at least that's what Brian Richardson said.

Hide and seek, rounders, skipping games, climbing trees and trying to climb over the orchard wall to steal apples! No not to steal only to consume.

A bad tempered boxer dog guarded the orchard. How many times did we win? Lots! On the one occasion we didn't win all the boys made it over the wall and I got stuck, climbing was never my forte. The boxer dog's teeth met my bottom and oh how it hurt. My skirt and knickers torn and blood running down my leg we all traipsed home. My father was furious and once I was patched up I was taken to the orchard keeper's house. My father explained very sternly about what had happened and after a few words it was agreed I would go down once a week and collect all the dropped apples. My Gran made lots of apple tarts and I would deliver them to many homes. Very happy times.

School was great I loved it. I had a terrible stammer due to me constantly living in fear of another beating (battering) although my mother put my stammer down to me having had German measles as a very young child, so I kept my head down and soaked up as much knowledge as I could.

People who stammer always sing beautifully and I was no exception. I sang at every opportunity and soon I was a singing solo at every school function.

I was eleven years old when my brother was born. The beatings gradually stopped because he was treated like the Second Coming. Attention was now all on him and I spent more and more time with my Grandparents. On one occasion I hid him in the bottom drawer of the chest of drawers in my parents room hoping he would go away, he didn't, my mother found him and I got a beating! Another time I left him in his pram outside the Co-op and took the messages home hoping someone would find him and take him with them. After another beating! I was sent back to fetch him and as I turned the corner there he sat in his pram smiling to everyone. I gave up trying to get rid of him because I always came off the worst.

Primary school meant so much to me; it was a safe haven away from upsets at home. My grandparents always shielded me but I had to escape to their house first. As my Dad worked long hours he always appeared to accept me staying at their house as a normal routine.

My Grandfather was a quiet man who was self taught so he instilled in me that education was an essential tool to enable one to grow. He spent many an hour helping me with my homework or some other subject matter he thought would

benefit me. He also insisted I read out loud to him to help me improve my speech without stammering.
High School gave me an insight into what I could be.
My English teacher, Miss Mercer had also taught my mother and her sisters and was known to be a tyrant. She introduced me to the Bard, Robert Burns. Her opinion of my mother wasn't very good but she never allowed that to cloud her judgment regarding me.
Nothing delighted her more than when I sang, "My love is like a red, red rose" she positively glowed and her eyes always told of some inner feelings she didn't acknowledge. I knew it was of a love that had gone to war and had not returned.
She also gave me my first book, 'The Jazz Singer' I read it twice, then she asked me to write an essay on how it made me feel.
Unknown to me she entered my essay into the 'Evening News Competition' When the results arrived Miss Mercer raced round the school telling everyone, and when she found me she danced me around the classroom, her usual staid self was gone and her kindness of heart shone through.
A new English teacher arrived who sang in a Folk Group. Soon he asked me to sing in a school folk group and now my confidence took a turn for the better.
Before I left school I had gained a good job with Timothy

Whites the chemist in Princes Street, Edinburgh. My singing was going well and life wasn't too bad.

Then I met Ian Mitchell at the Ice Rink at Murray field and I fell head over heels. I gave him my virginity; he gave me a diamond solitaire ring. We spent lots of time talking out our dreams. I thought he was perfect. He only worked when he wanted to so this made him unsuitable in my father's eyes. My father was a grafter so he couldn't' accept Ian lived off the family money so this led to many arguments. The arguments led to me becoming unwell and hospitalized due to thunderous headaches and soon I made the decision to leave home. I moved in with my uncle Alfie and his family.

My job was going well, Timothy Whites was now a part of Boots the Chemist, and our delivery schedules changed. Enter Ron, one of the drivers who made our deliveries. He was 6 foot 7 inches; dark hair, good looking and I didn't like him!

The shop's handyman was an elderly man called George Harley a war veteran; he was a great character, funny and very caring and he gave me a lift home every night.

Most nights we dropped into our local pub 'The Three Tuns' for one drink with some of our other work mates before we all went home. Ron began dropping in and joining the company. Always using the excuse he was meeting his mates for the football.

One night George took up Ron's offer to take me home; soon I began to think Ron was all right. He knew all about Ian, but that didn't stop him from asking me out continually.

My shop Manager who had become a good friend and father figure since I had left home and he arranged for Ron and I to go on a picnic lunch. Ron was a good laugh and I found myself melting towards. His first kiss on my cheek put my heart in a spin. Soon Ron was driving through every night in time to pick me up after work.

The situation between Ian and I had begun to deteriorate before Ron came on the scene so I decided it had to stop. I arranged to meet Ian in Princes Street Gardens to talk it over with him, my friend Ann came along to make sure he didn't get nasty. He looked so smart, dressed in his suit, shirt and tie, all clean and handsome. He laid out the newspaper he was carrying on the bench seat and I thought "oh how thoughtful," then he sat down on it!

We sat together and talked openly, I explained my feelings and I said our relationship was over. He was devastated, tears flowed and through our sobs he said "Don't marry him for the wrong reasons. He may be able to give you things that I can't but he won't love you as much as I do." I walked away, I didn't look back. Ann and I went for a

drink and after our second drink, in walked Ron. Ann left and I poured out my heart to Ron, I was numb, I needed time to be alone.
Ian sent flowers, and flowers and flowers soon the entire house and my friends' houses were bedecked with blooms. I spent many hours crying and eventually Ron asked me to take him to see Ian, and I agreed. After some boy talk Ian agreed to walk away. I also agreed to go back home to stay. Our romance blossomed and before long we planned to become engaged. My ring was a diamond solitaire set in an unusual setting and soon the magical day arrived.
My parents, my grandparents, Aunts Jessie and Margaret waited at home excitedly for us to arrive to show of my ring, a bottle of good wine toasted our special day. Their good wishes were pouring from their sincere smiles and kisses.
We then drove to Hamilton to give Ron's Parents and younger brother a look at our rings. We laughed all the way there, however our light hearted mood was about to change. As we walked into the sitting room his parents and Colin his younger brother were watching 'Dr. Who' on television. Ron spoke and his Mum's response was "Ssh, the young one is watching TV."
Ron grabbed my hand, hauled me outside, slammed the front door and headed for the car. He drove away on two

wheels and raced down the hill, he braked suddenly, stopped and ran into a small Off License and bought a half bottle of vodka.

He then drove us up through the back roads beyond Hamilton, narrow country lanes whisked by as he ranted about his family.

Soon he parked in a small entrance to a field; the view overlooked the layout of Lanarkshire to Glasgow. The twinkling lights made it look beautiful.

With each slug of the vodka his words spat out, it became obvious his relationship with his parents wasn't good, never had been. His outburst scared me but soon I recognized he was someone who was lost.

I listened and his words explained why he spent more time at my home instead of his own. My house felt welcoming, friendly and as my entire mother's family was forever popping in the atmosphere was nice to be around.

Before we returned to his parents house Ron asked me to put my ring in my purse, if they wanted to see it they would have to ask. During supper the idle chat was awkward and I sighed with relief, as I lay on my allocated bed upstairs. Usually when I stayed over I slept in his parent's bed upstairs and they slept on the sofa bed in the sitting room downstairs. Ron's bedroom was next door to his parents' bedroom and he usually crept in through the night for a cuddle.

As we made to leave next morning his Mum asked where my ring was. I looked at Ron, pleading with my eyes for him not to say anything nasty. I took the ring out of my purse and put it on. "Nice very nice" she said and turned and walked into the kitchen. No other works were exchanged.

As we drove to Edinburgh, Ron kept on apologising about their behaviour. I said not to worry, although within myself I didn't feel good about it.

Our engagement party at my home went well, two weeks later a date for our wedding was agreed, 3rd March 1973.Now we had nearly a year to make plans.

Soon the Church, hotel, flowers and dresses were all organized and plans all in place. My father was adamant no expense would be spared. As Ron didn't have any close friends my Uncle Sonny was the best man.

Ron didn't like me singing, and wherever I was singing he would always make himself scarce.

A few months before my wedding I was offered a year's contract to go to London to be groomed as a singer. Joy filled my heart, I was elated.

Ron wasn't too happy about this. After lots of time talking, we agreed to have three weeks apart, if we survived that period of time, I could go to London and come home every

month. This would give us a better future for our life that lay ahead of us.
Sounded so good at the time, Ron stayed away for three days! Three days, he couldn't cope at the thought he might lose me.
A decision had to be made, London wouldn't wait and I couldn't make Ron unhappy, so I gave it away. In one short moment my hopes and dreams scattered like clouds being blown by a strong breeze. Slowly I gave up my singing, and as I gave it up a part of me gave up too.
Again and again an incident that happened when I was ten years old ran around in my head.
My bedroom had a large bay window and one night a very large bright ball of light woke me as I lay in bed. Watching this light dancing around made me feel safe. I was in awe as I got out of bed to take a closer look. The huge ball of white light spoke to me about many things I could not understand however I listened. It said I would remember when I needed to. After some time I went to waken my Dad and tell him about the light.
He rose from his bed and accompanied me to look out of my window. There it was, still bright and still dancing around.
The stars had always fascinated my dad and we spent many nights stargazing. So his explanation that "Venus is talking

to you" was taken on board as being normal.
When I asked all my friends if they had seen the dancing light, one friend Brian Richardson replied "no one will see it", "why?" I asked, "Your light is special."
Now the ball of light was back dancing around outside my bedroom window, urging me on and making me feel safe.
I discussed it with Ron, he was sure to think I was daft."
No" he said, "The light is for you, only you, it's your special light."
Years apart, in fact ten years and here he was saying the same words as my Dad and my friend had said.
Days, weeks, months, sped along, soon it was pre-wedding time. We received lots of presents; the show of presents at my parent's home was a wonderful fun night.
Ron and Dad got on very well; in fact all my family enjoyed Ron's company, so he was never short of someone to join him for a pint. The only person who wasn't too sure of Ron was my Grandad. He said it was selfish of Ron to make me give up a special chance in my life and what else would he want me to give up. Ron spent most week-ends staying at our house; he said it made him feel wanted.
His Mother wanted a show of presents of her own. All was agreed and the packed boxes were delivered to be displayed. I agreed to stay over, as it would save Ron a round trip to Edinburgh and back.

Ron, his Dad and his younger brother of eleven years Colin made themselves scarce. Ron called Colin by the nick name Fred, don't ask me why but his parents seen it as a joke. As a show of presents is a woman's' thing! All the jolly Hamiltonians of the family duly arrived. Family, friends and neighbours sat and participated in small talk.

Tweed skirts, twin sets and lace up shoes somehow I don't think they took kindly to my short mini skirt, big hair and eye shadow, the same colour as my big earrings. Proper and staid don't take kindly to bubbly and funny. Hamilton born and bred do not take kindly to Edinburgh folk.

The next-door neighbour's son had married the daughter of the neighbour directly opposite. So Isobel the daughter of the neighbours directly opposite my In-laws to be was invited. She scrutinised every word and move I made. I overheard his Mum telling Isobel it wasn't too late, as Ron may still change his mind. An explosion went off in my head and I wanted home, home now. I went quiet and prayed silently for Ron to come home early. A short time later he appeared, his first words were "What's up?" This calmed me down.

We walked into the kitchen, closed over the door and I stammered out what I had heard. I wasn't feeling bubbly or funny now. I wanted to go home. "Take me to Glasgow and put me on a train," I continued to stammer.

I fought back tears; I wasn't going to give them any opportunity to see me like this. I went to sit in Ron's car outside; I left him to tell his Mother why I was going home. He did so in the kitchen. He was angry and she was left in no doubt about his feelings. Ron then drove me home.
I don't know how she explained my sudden departure, however I have never felt any need to know.
Through a friend of a friend of his parents we went to see a Factor who rented out flats. Living in Edinburgh wasn't an option, as Ron worked in Glasgow/Airdrie living in Hamilton was a better location.
We went to view a ground floor flat in Low Waters Road. One large living room with two recesses, one for eating and the other a kitchen. One very large bedroom with an open fire and a large walk in cupboard, plus an outside toilet. Both sets of parents viewed it and both were delighted.
As the wedding approached I found myself wandering around the places that I had ran around as a kid. I was going to miss my home city. I was giving up my singing, my hobby of skating, my job and my friends in fact I was giving up so much, saying Goodbye to it all, made me feel scared.
I spent time talking to my Granddad. He was a quiet man who had instilled in me a yearning to learn, to listen and to try. He was upset I had given up my London opportunity

however he gave me great words of wisdom, which I took on board. However one day I would hear them, truly hear them for their precious contents.

I spent time talking to my Dad. I was giving up so much and not seeing him on a daily basis made me sad. I knew we would both miss each other. I had always been the go between in my parent's turbulent marriage. My Dad was the one person who recognised who I truly was.

Since returning to live at home, my Mothers' love for my brother was more evident. Her whole world revolved around him.

I had a special relationship with all my Mothers sisters, they would make comments about her lack of concern over me, but all their comments always fell on her deaf ears.

They were all so very different as individuals however each one had a brilliant quality. Each one gave me something of themselves that I cherish. I plan to write about them all one day. Now as I write this they have all gone home to the higher side of life, but their love for me remains.

I was travelling down a road that was exciting yet scary and out of my control.

My leaving night with all my girly friends was a great laugh; however at the very end many tears were shed. A part of my life was over; the memories of those days are forever pleasant.

My wedding day arrived; my Dad carrying a tray of scrambled eggs, toast, tea and cheery words awakens me. I began to cry; he sat on my bed and joined me. "Come on, lets not be silly, this is the happiest day of your life," he said trying to be convincing.

Hairdressers next, Mum, Mandy my flower girl (who was the daughter of my Uncle Sonny) and myself. Jean my Bridesmaid was getting her own hair done elsewhere.

I was very quiet while the entire bustle around me was far away. I went into myself. "Nerves, just nerves" everyone was mouthing.

Everyone's hair beautifully coutured, we returned home where I promptly threw up. Eggs toast and all.

"Nerves just nerves," if another person said this I was going to scream.

My Mother had bought two outfits, the decision which one to wear was driving me nuts. Dad in vest and braces shaving carefully as not to nick himself was interrupted with our doorbell ringing.

As the bathroom was nearest to the front door my Dad answered it. There stood four adults all dressed up in their Sunday best, all smiling broadly. Half-shaved he invited them in, who were they?

My future Father in-law's sisters with their husbands! As they had arrived early, they asked directions to our house

and decided to drop by to say hello and to deliver our wedding present.
My Aunt Margaret took control, she made them tea with biscuits and then when she was due to leave for the Church, she took them with her.
Soon the house lay silent with only my Dad and me.
Minutes before my Mum had led him into my room to see me in my wedding dress for the first time. She left the room without a word.
Dad poured two large whiskies. His words filled the room, words I keep deep within my heart. My Father's love was bigger than the highest mountain, wider than the sky and as deep as the ocean, his words to me are special. Words to keep me safe within.
As we walked down the hall and out into the stairway a memory flashed in my mind. How many times had I flown down this route to escape blows from my angry Mum?
Now for the last time I was walking this same route to a new chapter in my life. I paused only a moment to kiss those memories good-bye.
As I emerged from the mouth of the stair a multitude of neighbours gave up a gasp then a loud cheer. My Dad's pride was plain to see. Neighbours all called out best wishes.
"Ah bonny lass, well Tam, who's proud today."

On and on came the words as we made our way to the car. My Dad then flung out handfuls of money into the crowd of children and adults. Only it was silver coins he threw and not pennies!!
He then asked the driver to go a tour around the neighbouring streets.
Craigmillar was a smashing place to be brought up. Everyone knew each other and everyone helped each other. The streets were soon lined with families all waving and cheering. Dad was as proud as a peacock and I felt safe within the cocoon of the car.
No expense had been spared. Today was a celebration, why did I feel as though I was outside looking in.
The date 3rd March 1973 time 3.00p.m. I arrived at the Church at ten past three.
Photographs taken, we stood at the top of the Aisle and I composed my nerves. The Church was a sea of hats, best suits, dresses and flowers.
As we stood awaiting the organ to herald the Wedding March my Dad took my hand, looked in my eyes and said, "If you want to go to London go, I'll take care of this. I'll back you all the way. Don't be worried or scared."
For a moment everything was still. As in slow motion I looked towards the filled pews, turned and smiled and said to my Dad "Too late."

All the way down the Aisle I gripped my Dad's hand, unknown to me I was digging my nails into his flesh. My Dad's Aunt Mary hissed as I passed "Get your bloody head up, walk tall." I did as I was told.

On taking his vows Ron's voice boomed off the church's cold stonewalls and his touch as he held my hand was very loving.

The rest of the day was a blur, kind words and best wishes, smiles and laughs, hugs and kisses.

Was I there?

The photographs say so. It's a day that brought happiness to so many, it's a day I find difficult to remember and at times without any emotion.

The Bride and Groom should leave the reception first! My Parents, Ron and I wished everyone good night as they all left. Then the four of us sat and had a drink, and then as my parents' taxi left, Ron and I walked across the street into our hotel, which we had kept a secret, to begin our married life.

Next morning before we set off on our Honeymoon we found my Dad's car, so we decided to decorate it with "Just married."

Colin, Tommy my brother and my Auntie's boys all tried to find Ron's car to decorate it. As the car was Ron's pride and joy he had hidden it well, no one found it. So when we

found my Dad's we decorated his for a laugh.
Our honeymoon was to be a few days in Inverness. Just before Perth Ron asked how much money I had with me. I told him and he growled, I should have had more. I sat silent and numb, a few miles up the road he apologised.
As Ron's work schedule had changed he now spent two nights in Inverness every week, and I thought I would be introduced to the people he stayed with and the people he drank with. No, it didn't happen.
We booked into a Bed and Breakfast near the Town Centre. After two days of driving repeatedly past his haunts, I was taken into the Pub on the corner down from his digs.
I met a lovely man called Charlie in the pub; he owned a local chemist shop. Ron conducted business with him but I wasn't privy to what exactly that business was.
Charlie bought me a drink, kissed my hand and said in a low voice how delighted he was to meet me. Before we left Charlie took Ron aside, I overhead him say, "Don't be a bloody fool, sort out your mess, this young lassie doesn't need this."
His words spun round in my head, as we lay in bed that night I plucked up courage to ask about what I had overheard. Somehow I knew his answer before he said a word. "I had got it wrong." How did I know he would say that?

As I rolled over, some honeymoon this! echoed in my mind. I heard myself saying, "In the morning we're going home," Ron didn't reply, but I heard his relief.

Once back in Hamilton, no explanation was given to why we were home early.

Our furniture was not arriving for another three days so we had no option but to stay with my In-laws.

I wanted to see my parents, so we went to visit. Dad kept on looking at me, pleading with his eyes to tell him what was wrong.

I went to visit my Grandparents, Ron and my Dad went for a pint. On their return from the pub it was suggested we spend a night in the newly opened Post Hotel beside Edinburgh Zoo.

A meal, a drink, a relaxed night would be special; my Dad had arranged it with Ron while they were having a pint. We had a lovely night; the residents of the Zoo also had a lovely night by all accounts of the roars, wails and screams of the animals.

Before we left Edinburgh we called into the furniture shop that was going to deliver our goods. The Manager was a friend of my Dad's so I used my charm and asked if our goods could be delivered as soon as possible.

We then drove back to Hamilton. The next day was spent cleaning out our flat. A phone call confirmed the furniture

would be delivered the next morning.
That night I slept fitfully, staying with your in-laws is not the best start to a marriage,
Walking into the bedroom without knocking was a habit of Ron's Mum, so when it happened again, this would be the last time. This night I would sleep in our new bed in our new home, come what may.

Low Waters Road

Low Waters Road was a one-bedroom ground floor flat with an outside toilet.

An outside toilet was a novelty but as the flat next door was empty so I set about painting the toilet from top to bottom and making it acceptable. As it was situated at the rear of a back alley, which led to the huge back gardens, it could be creepy at night.

Our coal cupboard was a huge black hole that was situated before the toilet, so the coal buckets had, and I mean had to be filled during the day. No way would I fill them when it was dark.

Our boxes and wedding presents were all piled into our walk-in cupboard in the bedroom, the living room and bedroom lay empty awaiting our furniture, which duly arrived that morning.

We were very blessed to have been given so much furniture as wedding presents:

A Three-Piece Suite, Dining Room and Bedroom Suite, Twin Tub Washing Machine and a Refrigerator. Our cooker was our first Hire Purchase buy. Everything was piled into the bedroom, while the carpet was laid in the living room. Next day with only the bedroom carpet to lay, I took time out to prepare our first Sunday dinner. I wanted it to be special, so I took time to make something Ron liked. Roast pork with applesauce, veggies and roast potatoes. All laid out nicely on the plate, with a glass of white wine at the side.

The fire in the bedroom was burning nicely, the small lamp was on, and the scene was set. I thought what a lovely romantic setting for our first meal together in our own home.

As I handed Ron the plate he said, "Oh, I don't think I'm going to like this."

I replied "Don't eat it then."

"Not the meal, it's the married bit I mean," he said.

My heart hit my boots and I fought back a rush of tears and sickness. I felt numb, what was happening? This was supposed to be romantic. Romantic my arse!

Ron touched my hand and I reeled back as though he had burnt me. "I'm sorry, I meant this will take a bit of getting used to," he said. I sat silently his remarks swimming around in my head. As he spoke on and on, his words bounced off my heart. As I lifted his untouched plate, I said in a whisper "You will eat those words, I swear one day you will."

I was about to put the untouched food into the bin, when he took the plate from me, went back through, sat down and ate everything. In fact he commented on it being "so delicious." After his second glass of wine, he snuggled up to me and apologised. I didn't think for one minute he didn't love me and I said it was all right, but my whole being felt numb.

Over the next few weeks I settled into a routine. Ron was now away two nights every week, so I had time to put our home together. I cleaned, polished and washed always making it nice and homely.

The back garden was a wilderness so I set about revamping it.

On the nights I was alone, I curled up in front of the coal fire lost in my thoughts or reading. As I had always enjoyed my own company, being on my own didn't bother me.

After a few weeks I began to feel unwell. I didn't want to get out of bed didn't want to go out at all.

On my arrival in Hamilton I had taken to walking in and around the town to find my bearings, now I wasn't interested.

I was missing my parents and my grandparents, my job and my friends in fact every bloody thing

I telephoned for a home visit from the doctor, maybe I was ill.

Enter Dr Alex Dowie who was to become a guiding light, my saviour.
When I answered the door and invited him in he looked taken aback. He introduced himself and told me to put on the kettle, how odd I thought.
He explained he could see why I was such a shock to the Pearson's. They never spoke or expressed their feelings to each other or anyone else. They were staid, proper and unemotional.
Here I was bubbly, outgoing, a good looker who wore short skirts, big hair, and eye shadow to match my way out earrings. He could understand why I was homesick. So my illness now had a name, homesickness. Remedy, get out and make friends, if I was going to wait till someone knocked on my door, I was going to wait a long time. So I began taking driving lessons; took up serious gardening and found myself a part time job in a prominent local business. I joined the Library and began dropping into the local branch of the Samaritans to find out about becoming a team member. Not long after I became a Samaritan. I spent many hours listening to people who were unhappy and I could identify with how they felt.
I also challenged myself to speak to one new person as many times as I could.
Marjorie and Charlie took over the flat next door; they were

due to be married in October, so they had a few months to get the flat in shape. Whenever Marjorie, who was a nurse, was around we would have a cup of tea and a gossip. I would say she was my first true friend in Hamilton.
Charlie was a schoolteacher and a fanatical Hamilton Accies Supporter, he and Ron soon become good boozy pals.

Ron would not go to visit his Parents, Why? I don't really know. After a few weeks of no communication his Mother arrived with his Dad in tow. "Oh you're still alive then" was her opening line. Oh no! Another sarcastic dialogue followed.

Why did they act like this?

Why did Joe my Father in-law say nothing?

What the hell was I doing here?

Had I really given up London for all of this?

Friday nights when Ron was home became his boy's night out. Every Saturday and Sunday we were out to dine and socialise. We fell into an existence; days became weeks, then months.

We went to visit my parents often but when I returned home I felt down and lonely. On one of our visits my Dad said, "If you're not happy come home" I smiled and convinced him I was fine. Oh to come home, my real home, would be to admit I was unhappy, I couldn't do that.

When Ron was away I began to get deep breathing phone calls. Then words asking if I knew where "he" was? When Ron phoned home as he usually did, I always tried not to be too upset.

It was also at this time Ron went off all physical and emotional contact. The first time it was for four weeks, in future the longest would be nine months. I was confused, what was wrong? The reply was "Nothing." What could I do? "Nothing." Was it me? "No." Was there someone else? "No."

Then he began to have problems with his back, pain meant no sex. Pain meant he went into himself, however when anyone, family or friend was around he was Mr. Happy.

I discussed it with Dr Dowie and he explained Ron was working too hard. Maybe he had fears or worries he could not cope with or confide to me. Well, he admitted himself he didn't like the thought of marriage, so maybe that was it.

During a chat over his lack of emotion he became angry, so I retaliated. I had kept quiet for so long, so I blew my stack. Ron grabbed a cushion and growled to get out of his sight. I knew he meant it, I didn't hang around, I grabbed my coat, keys and purse and flew out of the door.

As I ran out of our flat, memories flooded back, who was I running from now?

With nowhere to go or no one to run to I found myself

outside the local cinema. I paid and went in, in those days you could sit on through two showings, so I did. I was scared to go home. But where was home?

When I emerged from the cinema it was dark and as I walked up the road towards the flat, and got closer I recognised my Dads' car, and my in-laws car, what was up? When I walked in everyone began shouting at me "Where have you been? We've been worried sick about you" On and on they went. I know now it was out of relief, but at the time it was scary. Through my tears I let the words spill out, I wasn't loved and I wasn't wanted.

Everyone looked shocked by my words. I was only upset, feeling sorry for myself, I was tired, and our first tiff had really upset me. That was their explanation, and it was easier to go along with it.

My parents and Ron organised a surprise twenty-first birthday party for me, at my parents house, all my family and friends made it a great night.

Over the next three years our life consisted of holidays abroad to far away places twice a year, weekends socialising and coping with his problem.

The heavy breathing phone calls stopped when the letters began. Letters informing me of Rons' infidelity, which almost drove me to the brink of insanity while he always calmly, denied it. However when a work mate was accused of being the culprit the letters stopped. I tried not to dwell on it, but at times it was very difficult.

Marjorie and Charlie had moved to a two bedroom semi-detached in a fairly new estate at Low Waters. So once again I felt isolated but I kept up appearances and kept myself busy.

We had reached an acceptable routine. One week he was away Monday, Wednesday and Friday the other was Tuesday and Thursday.

The neighbours in number 10 and 12 all became friends and I also became a wonderful actress. I loved Ron when he allowed me to so the good times always gave me a reason to go on.

As I had passed my driving test within the first nine months of my marriage when he was away I would have the car. Freedom, freedom to drive into the country to star gaze and talk with my God, a truly divine spiritual being.

My granddad took seriously ill and died within a few months. He was a quiet man who always spoke to me about deep issues, he always took time to talk, explain and with his words and thoughts educate me and give me food for thought.

He always said, “One day you will recall all our conversations and you’ll know what they meant.”

Once during one of our long chats he explained that to speak to the man upstairs, God, you did not have to do so in a church or chapel, you could do it anytime, anywhere, He was always listening. My Grandfather was a deep thinker; he never used two words if one would do. I was devastated, my old pal was gone. But his words were full of wisdom. Throughout my life his words come to mind, when I least expect it.

My Mother worshipped her father, a few weeks after his death she suffered a nervous breakdown. She was admitted to the Andrew Duncan Clinic as a patient.

I began to come to Edinburgh every Wednesday, a train from Hamilton to Glasgow then another train to Edinburgh, then a bus to the hospital.

I always brought her a small gift or flowers. As always she never spoke or acknowledged my presence and as usual at 2pm in the afternoon she threw a wobbly screaming outburst. Her father had been cremated at that time hence the daily fit.

Each day my Dad would sit and talk to her, to try to catch one glimpse of acknowledgment but she never obliged.

After my weekly visit my Dad and I would go home and I would iron and tidy up.

My brother began playing truant from school and was out and about most of the day. Dad tried to keep tabs on him

but with his mind in turmoil it became more difficult.
One day after a visit Dad and I went for a drink. He opened his heart; their marriage was a sham. Yes, he played away from home because he couldn't live a loveless life.
Loveless, sounds familiar!
He stayed because of my brother and me. Now I was happily married he could stop worrying about me. When my brother was older, he was going to leave, but now with her being ill he couldn't.
The next Wednesday I suggested to my Mum's doctor that he hid her watch, if she didn't know the time, she wouldn't throw a wobbly. He agreed.
I was invited to join a Therapy session. All the inmates, sorry! Patients sat in a circle with two doctors present. I sat against the wall with a male nurse in attendance watching the session.
A young woman, whose whole family had been killed in a house fire, never spoke. Into the session the young woman spat at my Mum "Want to ken the time, it's past two, what's wrong not play acting today" Next thing all hell broke loose.
Chairs went one way, harsh words about her (my Mum) not caring about her family, treating me and my Dad like shite, boomed around the room.
I felt myself pinned to the wall. Hot breath against my face

as ugly harsh vile words were spat out. My mother was tearing at my skin and spitting out words of hate. Oh how I was hated. Arms grabbed me and I was pulled out of the room and taken into the doctor's room nearby.

As I regained my composure, tears flowed. They had phoned my Dad and he was on his way. He had phoned Ron, who thankfully was at home that night and he was also on his way.

I could not have made the full journey home.

Ron then phoned to say he couldn't come; he would meet me off the train in Glasgow. I had no option; somehow I had to regain my composure.

When Dad arrived he was taken aback at the state of me, who had attacked me? Who ripped my top? Who had scratched my face?

The doctor explained softly and quietly that I would always be at risk. Now that her true feelings towards me had surfaced her hate was now released and she would unleash it towards me at any opportunity so I would have to be careful.

I always knew deep within that she didn't love me, but now I had to take on board that she truly hated me.

Every unhappy event in her life was my fault. She needed someone to focus the hate on, my mother who had given birth to me, truly hated me.

As I sat on the train to Glasgow I was all alone in a crowded carriage. Her words ran through my mind, my feelings in turmoil, I withdrew into a space within my being.

I had been smiling when I left dad behind on the platform. I couldn't give him more to worry about. I shrugged it off but I'm sure I didn't fully convince him.

When the train pulled in to the station at Glasgow I couldn't find the strength to move. Lost in my mind I jumped when Ron spoke. He had asked a porter to allow him to board the train to look for me.

Nothing had prepared him for the wreck that sat before him. He was stunned by my appearance, why had no one explained fully to him? They had, he just wasn't listening.

On the drive home I was silent. I needed to be in bed where I could sleep away the day's events. Maybe, just maybe she'd love me in the morning.

Deep sleep consumed me. Ron spent a long time discussing the day's full events on the phone with the doctor at the hospital, and then he spoke to my Dad. He admitted he hadn't taken on board the full problem. He had no idea what to say or do, so he said nothing and went away the next night as usual.

Dr. Dowie gave me a sick note to stay off work and I concentrated on getting my emotions under control. I would not go and visit again, until she took on board her actions and the outcome. I was keeping out of the way; my survival was important.

Slowly she recovered and soon she was allowed home for overnight stopovers, slowly building up to being home full time. One condition was she had to attend as an outpatient three times per week. She never did attend.

A doctor from the hospital made arrangements to make a home visit to do an up-dated assessment. My dad asked me to be there for the visit.

The doctor, Mum, Dad and myself sat and pleasantly chatted about her progress. All was going smoothly. Dad and I decided to go out into the garden and leave Mum and the doctor time to discuss how she really felt.

While we weeded in the garden the voices through the open window became louder. All at once the doctor, looking very dishevelled with his brief case and his jacket wide open burst out of the entrance of the stair. He was in a tripping run, all his strength coping with trying not falling flat on his face.

When he regained his composure, he straightened up, reassembled his tie, jacket and briefcase and he looked over to where we stood looking dumbfounded at the scene, which had unfolded before us, he smiled towards me. That small smile told me he knew how I felt about her attitude towards me.

He spoke slowly "My report will not make good reading, she must be re-admitted, it's the only way we can help her. Although I must admit she doesn't want help. I'll be in touch." His many letters went unheeded; she never did receive any help.

Soon her illness wasn't mentioned and she got a part time job as a Bingo Caller. This was a position she was very good at, and she really enjoyed her time there. So the family was saved by the Bingo!

My marriage was an existence, sometimes I was happy, and at others I was glad Ron was away a few times a week. The nights I spent alone recharged my nerves for his nights at home.

Our flat was our home for five years; it was time to move. Our flat sold quickly. We only viewed three houses, when our next home fell into our sights.

I was excited, silly me, I thought new house; maybe all our problems will melt away. I packed up all our things praying for a new start.

Arran Gardens

Arran Gardens was a three-bedroom semi in a fairly new housing estate. Upstairs and downstairs played hell with our legs after living in our flat for four years. The stairs were exercise! And plenty of it.

In the front garden stood a very large apple blossom tree, I have fond memories of this type of tree, but I'll explain later.

The back garden was large, and backed onto a landscaped Bing, which was very peaceful. In fact so peaceful and quiet we couldn't sleep.

The flat as you recall was on a main road, so we always had noise from passing traffic. Now the birds singing in the early morning drove us nuts. However, it did not take us long to adjust.

Our first purchase was an MFI wall unit; you know the type you build yourself. Ron always thought he was a handyman; well the wall unit was about to try his patience. With German instructions, packets of screws and a multitude of different sized bits of wood, battle commenced. Four days later, countless bad words, blisters and sheer brute force, it was completed. As it was prized into a tight alcove on one side of the fireplace, it was in to stay, and stay it did. It was still in place when the house was sold.

Ron didn't want a family; the thought scared him, as he didn't like the thought of being responsible for someone, so it was a definite no. However the first summer in our new home found me pregnant. God knows how, as Ron was still going off sex.

I was elated, but scared to tell him. I wasn't scared for long. Early on into the pregnancy I miscarried. I felt numb and lost; as Ron held me close he couldn't hide his elation. I went back to work; it helped; keeping busy kept my grief at bay.

Our neighbours in our small cul-de-sac were friendly and I soon made lots of new friends and continued with my gardening.

Ron arranged a holiday in North Africa, exotic, warm and beautiful. Lots of excursions, camel rides and a couple of days out in the wilds in a mud hut. During the day was warm and serene. Nights were filled with constant screams and cries of animals doing whatever they do at night.

On our return relatives of my in-laws had arrived from Australia on holiday. As we had spare bedrooms they spent their nights at our house. Being a good hostess, I always

prepared them a full cooked breakfast, while I hung over the kitchen sink throwing up!
After three days I decided to phone the doctor. It was a wild, wet and windy morning when Dr Dowie popped in. The wind was swaying the branches of the apple blossom tree so much he nearly lost his head never mind his hat. He asked how our holiday went, while I relayed the details he took my pulse etc. and then asked me for a urine sample explaining that he had an idea of what might be wrong. I explained I only wanted a pill to stop me being sick.
Ron was still away two nights one week, and three nights the next so I was used to my own company. Along with my friends we went to sewing and knitting nights in each other's houses. In all the years I attended I never completed one item, so you can work it out, they were fun. All chat and no knitting

On the Friday Ron was away to Inverness as usual. I went to work, I worked as a cashier in Burtons the Tailors it was only part time but I enjoyed it. About lunchtime Dr Dowie phoned me and asked me if I was sitting down. I said, "I am." He then said, "Your flu bug has taken feet, congratulations."
I sat with tears running down my face as Dr.Dowie continued I was to come and see him the following week to

make sure this pregnancy went well.
My mind was in turmoil, how, when and where? I had to think... Wham!
Our one night of passion in that mud hut. Well, I would always remember that.
After work I went up to visit my in-laws and break the news, they were delighted. Out came the sherry and a toast followed. I felt their happiness was genuine.
I phoned Ron's usual digs at teatime and I explained as timidly as I could that he was about to be a daddy, silence, not a sound. Eventually he said that he was delighted and would phone me later. In fact he phoned my several times that night, each time a little drunker than before and happier about the situation. That night I prayed my baby would be fine.
Next day at work the hours sped in. I arrived home as Ron was soaking in the bath. I knocked on the door and popped my head around the door. I didn't hear his first words due to the fact that my heart was beating very loudly in my ears. Next thing he was pulling me into the tub beside him, he explained he was scared but if it was what I wanted then it would be ok.

It was at this time I made a friend of Cathy who lived a couple of houses beyond ours. She was married to Franco,

an Italian waiter and was also pregnant. She had two older boys from a previous marriage; she was a very serene person with a witty sense of humour. Our friendship grew with our bumps.
Marco her son was born early March.
At eleven weeks into my pregnancy I awoke to be taken aback at my appearance. You've seen the film about the woman who couldn't stop growing? Well my belly was huge. Margaret, my next door neighbour had to go down to Mothercare and buy me two dresses so I could go out, I was like a beached whale!
Ron arrived home and called out my name. I replied I was upstairs. As he stood at the foot of the stairs and gawped up at me, he said "Darling, I can't see the bathroom door for you." He laughed, I sobbed.
I had decided I was going to have my baby at St Francis Nursing Home in Govan, Glasgow. It was a private nursing home run by nuns, the place made me feel safe and at all costs I need to feel safe.
My huge increase in weight was due to fluid and a sugar imbalance. I travelled into Glasgow by train each month for my check-up's and had lunch at a cheap and cheerful upstairs café, then on by bus to Govan. I met lots of nice people and always found someone who I spent time chatting to. People are such a wealth of learning

opportunities. I had some brilliant conversations with complete strangers.

Towards the latter part of my pregnancy, my parents and in-laws would take me, sharing the trips, as I had to attend often weekly due to my health.

It was decided I would have a section, due to my sugar level and my size complications were expected.

For weeks Ron had began to arrive home late after being to the pub. I would phone him at the pub and tell him his dinner was ready, but hours later I would still be waiting. He was still away at nights as usual so I was a little scared being on my own, in case something happened. However, I wasn't scared for long, I was admitted on my next Wednesday visit. My blood pressure was causing concern. As it was my in-laws who took me in that day I asked them to contact Ron and my parents.

That night my parents and Ron all came to visit. I was flushed, my waters had broken and I felt out of sorts. Ron looked like a rabbit caught in headlights as I threw up all over the bed, he kissed me bye and said he needed a pint! That night I slept on and off. I was alone, due to the other girl sharing my room being taken away to pant, puff and push a new life into the world. Just after breakfast she was brought back. Her red hair cascading over her shoulders and a flushed look made her look angelic, however, her curses shattered the illusion. The nuns laughed with her and once settled into her bed they left. I laughed till I cried as she related the night's event.

At 1.20pm just after lunch, I thought I had been hit with a baseball bat. I was winded and as pain tore through my body I knew this was it. I had had a few false labour pains throughout my pregnancy but I knew this was business.

I was settled into Bethlehem the labour suite. Dr O'Reilly was at home having lunch and he would see to me as soon as he returned.

I had attended relaxation classes, a new way of repeating nursery rhymes through each pain had seemed ok during the classes. My chosen one was Mary had a little lamb. With each pain I was asking why did Mary or how did Mary have a fucking little lamb?

Still I kept on reciting as it was helping, not! For anyone who has experienced giving birth without any analgesic you will know what I mean.

Ron phoned twice to see how I was, imagine my replies. Sex and travel!! Fuck off was my reply number one. Number two reply was given as a HUGH contraction kicked in so I don't recall the words but I do recall the look on Sister Joseph's face.

Outside I heard lots of voices and the sound of a taxi's engine then rushing movements. Enter a woman with a shopping bag cursing loudly in her Irish tongue about her good for nothing husband. Puffs, pants, pushing, words of comfort, words of encouragement lasted for what seemed forever.

This woman was in the midst of delivering her NINTH child while her husband thought she was out buying bread and milk!

All the while I'm still doing my Mary had a little lamb routine. Next all hell broke loose. I interrupt cries of a new life, soft words, and congratulations by saying "Hello, hello I think I need some help here."

Dr O'Reilly came around the screen, took one look and pushed my two knees into my chest and out shot my baby. Thud onto the delivery bed and funny gasping noises filled my head. To be overtaken with the explosion of light, music, like angels singing, joy and love, pure love. As I write this, I can still recall that moment. Pure elation! I have a daughter, a beautiful baby girl.

I am convinced the speed of her delivery has broken her nose; soon my elation is overtaken with fears about the speed of her delivery. She is whisked away. As the Doctor stitches me up, I am convinced he is sewing the cheeks of my bum. This causes great hilarity amongst the Doc, nuns and myself.

Twenty past one till twenty past four in the afternoon. A

short, sharp and quick labour with no analgesic made me feel tired yet elated. Two hours later I am back in bed looking fantastic and numb from the waist down due to the numerous injections given while my lower body has been re attached to the rest of my body! Awaiting my visitors.
As Ron arrived Dr O'Reilly takes him aside and explains my sweet baby is in an incubator due to breathing difficulties and a doctor from Yorkhill Hospital is awaited. I had been ripped badly and I was about to go through a lot of pain as I recovered so I would need lots of T.L.C.
The huge bouquet of flowers my parents carried in made me cry. My brother looked petrified. Ron walked in, kissed me and said "well done." The morphine given to me while I was being stitched made me feel wonderful and with no pain I felt on top of the world.
Sister Irene came in and asked if we would like to be taken to see baby. Helped into a wheelchair, we set of to the side room off the labour suite. Dimmed lights made it appear magical. There she lay beautiful to my eyes asleep but making a grunting sound. I put my hand in and brushed it against her cheek. Love between us spontaneous as she moved to my touch. Into myself I vowed I would always take care of her, keep her safe and prayed she would be fine.
Ron plucked up the courage to put his finger beside her

hand. She uncurled her long fingers and held onto his finger tight. His eyes filled up with tears and I knew he was experiencing a moment of pure joy. The doctor had arrived from Yorkhill; he said he would speak to us after his examination.

Ron had chosen our daughters name. Lyn not Lynn or Lynne, just plain Lyn with no middle names either. So my lovely, beautiful baby now had a name.

The doctor spoke to us. He explained she was at least three weeks early and had swallowed a lot of fluid during the birth, hence the stomach wash he was now having done. This would enable her to breathe better and feed without problems, and her nose was fine he assured me. She was also suffering trauma due to the quickness of her birth however she was a tough little cookie so she'd soon be fine.

Four days later, late on in the afternoon Sister Irene walked into my room holding two babies. "Here, hold this wee bundle for me I'll be back shortly" she said handing me the baby.

The feeling was overwhelming this was my wee bundle; Sister Irene smiled and said she was now out of the incubator. I unwrapped her, kissed each toe and finger. Sung to her and told her my life story up to that moment. Her eyes followed my voice and her little facial expressions filled every part of my being.

My in-laws came to visit one afternoon and they told me Ron was very upset due to the fact I had not had a boy! In fact things may be difficult when I came home with the baby. I became upset and Sister Joseph asked them to leave. I was sedated and Dr O'Reilly was asked to come in and speak to Ron on his arrival at visiting time.

Dr O'Reilly spoke firmly but quietly about the day's events and explained his parents could not come to visit during my remaining days in their care.

Ron came into my room and apologised for his parents and promised to go to see them that night and sort out the bloody mess they had caused. He was genuinely upset and tried all he could to convince me it was lies. By the time he left I was worn out but determined that my baby would have all my love and my protection.

When my parents came to visit they knew about my upset from Ron. My Dad said, "If it's a problem having my Granddaughter home, you can come to ours." However, by the time I came home twelve days after her birth, I wasn't interested in apologies. I was home and settled into a routine with my baby.

The nuns at St Francis were brilliant and would become wonderful friends to me.

Ron's nights away continued so I fell into a routine to suit Lyn. I adored being a mum, I felt complete and my love for my little girl was over whelming. After every feed she would projectile vomit and it was worrying however once I understood it was due to her having a narrow gullet I coped. My washing basket was never empty. My in-laws wouldn't baby-sit at night no matter what, so my parents came through from Edinburgh most weekends to allow us to go out for dinner or to socialise.

When Lyn was eight months, one Sunday during a visit from my parents, we sat having breakfast as Lyn was sitting in her Moses wicker basket playing and giggling enjoying her toasted crusts of bread. She began throwing herself backwards and squealing at the fun her seesaw movements gave her. The phone rang and as I went to answer it I warned everyone to keep an eye on her.

During my phone call I heard a thud, then Lyn crying. Everyone was making a big fuss to calm her down. I hung up the phone and dashed to find out what had happened. Her Moses basket had toppled and her head had hit off the skirting board. No bump, no bruise and soon she was back smiling her usual smile.

However two days later after her bath, as she lay on her towel being dried I noticed a slight swelling on the side of her head. Lyn made no noise as I patted it gently; it felt soft like cotton wool. I wrapped her in the towel and phone Dr Dowie. "I'll be there shortly," he said. On his arrival he examined her bump, Lyn giggled. "I don't think it's serious but let's have the hospital look at it." He gave me a letter and by early evening we sat in a hospital room being quizzed about her injury. Lyn was admitted to the children's ward and we were ordered to go home. I protested, I couldn't leave her. A nurse told us to leave and her expression told us not to argue. For three days it was a nightmare. Continually being questioned as to who had hit Lyn and no-one listening to me about why her being sick was normal…

Leaving her each night was unbearable. I phoned Dr Dowie and sobbed out what was happening. The consultant of Lyn's medical team was off, and as soon as he returned he would decide what action was to be taken so I had to sit tight he explained.

A foreign doctor on the team was always rude and forbade me to hold Lyn. A psychiatric doctor interviewed us. She asked questions, Ron answered and I cried. Whenever we were near Lyn someone always watched us and we were not allowed to lift her up.

I had had enough; I demanded to speak to the consultant who was head of this appalling medical team. "You will see him when he is ready and not before" boomed the ward sister.

Lyn was crying, her nappy was soiled, and the clothes they

had on her didn't fit and were dirty. Due to Lyn's narrow gullet and sensitive digestive system I always had to be careful with what she ate. Now after every feed they gave her she was vomiting, I was enraged no way was this continuing.

At the top of the ward all the medical team I now loathed swarmed around a tall well built jolly looking bearded gent. The ward sister cooed and smiled sweetly up to him. As she eyed me marching up towards them her sweet smile left her, in fact all their smiles departed their faces. With Lyn vomiting over my shoulder and crying I presented myself a few feet from him, he smiled and said a friendly "Hello." "Don't hello me" I replied, tears cascaded down my cheeks as I let the words spill out. I pointed to each one staring at me and repeated their accusations. The Sister stepped forward to reprimand me. The consultant stopped her, his eyes never left mine and he slowly escorted me back to Lyn's room with the observation window; where an auxiliary nurse was peering in smirking however she soon moved when he sat me down and asked me to explain fully. As I did Lyn snuggled into my breast and slept. He listened, he patted my hand and said he would return shortly.

A door slammed and loud words echoed towards the room where I sat emotionally exhausted. Ron appeared looking bewildered. The consultant had phoned him. What was going on? I explained what I had said and done, he sat down shaking his head, my outburst would only make this whole situation worse he spat out. I chose to ignore him. Sometime later the door opened and they all walked in, I tensed up and Lyn wriggled in her sleep, the consultant towered above them. “Well who is going to start?” he demanded. Each one in turn apologised for their accusations and behaviour. “Not to the bloody floor, to Mrs Pearson sitting on the chair” he boomed. “Get out, the lot of you” was his final demand to them. Out they shuffled, he closed the door and sat on the bed. He was deeply sorry for our treatment, a letter of apology would be sent to our doctor and to ourselves. Each one would be given a disciplinary warning. He reached over and stroked Lyn’s hair. “I don’t have a daughter, only four small sons. Take her home Mrs Pearson,” he said. Through my tears I thanked him. As he shook Ron’s hand he said “Your wife reminds me of my own mother, no one does anything to her own.” Ron agreed and as a wrapped Lyn in her favourite blanket we drove home. Once home I filled the bath, undressed, stripped off Lyn and we both soaked in the bubbles. As I held her close she was contented, I could feel she was safe.

Lyn walked at eight and a half months. She was very tall

for her age and she always looked older. A bundle of pure joy. She brought pure love into my life and we shared many beautiful days having fun.

Lyn was fifteen months old when we were invited to Canada to visit and stay with Ron's uncle. His mother's only brother and his second wife. For nine months Ron and I had had no physical or emotional contact, so I was now a wreck. This had been the longest period and I didn't want to go and play happy families so far from home. Up until the night before, I wasn't going. My dad had a lengthily talk to me and I agreed, but it was under duress.

The holiday was ok but too long. Canada and the USA were fine but I was homesick. Fed up being an actress I only wanted home.

An ultimatum two nights before we left for homemade Ron respond and make love to me and afterwards I was left with an enormous empty feeling. Later I realised I should have waited until we were home. On the flight home I'm sure it didn't take the usual time as I was willing us on faster.

Back home our usual routine settled in and my days with Lyn became bliss again. No more nervous tension playing with all our emotions.

I was now pregnant again and I was slightly apprehensive about breaking the news, so I kept hush for the first few months.

At Christmas I always had my family and sometimes Ron's family joined us. Ron would always sigh and moan about the arrangement while I always kept busy in the kitchen speaking words to soothe him. When all the family was around I felt calm and safe.

While mashing the potatoes for Christmas dinner I whispered to Ron that as I was pregnant we should announce it now, today. His emotion was totally void so I said I was going to tell everyone at dinner, so he had better smile and act pleased for our baby's sake. The mashed potatoes were pure brilliant! Words of delight spun around the table. Lyn came and hugged and kissed my tummy. My dad gave a toast, and I visibly relaxed.

Four days later I awoke during the night feeling on edge with niggling pains. I moved to the bed in the spare room to save annoying Ron. Up, down, tossing one way then the other. At 7.20am I sat on the toilet as I lost my baby. Blood everywhere, tears cascading and fear rising from deep within. I struggled to the bedroom door and called to Ron, I didn't want to wake Lyn so I motioned him to get up. His unpleasant look changed when he saw the blood. For the next few minutes he ran up and down the stairs, so I telephoned the doctor and spoke to his wife Jenny, whom I knew.

The doctor was out on a call so I was to lie flat with my legs raised and she would send him ASAP.

I then phoned my dad and all I could cry was "My baby, Dad, my baby."

"I'm on my way" he replied then the line went dead.

Ron phoned his parents from downstairs, they arrived very quickly. Joe stayed downstairs; Jess came into the bedroom, looked and said, "What did you do for this to happen?" Gripped with pain I told her to "Get lost."

The doctor arrived, spoke kindly, examined me and looked in the bathroom and telephoned the ambulance. He took my hand and said he was so sorry; he would let Dr Dowie know. Through my tears I thanked him.

When the ambulance arrived the medics were wonderful. I wanted to walk downstairs and out to the ambulance. No way they said so we agreed on a chair type contraption. I was concerned about leaving Lyn, where were my parents? I was on the last step into the ambulance when my dad's car screeched to a halt. Half shaved, wearing his vest, braces and slippers he couldn't say a thing as tears choked him. My mum said "Go on, Lyn will be fine Dad will drive Ron to the hospital and Tom can amuse Lyn."

With sirens sounding and lights flashing we took off. Oh, to sleep. The medic spoke to me about all his family, his daughter in Canada, on and on he droned. I closed my eyes and he nipped me. What a bloody cheek, he nipped me! He took my hand and spoke gently. "I can't let you sleep, you are bleeding heavily, so heavily that you need urgent, medical help to stop you from dying." Blunt or what! What do you want to talk about; he asked "Any bloody thing" I replied.

Once at the hospital I was transferred onto a trolley and next thing the Olympic trolley race began. I was then sedated and whisked into the theatre without anyone speaking to me.

I awoke sometime early evening, alone, feeling numb, with hands protecting my tummy. I allowed my mind to wander over the day's events. I rolled onto my side, still protecting my tummy. Someone would soon come, maybe Ron, and tell me I was fine. No, it was a grumpy nurse. "So you've decided to wake up." "Everything happened so quickly, I didn't have time to explain that I react to anaesthetic," I said.

Tea and toast appeared. Most hospitals give you tea and toast after giving birth. Maybe I was fine. I ate the toast, drunk the tea and fell back to sleep. Next morning the noise of the ward awakening brought me to my senses. Why had no one come to visit? Why was I alone?

I eavesdropped on the other patients termination, D & C, sterilisation. As my mind spun around a doctor appeared. He stood at the end of my bed and spoke at me, not to me. All I could make out was Lost, Lost, Lost.

I wanted home and with an inner rage rising I was determined to go home. I asked for a phone.

Ron answered. "Come and get me now!" I said in an angry manner before I hung up. I was sitting on the side of the bed when the doctor returned and explained I was to stay another night before being discharged the next morning. Through clenched teeth I said "No way, a ward full of people who don't want babies, how insensitive!" He looked at his feet and mumbled an apology. As he walked away Ron arrived "Well, you'll be happy, as there is no more baby." I growled. "You couldn't even come and visit me last night" I seethed.

My dad and Ron had come to visit, but as I was deeply asleep they decided to leave me to sleep however they had left a message. No one had passed it on.

I didn't bother getting dressed. With slippers and dressing gown on I left, feeling empty and very unstable on my feet. Back home with my parents around the house and Lyn playing peek-a-boo with Tom behind the couch, I felt safe. As I sat on the armchair the flashback of bathroom, blood, my baby, the words echoed in my head. My dad appeared with scrambled egg on toast on a tray. His usual comfort meal, as he placed it on my lap he said, "Everything upstairs is ok, the baby's gone pet, we'll stay as long as you want."

I was safe, no need to worry.

Next day Dad drove home to check on his house, they had left in such a hurry, and he could also pick up clothes to last over Hogmanay and a few days into the New Year.

Ron went into work, to be on his own I suspect. Weeks earlier we had been invited to a Hogmanay party. I thought 'Life goes on', so I agreed to go.

My girl friends were all so kind. It was a good night. I sat and people watched, unusual, because I loved to dance whenever we went out!

Someone took a photo of us and I was amazed how good I looked.

A few days later Ron went back to work and my parents returned home, promising to return next weekend.

Lyn and I spent days snuggled up, playing games, painting, reading stories and explaining baby had gone to Heaven.

Late February I was pregnant again… This time as soon as I found out I didn't keep it to myself. St Francis was informed, I was in need of some gentle T.L.C. This baby would give me two adorable children.

On my walks into town with Lyn we always passed a large run down Victorian red sandstone semi-detached villa.
I knocked on the door and enquired about the run down house next door. I must have called at the right time because the young lady of the house was in a right state. Crying and bedraggled she invited Lyn and I in to meet her wee boy. Over a cup of tea her life story unfolded. She had to sell; she had to leave; her divorce was acrimonious and she had to get her life back. The house was very run down, but I was hooked.
High ceilings, big rooms and lots of space; to me the ideal family home.
Ron agreed, or at least he went along with the move to keep me happy!
Our house sold very quickly and an entry date into the New Year was set for our mutual move.
Ron was still working away on his usual pattern, so Lyn and I made plans for our new baby. I had attended the W.R.V.S mother and toddler group since Lyn was 6 months old. Now two years on and I was an active member on the committee, so Lyn and I had very busy social life… toddler group most mornings, lunch with friends at their homes on a rota basis. The nights Ron wasn't coming home, were filled with bubble baths and cosy bedtime stories… Bliss.
Ron found it difficulty being a parent. The responsibility

was a great strain and he was at times clumsy around Lyn and this scared him, as he didn't want to hurt her.

At six foot seven inches he was huge, but such a gentle giant. He tried so hard to be natural around her. His apprehension was picked up by Lyn very quickly and she would be impish or naughty. This would make him on edge so I'd be referee or go between.

So much love for each other plain to see, somehow at times never felt or shown as it should have been.

Baby was due early December so I was well ahead with packing boxes for our move plus all the Christmas gifts wrapped and hidden.

During this pregnancy I had a passion for lemon sorbet ice cream. With Lyn it had been bananas and once again Ill health dogged me. The beached whale look was back again but I was happy.

Ron was still having weeks of no physical or emotional contact but by now I could cope.

Early November arrived with niggling back pains moving to my pubic bone area. Constant checks at St Francis eased my fears.

22nd November I phoned my parents and asked them to come with the expectation of staying. They agreed and duly arrived later that same day.

As I sat splay legged on a wee stool with my back against

the radiator, I demanded a tub of lemon sorbet ice cream. Ron set off on his mission and I phoned St Francis. I explained through tears that I felt awful. I couldn't explain fully, just not ok.

Sister Magdalene told me to come; and agreed I might be ready.

Ron arrived back with a tub of orange sorbet. I cried all the time I ate it. I wasn't going anywhere until it was finished. Once done, Dad and Ron drove me to St Francis' nursing home. Mum and Tommy stayed behind to look after Lyn. Mum phoned my in-laws to explain what was happening. Sister Magdalene was gentle as she examined me. I was on my way.

Tucked up in my usual bed in the room I loved, Dad and Ron crept in to say goodnight.

I was safe. After a good nights rest with my usual hot water bottle clamped to my back I felt a little better.

Not my usual doctor came in to examine me. "No, no, not at all ready" he said as he left.

I was still crying when Sister Annunsiata came into my room. She felt my expansive tummy, listened to the heartbeat and gently examined me.

Quietly she explained I was dilated. Rest and do as I say and you won't have a caesarean section you'll cope like you did last time.

Rest I did, at one twenty pm while I was speaking to Ron on the phone the first contraction hit, and hit it did.
An hour later labour was in full swing.
By 3pm Sister Annunsiata asked me to trust her as she began guiding baby's head slowly down the birth channel. No analgesic, nothing. Pain shot through my body continually. Three twenty pm, head out, gasping noises. Sister Annunsiata's gentle words need to cut, lots of mess. Pain, pants, push, rush of fluid, baby whisked away. The unbiblical cord had been wrapped round her neck twice and as she was being born she was being strangled. However gentle hands guided her out.
Placenta in bits, urgent care going on to the lower part of my body.
No pain just pure relief and the explosion of sheer joy, happiness and love filled my soul. Angelic fireworks all around as my baby girl is placed in my arms.
Beautiful, I have two, not one, but two beautiful daughters.
Oh, where is Lyn.
We shall all have such happy times.

Early evening visiting arrives; I am elated, flying without wings.
I have no stitches this time. Tired no, elated yes.
Lyn runs in ahead of everyone. We both cry as we hug, oh

I've missed her.
"Where is baby" she squeals and as her squeals of delight get louder, Sister Joseph comes in to join in our happiness. As I've been very good we can all go to see baby.
Ron began to help me out of bed and the look of shock on his face was a picture. After Lyn had been born it took me twenty minutes to get out of bed due to the stitches, this time it was easy. He hugged me close and said a genuine "Thank you, I love you so much."
Baby Louise slept peacefully as both of our families said hello. Ron's parents were present, as he did not want a replay of Lyn's birth comments.

For the next eight days, I rested. Visiting times were fun and after everyone's visitors left I would hold a tea party in my room. All the goodies the visitors brought were shared out. The nuns would join us after prayers and on many occasions lights out was later than usual. On the 2nd December we both went home.
Ron decides within a week of me being home, he was giving up going away nights. He wanted to be home every night.
One night as we lay in bed, both girls asleep, he whispered he might be ready to take on this family, our family as a responsibility. As I kissed him gently I reassured him it was

a task he was capable of.
Christmas and New Year was a wonderful, happy time. Having Ron home every night was a strain.
Since we got married, he spent two nights one week, three nights the next, either in Inverness or Aberdeen. Now, meals every night, making sure all chores were done before he came home, no quiet time in the evenings for Lyn, made me tense at times.
Ron liked to chill out, watching TV without many interruptions. So I devised that I put Lyn to bed while he fed Louise her last bottle. This made him feel useful and eased his strain.

We had employed a lovely lady two days per week to help with the housework; after Lyn was born and she was a Godsend.
She left when her husband took a nervous breakdown due to his business going bust. Here was a very intelligent, well-educated woman who wasn't afraid to slum it, as she said, for extra money. We had great lengthy chats. I was sorry to see her go.
I was six months pregnant with Louise when Aggie came to work for us. She was a small, buxom blonde, who was bubbly with a downside; she liked a wee drink. Aggie walked splay footed like Mary Poppins, however the

similarity stopped there.
She was a good laugh and her life was interesting. She was divorced with one daughter, who chose to live with her dad. Aggie had been having a torrid affair for years with her brother-in-law. No matter how her life was going, once at our home all her worries left her and she gave her all.
My parents and in-laws liked her a lot, so it was never awkward and she was a great help getting the house packed up for our move into the run down Victorian villa.
Cathy was sorry I was moving, but as it was only a stone throw away we would continue to see each other as usual. Marco and Lyn were such good playmates, so their play days had to go on.
Six weeks in to the New Year, we moved.

Arran Gardens had been a lovely home, a place that will always hold a special love due to my daughters being born during our stay there.

Time to move on.

Woodside Walk Part 1

Our new home was a Victorian red sandstone semi-detached villa, which needed lots renovations.

A new kitchen was installed and it was redecorated from top to bottom. The small dingy bathroom was transformed into large luxury bathroom by knocking down the adjoining wall to a tiny box room. Changing rooms from total mess to a beautiful and welcoming home.

Woodside Walk was to become known as 'the big house'. The roof needed completely overhauled so it meant lots of banging, and the workmen who worked on all our renovations were always amazed at how Louise slept on and on. One of them plucked up the courage to ask if she was deaf.

Next time she was awake they all piled in to see her, gooing and gaahing like big Jessies!

Louise ate, slept, lay quietly when awake so you would've never known she was there. Completely contented.

While Lyn ran off with the workmen's tools, tried to climb the ladders to the roof and in general whisked around, you

always knew where she was!
With arrangements in place for Louise's christening, I asked Cathy to be her Godmother.
By now Ron's brother Colin had a girlfriend called Shona. His parents weren't too happy about it, but as it had been the same with me, I could sympathise with her.
When the outer storm door was closed, I was out or didn't want visitors. When it was fully open, the small vestibule displayed an ornate half glass door, which meant I was at home to visitors. However, no one could ring our bell after seven pm in the evening.
This may sound awful, but as we had so many friends, our home was similar to a busy fun fair some days. It was a system that worked.
One evening, with the girls tucked up in bed the doorbell rang. In the evenings I always liked relaxing in my nightdress and soaking my feet in warm soapy water. Soaking and washing my feet this way had been a ritual I had done since a child. As I took my feet out of the basin of warm bubbly water I was enjoying I cursed to myself at who'd rung the bloody bell!
There stood Colin and Shona. I invited them in, made tea, chatted politely and apologised for Ron being out. Some time later they left. Only when they had gone did it strike me that I was wearing my nightdress. My nightdress! What

an impression!
Colin worked shifts so he would pop in often during the day. Ron began to joke in a serious way that his brother liked me a lot. Colin and Shona soon became engaged and my in-laws moaned to me about it!
Cathy had complained constantly after having given birth to Marco, about her back always being sore. After lots of tests she was informed the big C had struck.
During her hospital appointments I would have Marco.
As there was only three months age difference between Lyn and Marco, they were great friends, so it was a pleasure to have him.
Newly built detached villas on an estate around the corner from our house caught Cathy and Franco's attention. Soon their house was sold and the move into their brand new home went smoothly.
After a few weeks, Cathy's health began once again to cause concern. Another hospital stay meant serious surgery was needed and fast.
After her surgery she was tense and something within her began to give up.
A full hysterectomy, removal of both bowel and bladder plus the big C growth made the thought of coming home impossible to her.
To celebrate her birthday I organised a singing telegram.

All the staff and doctors knew plus all her family and friends. The day arrived and we sat around her bed in anticipation of who was about to arrive. The ward sister asked to speak to me. Cathy, as sharp as a razor asked "Why?" A feeble excuse passed my lips as I made my way down the ward.

Before me stood a very tall, good looking young man, dressed in top hat, tails, plus evening cape, with a small bouquet of red roses.

Visitors and staff fell silent as he entered the ward singing in a beautiful voice "I'll take you home again Kathleen." The song had been her late father's favourite and he sung it often to her when she was a child. When he had finished, he kissed her hand, delivered his roses and bid her farewell as he rendered the song again as he left.

Not one person had a dry eye in the ward and as tears blinded me I knew this would be her last birthday but the memory of this day would always be with her family and in her heart.

She accused me of embarrassing her, but I paid no heed. I knew what it meant to her.

A few days later she came home.

Unable to be Louise's Godmother, Shona agreed to stand in.

Ron wouldn't take the vows taken by parents during a

christening service due to the fact he couldn't answer whether he did or did not believe in God. So once again I took the vows while he stood beside me. I always admired his courage at standing by his honesty on the subject.
Back at the house, the day went well.
As a baby, Lyn had been constantly sick however Louise never parted with anything so it was a shock when she threw up over Shona's shoulder and onto her dress. She was not amused, however, these things happen.
Ron wasn't too keen on Shona so he found it difficult to talk to her. Ron's parents still moaned about her and I kept quiet.
Life went on and our home began to take shape.
Ron still went off the physical side of our marriage but I was so busy with the W.R.V.S, friends and the girls, I rarely complained. Life was easier when I didn't go on about my lack of affection from him. Other times I blew my stack out of sheer frustration, sexual and otherwise.

Colin and Shona planned to get married on the 20th November, three day's short of Louise's first birthday. Lyn was invited to be a flower girl and Ron an usher.
When Louise was six months old, I was being treated at St Francis for cervical erosions. Cells in my cervix had been diagnosed as out of sorts! So trips to have treatment became

part of my routine.
During this time, Cathy's illness was causing concern, so I was doing all I could to be of help.
Arrangements for Lyn's flower girl dress caused a hick-up. I had assumed we would pay for the dress, hair band, shoes and Shona would arrange for her posy of flowers. The way in which this was discussed showed up the other side of quiet Shona! Her manner took me aback, it really upset me. When I told Ron, he roared "That's it, we are not bloody going."
As the wedding drew closer, Ron's emotional past leapt to the front of his mind, paling everything else.

As my treatments were becoming more painful, coming home afterwards became more difficult. Ron would pick me up at St Francis; I'd curl up in the car on the way home, stagger into the house and drag myself upstairs before collapsing into bed. Aggie would help my parents with the daily running of the house till I was once again on my feet. The cleaning lady I found for Cathy was a Godsend. She looked after Cathy's household like it was her own. Her being there most of the day Monday to Friday eased the pressure on Franco and myself.
Dr O'Reilly agreed to stop the treatment for a short time to see how my cells recovered. As the wedding was coming

closer I was relieved.
I had been giving Colin dancing lessons to prepare him for the wedding Waltz. He was really a nice young guy and I hoped within my heart he didn't hold emotional trauma like his big brother. With eleven years age gap between him and Ron, they weren't very close. Ron desperately wanted to be his pal but their worlds seemed miles apart, as far as his mind told him.

Fat, frumpy and feeling like shit, I began my hunt for an outfit for the wedding.
Bloated, tired, feeling sick, drained and with constant moaning in my ear from my in-laws – Wedding! I felt like running away.
"Could I change the young yin's mind?"
"Would I try and talk him out of it?" On and on it went.
I was only married in to the family, not real family, as I had once been told, so why didn't they speak to 'the young yin'? Why?
Because, as a family they did not communicate. They all spoke at each other but not to each other.
The night of the showing of presents at Shona's parents home was a delight: not. I was made to feel like a piece of shit on all their shoes. I smiled sweetly, chatted pleasantly, clenched my teeth and made my good-byes early into the

evening.
They all came across as so sanctimonious. I drove home emotionally shattered and kept hush. To say anything would only wind Ron up more, and at present he was so wound up that if anyone shot a starting pistol he would have become Britain's best Olympic runner!
However, I did chat on the phone to my dad about it. His answer, always the same, "Rise above it, you are better than all of them put together, listen to your heart."
The night of the stag 'do' was even more interesting. The 'do' was being held in a local pub that the local police used, and as Colin was a police officer, so it began.
Ron didn't know many of them so he felt a bit left out to begin with. He watched and listened to Colin with his mates and realised he really did not know his brother at all. Brothers with the same parents, but nothing else.
The feeling of emptiness swamped him; he made his apologies, left, and headed for his local, the football social club.
What a welcome. His mates had wondered where he was. In the wee small hours he came rolling home, drunk as a skunk at first in a happy, jovial mood, soon to be overtaken by his inner emotional turmoil. Tears, endless words comforting him as best I could. As usual, slumber overtook this drained giant and I prayed his drunken snores would

carry off his phantoms.

Louise's first birthday party was a huge success. We decided to have it before the wedding due to all the preparation. All her wee friends from mother and toddler group, grandparents, friends and family had a wonderful afternoon, to be rounded off with a family sit down meal. Girls tucked up in bed, the house fell silent and I counted my blessings.

Next day outside the Post Office, I met Colin's best man's wife Carol, along with her sister-in-law also called Carol, who was the best man's sister! Complicated, read again! They said they were so happy to have bumped into me. "Oh yeah," I thought. Carol, the sister-in-law I liked, she was down to earth and easy going, a likeable person. The other, Rottweiler springs to mind.

"Did I know Shona was attending the hospital with a very personal problem?"

"No," I said.

"Did I know if Colin knew?" "I don't know," I said.

"We think you should tell him. After all, he has a right to know!"

"What is exactly her problem," I asked. They explained. What sprung to mind immediately was, some friends!

"You really do need to tell him, it will ruin their marriage," they insisted!
I excused myself, forgot about the Post Office and set off home with haste.
Lyn was confused. She was looking forward to going to the cake shop, now we were going home.
As I breezed in the back door into the kitchen, Ron commented "That was quick." Breathless, I spilled out the conversation I had had. Without saying one word, and listening intently, he put on the kettle then said "Promise me you will say not one word of this to anyone." I promised.
I explained I was upset, not about Shona's problem, but the fact that her best friend was in no way keeping the problem quiet. I was more intent in telling Shona, but again Ron made me promise, so I promised.
The wedding day arrived and I felt so ill. My parents were as usual through to stay.
Louise had not been invited to the wedding however, my parents were attending the marriage service with Louise so she could present the couple with a lucky horseshoe. Shona wasn't too pleased, but Louise smiled and felt part of the day.
Arrangements were made for my dad to come to the reception to uplift Lyn early evening.

The meal was pleasant, Ron's face left a lot to be desired, and I just let the time wash over me.

I was quite pleased; Colin's dancing was passable. I approached him and asked for a dance. "Fuck off," he replied. I was shell-shocked. I came over numb. What had I done to deserve those words?

Ron, who unknown to me, had been watching, walked over to me and led me over to a quiet spot, hugged me against him and asked "What did he just say to you?"

"Oh, it was nothing," I said.

"I'll ask again, what did he say to you?" He asked.

"I'll tell you shall I?" He said. "He told you to fuck off." I could only nod my head in agreement.

Ron's inner phantoms arose and as he held me closer and closer, his fears, insecurities and frustration grew and he announced he was going to speak to Colin about his disrespect for me.

"Who the hell does he think he is?" He growled.

"No one tells my wife to fuck off" he whispered in my ear.

"Leave it Ron, please, not now, not tonight," I begged.

The excitement of the happy couple about to leave froze Ron's reactions. With them cosseted in the taxi outside and everyone biding the happy couple goodbye eased the moment.

The taxi behind theirs' was empty. Awaiting his hire, the

taxi driver called out a name and before I knew it we were sat inside it and off home. Or maybe not!

I heard Ron say "social club," as he tore off his bowtie and stuffed it in his pocket. I knew best to stay silent.

Dad was still up when we eventually got home. Ron's phantoms had returned, so I was pleased to see Dad waiting up. I went to bed sore and exhausted. Dad and Ron were in deep discussion as I bid them goodnight.

A few weeks later, Ron and I were invited up to the happy couples' home to look at the wedding photos. Shona had also invited her brother and his wife.

Ron felt awkward all night. I spoke too much to compensate, and when we left, you could visibly see the others relax.

Once again, Ron's phantoms arose and we hadn't even reached the car!

The usual routine followed, social club, too much booze, home, dad's kind words and bed for me. When exhaustion took over he would fall into bed beside me and hold me tight. I was his safety net.

Colin still continued to drop by like he did before he was married, however, I never said a word about Ron's feelings. The girls were always delighted to see him, their delight chased the idea out of my mind, and anyway, I had promised.

Our next visit to their new home was with the girls. Shona had laid out a large towel on the carpet where the girls had a drink and a biscuit. We didn't stay long because Ron was furious. We had taken the girls since they were babies out to eat and Ron was proud that his young girls knew how to behave and dine out.
As we strapped the girls into their car seats, Ron vowed he wouldn't be in their house again.
How right those words would be.

Cathy's condition was now serious. Stobhill hospital laid aside a small side room and we sat, Franco and I, and waited. Visitors did not linger long.
Franco's sister and husband had arrived from Italy. Their small son was ages with Marco, so he had a playmate and his aunt took over Cathy's role as best she could.
My parents and Aggie took over the running of my home, looking after the girls, and my dad spent time with Ron.
I promised Cathy she would not die alone. I wet her lips, I held her hand, I read the papers out loud to her and I watched her life force slowly but gradually leave.
Cathy wasn't alone when her time came.
I lost a good friend, a beautiful woman who had a warm

heart. I was glad to have kept my word.

I arranged her funeral and the purvey back at her house. It was then I met Father Devany, a priest who was to become a friend. It was left to me to tell Cathy's older sons about her death. Franco couldn't cope, he was lost.
So it was arranged, Marco was to return with his aunt, uncle and cousin to Italy.
Franco needed time to grieve. As I was ill again, I couldn't take on Marco. I felt helpless but it wasn't my decision that was Franco's.
Late afternoon after the funeral, they made ready to set off on the drive south for the Channel ferry and the long drive home.
I helped pack up Marco's things, held him close and told him with smiles about the journey he was about to go on. Strapped into his car seat, many friends and family waving to him, he looked bewildered.
Someone took my arm, I turned. "Your husband is in the kitchen, you better go and see to him." "Why?" I replied. "He is in a terrible state," she said.
Ron stood against the sink, tears streaming down his face. "What's up?" I said.
"How can you do that? How can you show him so much love, compassion, smile and ease his fears?" He blurted out

to me.
"Why? I have to. I'll deal with my feelings later, but for now we are both going outside to say goodbye to a beautiful wee boy who will always have his mother's gentle ways and lovely eyes. I owe it to Cathy," I explained.
I did deal with my feelings a couple of months later.
The singing group 'The Three Degrees' were on a TV special singing for Prince Charles. As I snuggled up to Ron on the sofa watching, they began to sing 'When will I see you again'.
Cathy stood before me smiling as the words of the song washed over me. Tears came. Now I dealt with my feelings.
Franco wasn't coping and he decided to return to Italy. The oldest of Cathy's sons moved to Glasgow near his real fathers family and David who was almost in his final year at high school was left in my care. So I organised him accommodation and coped with him the best I could. He was a real handful but I had to take into account he had just lost his beloved mum.
Ron was angry with Franco copping out however I took time to explain to him that Franco was like a little boy lost and being back home would hopefully heal his breaking heart.
Time flew by and from time to time my health caused a hick-up.

At our local social club an older woman called Mary was causing problems and her reputation was widely known. Her husband had divorced her then he married a younger woman. Six months later, he died from a massive heart attack.

Since then she went out of her way to come between happily married couples. Her friend Margaret and her partner Pete felt sorry for her and always made excuses for her.

Ron knew what a reputation she had so we always gave her a wide berth.

Margaret had had a very difficult phase earlier in her life. It led to her drinking more than she should from time to time. She approached me and asked me to counsel her. I refused, but did suggest a close friend who was capable and willing to do so.

I arranged to drop her off at Marion's house on a Friday evening. She brought a small bottle of booze to take with her to help her relax. I arranged to go and pick her up later. Aggie had agreed to stay on so I could go out if I wished and I dropped in on a close friend for a coffee and a chat. When I arrived back at Marion's, Margaret was truly drunk. She had finished off her bottle and most of Marion's brandy, so words and emotions poured from her.

As I sat down beside her, she took my hand and kissed it. "You're a good person, someone who has always been kind to me," she slurred. "You don't deserve it," she went on. "You need to know because it's not right and you'll stop it," she continued.

I didn't say a word; I could only look at her in bewilderment.

After another swig from her fast emptying glass, she began her explanation.

"You've been ill for some time. Ron's been drinking more and more and always in the social club on a Friday during the disco nights. Always alone, so Mary has began talking to him and sitting beside him and sometimes they dance."

The word 'dance' bounded off my head. Ron was 6'7'. He never danced because he always felt embarrassed. Now he was dancing with a slut! I remained silent and continued to listen.

"He always drives her home, as she doesn't stay with me and Pete on those nights," she continued to slur.

Ron had been coming home later and later on his Friday nights out. Still I remained silent.

"He's having an affair with Mary and she wants everything you have," she slurred.

I growled to Marion, "Take her home."

I jumped in my car and drove to the social club where I

knew Ron would be drinking after hours. I banged on the locked doors. The Convenor opened the door and jumped out of my way as I strode in. Ron and his mates turned around, stared at me and fell silent.

"Pearson, outside now," I roared.

As I turned to march out, I heard them joke "Oh, Pearson, what have you been up to?"

Under my seat in the car I kept a very large heavy wrench and I reached down took it out. As Ron came out towards me, I lifted the wrench and swung it at him. It missed him and hit his car, only because he ducked. His first words to me were "I'm sorry, it didn't mean anything, it's over, please, believe me."

I yelled in return "I want you out, out by tonight."

As he got into his car, I had already sped off. I had an idea where Mary lived so I headed there. It was now well past midnight. I knocked on the door where lights were still on and asked where she lived. Third time lucky.

I banged and banged on her door, her curtains twitched but the door remained closed. I continued to bang on her door. Next, Ron drew up in his car.

He got as far as the garden gate and I growled "So you know your way, hope she's ready to give you a place to stay. Got your things with you?"

"You're both bastards," I screamed.

Two policemen walking the beat turned up. One spoke to Ron and the older one stepped forward and took my arm as he said "Calm down missus. We know her well; she's not worth it. You look a decent lassie, go home, you shouldn't be here."

He escorted me to my car. To Ron he said, "You're a foolish man, not the first but this young lassie doesn't need this."

Ron got into my passenger seat. "Please, forgive me. It was stupid, it was over, trust me, it was over" he said.

"Trust you, trust you? I have given you my life and time after time you have hurt me and I always keep trying, well not anymore, not anymore. Get out of my car," I screamed.

As if frightened by my outburst he did. I drove home like a fiend.

As I walked into the hall Aggie met me. Ron had been home earlier and when he realised I wasn't in he guessed where I was. I now growled "Aggie get a taxi," she flew. I sat and waited patiently for Ron's return.

He begged, he pleaded and tried to explain it meant nothing.

I had been ill and he couldn't cope with losing me!

I was emotionally exhausted, I was numb, and I needed to sleep. With my nightdress and dressing gown on I slipped beneath the quilt and curled up. Ron lay on top of the quilt and tried to get close, my silent answer told him to back off.

Next morning I telephoned his parents.
"You have to look after the girls as we have a situation here which needs sorted," I said. The situation I explained to them. Soon after they arrived my father-in-law went into the kitchen with Ron and I heard raised voices, while my mother-in-law asked me what had I done!
Her statement did not merit a reply.
The girls giggled their good byes, I smiled, waved and blew them kisses as they drove off.
I was shattered, in the cold light of day I knew this situation had to be sorted once and for all!
Ron made me lunch, I wept and played with the food on the plate. He made me cups of tea, I wept and the tea turned cold.
How could he hurt me so much? Why her, of all people? What did she have I didn't?
"Big boobs" he laughed trying to lift my mood. Guess what, it didn't.
I decided to go for a bath. Aggie phoned and Ron told her to come as usual because we were going out for a meal.
After my bath Ron tried to become amorous but I told him to leave me alone. He continued to be very loving towards me and I eventually gave in. I wept continuously as he

lovingly soothed my mood. I also agreed to go out for a meal that evening. He wanted everything to appear as normal that way he wouldn't have to deal with it fully.
Aggie arrived to baby-sit. I needed tights, so Ron offered to take me down to the rear entrance of our nearby shopping mall. I left him in the car while I made my way to Safeway in the Mall, not for tights! I had lied. Mary the slut was a cashier there. A pleasant faced male assistant informed me the shop was about to close.

"I know, can I speak to Mary its rather urgent" I pleaded,

"Hold on a moment" he said.

A young lad was lining up all the trolleys ready for next day's business, I stood ready for my next move. As she walked around the top of the food aisle smiling at her boss, who was in an animated conversation, my fist connected with her face. It felt brilliant! Back she reeled into the line of trolleys, which in turn went trundling down the aisle. What a sight! Gawping stares, looks of amazement and muttered words. As I stood towering over her I dared her to get up. The boss took my arm and escorted me to the door and said "Due to your behaviour I'll have to bar you from these premises."

I laughed, told him to "Fuck off" and said, "I didn't think a large well known establishment would employ husband stealing sluts."

As I walked back to the car my hand hurt but oh, I felt good.

Ron asked where my tights were! I laughed as I recalled in full detail my trip to Safeway. Ron's face was a picture but he remained silent.

Seated in our usual Italian restaurant I spoke very quietly but firmly "When we leave here we are going to the social club. As you seem to like the place so much and everyone now knows your indiscretions better than me, I don't intend to hide away." He looked at me, opened his mouth to answer and I looked him directly in the eye and said, "Do not push it." He didn't.

We walked into the social club and our friends invited us to join them. Margaret, Pete and Mary sat a few tables away. I took Ron's arm and whispered in his ear "Look at her and I'll blind you." My usual outgoing mood was missing.

As the bingo was being called Mary went to the ladies. I went too! I burst the door of her cubicle, grabbed her by the throat and demanded "Was it good? Did he excel himself? You want my home? Just how long have you both been screwing around?"

All answers were yes, the last was "For some months." I totally lost the plot, I became manic as my fists punched and my hand slapped her. I came to my senses when a knock on the cubicle door broke into my thoughts, it was

Margaret. "Please stop this, it won't help," she said.
I let Mary go and growled at her not to move. I then picked up Margaret and sat her in the wash hand basin, told her not to interfere and went back to finish my confrontation with Mary.
As I came out of the ladies, the bingo had been halted as everyone could hear me and much to my surprise everyone began to applaud and cheer. Nobody had ever challenged her about her actions and the committee knew of her reputation but had turned a blind eye to it. Well I wasn't and wouldn't, so I found my solution and applied it.
With all the drinks I was bought that night I went home very tipsy.

A few months later my health problems returned and more hospital visits began. I felt emotionally drained, time was as ever moving on, but I felt I was sinking into an abyss with every tick of the clock.
Ron went about his business as usual. His Friday nights out with the boys continued, however, I wouldn't let him take his car. With no car he wouldn't or couldn't take Mary home. He continually apologised and I in turn coped with my broken heart.

Ron booked us a long weekend at Lake Windermere in the

Lake District and my parents came to look after the girls. I hadn't told them about our problems and my Dad thought the break was a good idea because I was unwell.

The hotel was lovely and the first night went ok. Next day he retook his marriage vows in a quaint little church, and I hoped and prayed he meant those hallowed words.

He also told me of the two nights he sat outside his parent's house and Colin's house trying to find the courage to go in and unburden his fear of me dying and leaving him with the responsibility of the girls. He was clearly in a lot of emotional pain and I reassured him that he couldn't get rid of me that easily. I would be fine and he wasn't to worry. I had to find a solution to ease his inner pain.

Later that evening as I soaked in a warm bath, the bedside phone rang. I heard Ron talking; as he popped his head round the door his expression spoke volumes. It was the doctor from St. Francis with my results of tests I had taken a short time ago. I felt his phone call was ominous. He explained in detail, "transmitted infection," "not good," and "I need you back here at once," was all I took in.

After a sleepless night we drove home in silence.

After several bouts of ill health I thought I was on the mend, Ron's indiscretion was about to take its toll, and he had to be seen to as well. The treatment was awful and the pills made me vomit so I wasn't a happy bunny. However, I picked myself up and to everyone outside our bedroom door life was 'wonderful'. 'Business as usual' was the sign pinned to my head.

St Annunsiata suggested we had a holiday at her home on Barra, on the Outer Hebrides. It was quiet, somewhere far away where time froze, and as I needed time to convalesce, the arrangements were soon made. The holiday was brilliant, the girls had such fun and I felt I had come home. I spooked Ron on several occasions when I would explain events in detail on the day-to-day life on the island from many years ago. The overwhelming feeling of being home was indescribable and taking us to visit places I had been once before was bewildering yet wonderful.
An old man sat on the same spot on the shore daily looking out to sea as if he was searching for something or someone. One day when Ron took the girls for ice cream I wandered down to the shore, and as I tiptoed barefoot among the rock pools the old man spoke.
"I knew you would return in my lifetime." As he continued to speak to me in his native Gaelic his words melted into my heart and I felt an overwhelming love for him. I sat beside him and held him close. Why? I knew it was meant to be.
Ron stood for some time watching us and he admitted later

that the old man had looked at me with a deep unspoken love. "How do you know?" I asked.
"I know because I want to look at you like that and tell you things but something always makes me feel I don't deserve you" he replied.
I kissed away his fears and told him I didn't have to be told. He visibly relaxed and our pleasant day continued.
The island brought me a comfort I had never known. On the day we sailed out of Castlebay I cried until the island was out of sight. I would return.

Home again I thought normality would return!
On a night out at the social club my parents joined us. The place was very busy and once again Margaret, Pete and Mary were in attendance. An hour after we arrived Ron whispered in my ear "Don't you dare cause a scene tonight." I ignored him and moved to sit beside my dad. I came back from the ladies to see Mary chatting amicably with my Dad. As I approached my Dad said "You've never introduced us, as they are friends of yours I've asked them to join us."
"She's no friend of mine" I replied, as my Dad looked at me with a puzzled look her hand came from nowhere and slapped me full force across my face. I reeled back, the taste of blood in my mouth and the pain searing through my

face made me feel giddy. My Dad steadied me as Ron growled "look what you've done." Was he growling at Mary?

No he was growling at me!

As I looked over to him he was speaking gently to Mary. I grabbed my cardigan and handbag and flew out into the night.

As I stumbled up the long dark lane to the main road my thoughts reeling, my face on fire from the slap and blood oozing from my burst lip I didn't know where I was going. Arriving at Marjorie's flat nearby I looked a sorry state as she let me in. Marjorie had been having a few problems of her own and I felt awful for turning up on her doorstep but I truly didn't know where to go. As I blurted out the whole story, she kept re-filling my glass. Her phone rang and I froze, I heard her speak and I knew from her replies it was Ron. I was waving my hands franticly and mouthing "I'm not here."

Sometime later I decided to walk home. On the way Ron drove past me twice, he would later deny seeing me. I walked in the back door and the look of relief on my parents face was plain to see. I quietly set about making a cup of tea as their questions about the night's events rained down on me. How could I tell them? They held Ron in such high esteem, what could I say? As my mind was trying to find a suitable or acceptable reply Ron burst in and he didn't lose any time in his verbal onslaught. After some time I could hear screams, a raised voice, bewilderment and fright fill the air and it wasn't until my mother grabbed me that I realised, it was me!

I was screaming out my hurt, soon to be replaced by my sobbing. I sobbed like a wounded animal, nobody could console me and I asked them all to go to bed and leave me alone. They did, probably glad to be away from the wreck that stood before them.

As I lay curled up on the sofa the house now silent, my sobs exhausted, an inner glow descended and my Granddad's words came into my head. "Every situation has a solution, find yours."

Mary and I were both barred from the social club, although a few weeks later she was allowed back in, me I had no intention of ever stepping foot inside the place again.

Business as usual and Ron became more attentive towards me. He found it very difficult to live with his guilt and he was always apologising and asking me to forgive him. Forgive him I could because I still loved him. Forget, no, that would take time.

Something inside me changed, strength from deep within began to emerge and I took the following steps.

Windmill Road

Windmill Road was a huge detached sandstone Victorian villa that stood in very large and impressive walled garden. The house had lain empty for some time and I liked the feel of the place and it had great potential as a small hotel.
As I was still coming to terms with Ron's affair and previous numerous one night stands to which he had confessed I needed to know within my heart I could survive and provide a stable environment for my girls.
Who said "confession is good for the soul?" It may be for the one doing the confessing but not for the one who is being confessed too. With my married life in tatters and my heart feeling as though it had been ripped apart, I found an inner strength that made me feel twelve feet tall. I felt I was not walking alone.
I needed desperately to find a place to make my own and give me an income so I could be financially independent. Should I divorce or not was a question running around in my head.
Ron had pleaded forgiveness, renewed his marriage vows, and thought I would bounce back forgiving all he had told

me. Maybe I would, but in the meantime I had to plan my own survival, the girls deserved it.

An offer was

made on the house at Windmill Road and accepted. I only had four thousand pounds as working capital to find. The four thousand was to carry out repairs, any renovations and fully furnish the place, ready for business.

My parents were having another crisis in their marriage so I had the idea of them becoming live-in caretakers. That would give them a home, a purpose and a fresh start. It also meant they would be close to the girls, something that made me calm. They agreed.

My brother also decided to move to Hamilton with his girlfriend Caroline. Tom got a job and Caroline became a playgroup assistant at the local playgroup where I was Chairperson, and I helped them find a small rented flat.

Although I desperately wanted to trust Ron, a part of me questioned and questioned time and time again, why?

Why did I want to trust him?

Why should I trust him?

I loved him; it was as simple as that. Love has no boundaries and I loved him. Maybe one day he would come to know how much.

A local business man who owned a chain of well-known stores was more than willing to help fund my idea. I was offered advertising boards at the local football ground, as it was very close to Windmill Road and it would generate custom so I agreed.
An offer of an entry into the area Tourist Brochure for a greatly reduced fee meant the 'Wellington House Hotel' was about to be born.

Six weeks before my entry date my parents moved from Edinburgh. Their house contents were stored in our large garage and outside storage sheds, and they moved into our large spare bedroom.
My excitement grew, however Ron's did not. He became only too aware that I meant business and I would leave him and go it alone if I had to, the worm had turned. I had given years of my life to a man I thought I greatly loved and he had betrayed me more than once due to his insecurities.
I did not deserve it and I would no longer accept it.
I had been very ill, scared I was going to die and he had played away from home by having an affair. Making the excuse that too much booze had clouded his judgement.
Ron's constant badgering was beginning to wear me down.
One night after a shouting match in the bathroom, with all the taps gushing water to drown out our loud words, I

finally agreed to put it into joint names.
The four thousand pounds I needed he insisted he would find for me, he was experiencing cash problems but as they were only temporary I wasn't to worry. Ron asked me to go to his parents and ask for a loan of the money. He would have it repaid ASAP, they could afford it and as their younger son had had money from them, why couldn't he? I didn't want to and I was nervous because he insisted I went alone. His excuse for not going was that they wouldn't deal with my request fairly because of him.
I went and asked, they refused, he got mad then very drunk. He still insisted he would get the money for me. I had been given a set of keys to Windmill Road a few weeks before my legal entry date to allow me to have workmen in to provide estimates for work needing done and as the house had lain empty for some time the owners approved of this arrangement. Having my parents living at our house was proving a problem. My dad was a great help but my mum was a pain in the a…!
Ron began to help out as much as possible and began to look at me with a new set of eyes after he took on board I was determined to achieve my goal.
As the house was huge my parents would have their own sitting room and en-suite bedroom
The kitchen and utility room was a very large area so they

had their own space. With free heating, lighting, and phone they would only have to provide their meals themselves. I thought this was a generous offer however Ron thought I was mad and he was adamant it would back fire on me. However a situation was about to blow up.

My brother and his friend George who came through from Edinburgh to visit often had continually joked about finding me the money I needed and I always joined in their rapport because I truly thought it was their bravado. They had mentioned they could do a robbery somewhere and I decided to humour them instead of taking them seriously. One day they asked me to pick them up from the car park situated near the old part of town the following morning and I agreed. On the way to meet them I was held up by a huge livestock wagon trying to make a difficult manoeuvre into the local market place. As I sat and patiently waited thoughts ran through my head that they would be annoyed I hadn't turned up. I eventually made the car park but as I was very late they no doubt had got fed up and decided to take themselves off to wherever they were going. I sat for a few more moments then went home.

Caroline was in when I arrived back home and the look on her and Aggie's face meant something had happened. She asked if I had seen the boys and I explained I had been held up on my way to meet them and asked where they had been going.

"To help you," she replied.

"In what way" I asked.

"They've planned to rob the post office to get you the money," she said.

The next hour passed in a blur as my head was swamped with all the conversations we had had. I had joined in their joking and now my mind couldn't quite take in the facts. I decided to send Aggie down to the bakers shop opposite the post office to find out any gossip that was going around. Should it be true then it would be the talk of the place. Deep within I prayed and hoped they were of somewhere else safe and sound totally unaware of the panic that was absorbing Caroline and myself. Too soon Aggie returned and her face told us before she uttered a word.

Yes they had committed the robbery and they place was swarming with armed police with dogs and a helicopter was circling around the nearby Palace grounds looking for them. I decide to drive down to the park to see if I could see them and try to resolve this terrible mess.

On arriving at the park the place was deserted. I drove around saw nobody and decided to drive home.

On the television lunchtime news it was announced a robbery had taken place and two youths were in custody. My heart sunk, my mind raced and I fought the waves of nausea that now consumed me. Caroline was as white as a sheet and Aggie kept on saying the same things over and over again.

I still held firmly onto the idea it may have been other youths and not them. I kept hoping that any minute they would walk in and all our fears would disappear.

A knock at the back door made us all jump. When I saw the two plain clothes men standing before me I knew my worst nightmare had come to call. I invited them in and the detectives introduced themselves and explained why they had come. The younger of the two was so pleasant and I was as helpful as I could be under the circumstances. He said he would arrange for me to come down later to the police station to see my brother. He then asked to go to Tom and Caroline's flat to carry out a search. I agreed and Caroline went with them. I had to make a phone call to Ron and then try to contact my parents who were visiting friends in Edinburgh. After they left with Caroline I allowed my feelings to come to the fore. I cried and threw up several times before I was able to stop the shaking.

I couldn't reach my parents so I decided to wait until they returned.

I them phoned the depot to get a hold of Ron however he had already left so I then phoned his usual pub he dropped into before he came home hoping to catch him. On hearing

his voice on the other end of the phone I began to stammer uncontrollably which by this stage in my life was no longer a problem to me.
“What’s up darling? Are the girls’ ok? Take your time it can’t be that bad,” he said softly. I took a deep breath and blurted out “Have you heard about the armed robbery that took place today in town.”
His tone changed as he asked, “Yes, why?”
“It was Tom and George” I stammered.
“I’m on my way and he better keep out of my way,” he growled. The line went dead and I paced the floor until a short time later he burst in through the front door.
Aggie took the girls down to the swing park while I relayed all the details and facts that I knew. Ron kept silent as I spoke and the warmth from his hands as he held me close kept me from falling apart. However when I told him about me going down to meet them and how I had been delayed he blew his stack. His anger frightened me and I knew within that no words would help calm him. The back door opened and as my parents walked in Ron continued to rant and rave. While he went on I tried to inform them about the day’s events as gently as I could.
My dad was furious and through his anger he said he was washing his hands of him due to this. My mum turned on me and growled at me it was my entire fault. On hearing

her words towards me Ron stopped his ranting and turned on my mum.

"How dare you talk to her like that? Shall I tell you what I think of you?" He said.

I walked out of the room and left them all to exchange as many words as they wanted. I was totally drained I needed some space so I took myself off on a walk down to the swing park to meet Aggie and my girls.

A few hours later my dad took his sleeping pills and went to bed.

My mum sat in the kitchen continually crying and repeating the same things again and again. Ron was upstairs bathing the girls and I was on the phone making arrangements to see Tom. Aggie had gone down to see Caroline and arrange for her to come to our house to stay the night.

Once the girls were settled Ron and I went to see his parents to allow me to explain what would soon be public knowledge that my brother and his pal had held up the post office. They were kind and lost for words.

Next we went to Colin's house were Ron insisted on waiting in the car. I went in alone to ask advice on police procedures. Shona's look of disgust spoke volumes however Colin was as helpful as he could be and spoke kindly and his calm response washed over me. Once back

in the car I told Ron about Colin's warm and kind help.
"I've told you repeatedly he will always be there for you. No question about it I know he will always give you his time no matter what," he said. He then reached over and hugged me close. "He loves you as much as I do" he continued.
At the police station I went in alone while Ron sat outside and waited. The detective was kind and informed me the guns they had were fake however the ladies in the post office didn't know that so it was a very serious charge and all the money had been recovered.
"How much did they take?" I asked.
"This is what is strange out of all the money in the post office they insisted on only being given four thousand pounds" he replied.
I felt a huge surge of love for my brother overwhelm me. He would need a very good lawyer and he would be held in the cells until Monday where he would then appear in the local court. He would then be remanded until the High Court in Edinburgh dealt with his case.
He then asked, "I need your help. An officer has beaten up your brother and I need to know who it was. Can you ask Tom to tell you?"
I agreed then he led me down to the cells where he was locked up.

Sitting as far into the corner of the cell as he could get sat my brother. His appearance shocked me and anger rose from deep within me. We were left alone and within a few moments out he spilled all the details and more.

"I only wanted to help you sis. I'm so sorry, don't be angry with me," he sobbed.

"Is Ron mighty pissed off?" he said. "How did mum and dad take the news?" he continued.

I convinced him nothing would be a problem to me in connection with family and friends and anyway it would be a nine-day wonder. Before I left he gave me the name of the bastard of an officer who had beaten him up.

After another long conservation with the detective I was about to leave when I asked to speak to the said bastard alone.

He was a big ugly burly brute and as I smiled at him sweetly he asked most kindly if he could be of any help.

I walked over to the seating area and he followed. I turned around and through clenched teeth an animal sound of snarling spat out low growls. I don't recall any words that passed my lips but the look on his face was of pure fear. I held his frozen stare and as he changed before my eyes I knew something was taking place but I felt outside looking in on the scene. I then politely thanked him for his time and left him standing staring at me.

With the household all in bed I sat long into the night in our darkened sitting room taking in the day's events. My brother's deed had been done for me. With only the thought of helping me he had not thought about any other outcome. I couldn't be angry with him, I was only sad.
Ron had awakened and came to find me. As he held me close he told me of his fears. Had I thought about the different outcome if I had been on time to meet them?
I was continually sick for the rest of the night. Every time Ron's words echoed in my mind I would be sick. By morning I was exhausted emotionally and physically.
The weekend flew by with Ron very rarely leaving my side. I made a few phone calls and soon a lawyer was arranged for Monday.
On Monday Ron went to work as my parents, Caroline and I went to the local court.
Tom and George were remanded in a detention centre an hour and a half drive away. Now my relationship with my brother would have to be by letter and a once a month visit split between my parents and Caroline.
The atmosphere around our home was awful so rightly or wrongly I decided to move my parents into Windmill Road the week before my official entry date. The move was carried out swiftly and with very little fuss. I never told anyone I had made the decision entirely on my own so if

my decision back fired then I would only have myself to blame. It was a risk I was prepared to take. The decision gave them their space to come to terms with what had happened. I also prayed it would bring about a closeness in them that had been missing for many years.

As they faced the first night on their own in their new abode I was preparing a meal for the two of us at home.

Woodside Walk Part 2

For the first time in six weeks we had our house back to ourselves. With the girls tucked up in bed Ron and I enjoyed a delicious meal with a welcomed bottle of wine. Later as we snuggled up in front of the fire Ron's words soothed over me and I felt safe and sound. He constantly reassured me how he felt towards us as a family. He would never leave me and that he would always be close to keep me safe and for any reason should he be away Colin would take over and help without any hesitation. That night his words touched deep within my heart.

Next day Ron came home for a short time in the afternoon to speak to me about an important matter and as the girls and Aggie were out I knew we wouldn't be disturbed. He lay on the bed and began by saying it was serious and I wasn't to ask him any questions until he had finished. His manner slightly alarmed me but I managed to keep hush as he had asked. He explained he was involved in something very serious and that he would no doubt be arrested on the Monday morning once the thing he was involved with was discovered. I was to arrange for the best lawyer we could afford and I was to keep my head held high and I was to promise to enlist Colin's help. His words began to scare me and I visibly crumpled into a heap onto the bed beside him. He was adamant in not telling me what the matter was because what I didn't know would be in my interests. His loving actions towards me made all my fears melt away. Melt away for at least the rest of the afternoon as he continued to love me in a way that made my whole being feel alive.

My friend Ronnie had given birth to twins very unexpected at St. Francis and I was due there later for a small celebration tea party to welcome the new arrivals. Trying to get ready with my head swimming with the afternoons events made me feel slightly unreal.
On my way into Glasgow Ron had asked me to call into his local to share a drink with his fellow drivers.
When I arrived he was in a very jovial mood and as he held me close and showed his feelings in front of the others I was taken aback as Ron was always reserved and respectful towards me around company. He called for order and asked the assembled company to join him in a toast. I looked on bewildered.
He began "This woman is my beautiful wife, a wonderful

mother and a very special person who has made my life worthwhile and I shall love her now and forever. I have been a shit at times but she has never stopped loving me or left my side and I am a very fortunate man who at times does not deserve her. Join me in a toast to her."

After a short space of time I made my leave and Ron walked me out to my car. I had managed to compose myself and as he held me close he whispered, "I meant every word in there and more."

"I know and I am very touched by your unexpected words" I replied.

"I have more than words to give you but you'll have to wait until the time is right and when the time is right you shall have everything you shall need" he continued.

He hushed my questions with a lingering kiss and then told me to get going or else I would be late.

During my drive to St Francis the words I had whispered during our very first meal came to mind. I had promised he would eat those harsh words he had said to me. His words and actions tonight had erased those first words.

I had a lovely night at St Francis welcoming Ronnie's unexpected twins. Being around the nuns and catching up with lots of chatter and laughter made me feel very relaxed. Then home to bed feeling good for the first time in many days.

The time on the clock stated it was 3.40am and the noise downstairs heralded Ron's arrival. His boys' nights out were becoming later and later. As I stood at the top of the stair his drunken state took me aback. He was so drunk he was finding it difficult to stand up and his slurred words made no sense. My anger had no impact at all as he only continued to slur and fall about the hall. I was concerned his noisy behaviour would wake the girls so I growled at him to shut up. He made the fourth step, fell backwards and landed in a heap knocking over the hall table and breaking the lamp that sat upon it.

When one is angry one finds incredible strength and I was no exception.

I hoisted him up the stairs while he draped his six foot seven body over my shoulders and back. As he landed in a heap on the bed his drunken state was being overtaken by a drunken slumber.

When his alarm went off two hours later it took a further twenty minutes for him to surface totally.

He was due in at the depot to conduct a little business and he asked me to meet him later with the girls to have lunch. I informed him about his antics and the breakages he had caused and he cheekily laughed it off.

I couldn't stay angry and as he rolled over beside me he loved me and kissed me as though it was the last time he ever would. When I commented on his warm deep passion so early in the morning he replied “I shall take this moment with me.”

Later that morning the girls and I met Ron and he decided to take Lyn with him on his last run to the depot. They would meet up with Louise and I later at our usual Saturday eating place for lunch.

Louise and I went to the local supermarket to pick up shopping to pass the time before we all met up.

Lunch was fun; the girls had a great time and Ron was completely at ease.

With the girls strapped into their car seats, outside the car Ron held me close.

“I will always love you. All of you are my life.” He whispered in my ear.

“One day you will know how much you mean to me. You have given me so much and I have not returned what I should have but one day you’ll know,” he continued as he held me so close.

Somehow I knew he was speaking the truth and at that moment I loved him more.

We drove out the car park leaving Ron to continue with the business he had to finish, he clowned around dancing, waving and making funny faces. The girls’ excited giggles about funny daddy remained until we reached home.

We had a big night out in Glasgow planned and as I had a hairdresser's appointment that afternoon, it was arranged my in-laws would baby-sit the girls as my parents were visiting friends in Edinburgh. Ron had forgotten his house keys so Caroline offered to stay at our house, so he could get in.

I also left word for Ron to uplift the girls from his parents' late afternoon.

Aggie and Caroline were looking forward to babysitting that night. They were so good with the girls that I never worried about them. They always had fun.

Ron arrived home and as he still had unfinished business to do he couldn't uplift the girls.

My parents, upon their return popped in to see the girls, and saved him. Ron explained he couldn't pick up the girls and begged my dad to do so.

As my dad had a soft spot for Ron he agreed, Ron was delighted. He hated going up to his parents alone, so my dad agreeing saved him an unpleasant task.

When I returned from the hairdressers, the house was full. My parents, the girls, Aggie and Caroline all talking and having fun.

My dad explained Ron had had to go out to conduct some

business he hadn't finalised and he would be home before we were due to leave for Glasgow. The business must have been connected with what he had already given me a hint of. I tried not to feel worried. Maybe tonight I would find out more while he had a drink in him.

After their bath time, the girls sat down to have tea with Aggie and Caroline.

My parents had left but had promised to call in later to spend time with the girls before bedtime.

Time ticked by with no sign of Ron and I was becoming slightly annoyed because we were going to be late for our night out. I was standing next to the wall phone in the kitchen when it rang, startling me.

"Hi darling, I'm running a little late but I'll be with you soon, be ready and don't keep me waiting for you." He laughed as he went on, "have I told you lately I love you? See you soon," he finished.

"I love you too, so move your butt," I replied.

As I stepped out of the bath I was hit with a tremor of pain shooting through my body. Very winded, I tried to pick myself up from the floor but was unable to do so. I crawled on my hands and knees towards the hand basin and with the pain easing I pulled myself to my feet using the hand basin to give me support. Sweat was lashing out of every pore and my breathing was very laboured.

I sat on the toilet and waited, this feeling would soon pass I prayed – and it did. Twenty minutes later, I was back to normal.

I dressed slowly, put on my make-up and made sure my hair was fine.

As I walked downstairs I felt caged and uneasy. Ron still wasn't home. Caroline and the girls were busy reading a story. Aggie noticed the change in me and said, "Why don't you phone the pub, he may have been held up." So I did. He had left shortly after he spoke to me, earlier.

I now paced up and down trying to keep calm. I felt like a caged tiger. I remember visualising a large White Bengal Tiger pacing with me.

The girls ran to the sitting-room window and looked out. Outside our neighbours' house next door sat a police car. The officers knocked at the door, no reply, they went on to the next house again no reply. Lyn asked where the policemen were going.

I replied, "To speak to someone, to help them."

At the end of our short street lived two spinster sisters. The younger of the two now walked along the street with the two police officers.

As they passed the police car I knew they were coming to

our house.

I turned to Aggie and with a strange tone in my voice I said "under no circumstances do you leave my girls tonight, no matter what. Promise me you'll take care of them." "I promise" she replied.

As I opened the front door Miss Stewart, the old lady walked past me without a glance into the sitting room.

The two officers now stood and shoe shuffled.

"Has there been an accident?" I said.

They nodded.

"Has Ron been taken to the Hospital and is it serious?" I asked.

They never raised their heads but their overall appearance spelt out doom.

"Are you trying to tell me he's dead?" I said.

They nodded.

Calmly, I reached into the nearby cupboard for my coat.

Aggie screamed and screamed. Caroline held the girls tightly and a black cloak of calmness swept over me.

I needed to be calm; to take in the events of what was happening. As we approached the police car I said "I can't sit in the back seat, I'll be sick."

So, as I safely sat in the front, we set off for the police station.

How? When? Why?

Was he badly hurt?

Was he badly marked?

Can I see him?

I must see him!

Their muffled replies did not ease my fears.

Does no one prepare police officers for this task?

Once at the police station in the waiting area, I was asked to sit down. I sat and answered their questions.

What was his full name?

What was his date of birth?

What he was wearing?

What colour and make of car did he drive?

Did he have any distinguished identifiable scars?

On and on their questions came.

"Please, let me see him" I quietly said. As they both walked away I said, "Is he badly hurt?"

"No" one replied.

Left alone, I heard screaming. A loud screaming that vibrated, where was it coming from I wondered. I looked around and I was truly alone yet the screams continued. The screaming was inside me yet outwardly I looked calm.

I began to walk around the large emblem that was printed on the floor tiles.

Round and round I walked.

The C.I.D. officer who had arrested my brother the week

before appeared. "Don't touch me," I hissed. He joined me walking around the floor emblem.

He asked many questions. I remember the look on his face clearly; it was a look of shock and disbelief.

He spoke calmly.

The police station doors burst open and my dad stumbled in. As he headed towards me I hissed, "Don't touch me."

"I won't, but don't shut me out!" he replied in a hushed tone.

We must have looked a strange sight as we all walked around the emblem on the floor.

The C.I.D. officer and my dad exchanged questions and answers while I could only hear the continued screaming.

A tall police officer with lots of gold braid on his hat and lapels joined us.

I shall call him the Hat!

With a disgusted look he explained they were now ready for us at the morgue.

I asked, "Is he badly marked?" "No" he replied.

So this procession headed out towards the morgue building, which was situated at the rear of the police station in a separate building.

Once inside the small waiting room within the morgue building, the gold braided Hat spoke!

"As we are short of staff and there is a lot of blood, I don't think it would be wise for you to see him."
The room was tightly packed with fluorescent-jacketed police officers and he had just said, "We are short staffed!"
With a sharp intake of breath I said, "I'll clean him up as he's my husband and it won't put your staff under any pressure. I looked around and continued saying, "it's very obvious you lack staff as they all want to be in this room and not next door!"
My dad stepped forward as he could see I was becoming a tad agitated and said, "I'll go in and if I think it's okay I'll tell you." I agreed.
He went with into the next room with two police officers wearing matching fluorescent jackets.
Gold Hat said, "Take a seat."
"No." I replied.
The others all made small talk and I backed myself into the corner furthest away from the door my dad had entered.
Time appeared to have stood still. I could hear everyone's small talk and the screaming still went on.
The door to the morgue opened and the two police officers supported my dad with his elbows.
He lowered the hankie he was holding over his mouth and pleaded "please, don't go in, don't go in pet."
The ashen look of horror etched upon his face will stay with

me to my grave.
Before I could reply I was hoisted up by my elbows and marched outside onto the pavement while the Gold Hat said "Now, now, don't cause a scene!" again before I could reply I was sat in the front seat of the police car that had brought me here. With my dad in the back seat along with the other police officer, they took us home. The lights on the dashboard of the police car shone like an aircraft control panel. Oh to fly away.
The car stopped outside my house, I got out. The front door of my house opened and out rushed my mum.
"Don't touch me," I hissed.
"Ellen, don't go near her, give her space," my dad shouted.
The house felt like a cocoon, my safe haven and I knew Ron was home.
The officers came back a little later to ask more bloody questions. I gave them their answers and they left.
Aggie informed me there was a problem with Ginger the cat. She was sprawled over the top landing step and wouldn't let anyone up to check on the girls. Ginger was never allowed upstairs so I went upstairs to check on the girls. Ginger purred and followed me into their bedroom.
Both asleep in gentle slumber land, carefree and contented smiles eased across their faces both safe and secure wrapped in their duvets. Too soon the morning would

arrive that would change their lives. As I made my way back downstairs Ginger took up her sentry duty yet again. Ron's parents needed to be informed so I decided the task was mine and mine alone.

My dad insisted he drove me there. I agreed.

On arriving, I braced myself and rung the doorbell. My father-in-law opened the door with a look of surprise.

I stood in the middle of their living room and explained as gently as I could that I had bad news for them. "Ron has been involved in a serious car accident and he's dead, I came to tell you personally because I didn't want the police to do so." I said softly.

My father-in-law walked past my dad and myself as though we didn't exist.

"I'll get Colin, he'll sort this out," he said.

"I take it Ron had been drinking?" said my mother-in-law.

What did it matter if he had been drinking, he was dead and these were the only words she could say to me.

In the background I could hear my father-in-law continually dialling the phone, obsessed with finding Colin.

I tried to find words but somehow they wouldn't come. They wouldn't have helped as they were on their own course of trying to take in what I had told them.

Somehow my word wasn't good enough; only Colin's word would be acceptable.

I turned to my dad and said “let’s go, get me out of here.”
As we left neither of them spoke to us.
Back in the car I said “she never had a good word for him when he was alive and it’s the same now he’s dead!”
I was angry at their response. He was their first-born. They should have shown some emotion. Not to worry, Colin would put it right!

As we drove home we made a detour to Marjorie and Charlie’s home to tell them.
I drank two large whiskies while I relayed the nights’ events.
During our friendship we had had some brilliant times together so we sat and recalled some funny events.
On leaving, Marjorie told my dad to phone the doctor, as I would need something to make me sleep.

We were only home a few minutes when my friend Elizabeth or Biff as our Louise called her, arrived breathless as she had ran from her home to mine.
She asked questions with a look of disbelief and she tried to hold me but I recoiled as she touched my arm. “Please, don’t touch me” I said softly.

The doorbell announced the arrival of the doctor. Dr

Sandilands had gone to school with Ron; he had the look of wanting to be anywhere but here. He spoke kindly and asked the questions that by now were the usual ones and suggested I received an injection to help me sleep. I was given the injection and the doctor escaped.

I didn't want to sleep. I wanted Ron. I knew he was close by waiting for me to be alone so he could come home.

A thought came to me...

Ron's wallet, loose change, belt buckle and watch minus its clip had been returned to me but where were his clothes? I asked.

"In a black plastic bag in the garage" my dad replied.

"Bring them here now" I insisted.

"If anyone is squeamish at the sight of blood leave now" I continued.

Ron's jeans, socks and under pants were intact. His shoes were clean with shreds of glass embedded into the soles. His sweatshirt was torn high on left shoulder with a dark green stain around the tear.

One thing puzzled me.

Why no blood? Not a blood stain on anything, so why had I been told that due to his blood loss and the mess I couldn't go in to identify him? I was confused.

Why had they not cut off his clothes?

Had they washed and dried them before returning them?

No answers or explanation were ever offered.

Aggie left promising to be back early morning. Caroline slept on the couch and my parents slept in the spare room they had moved out of a few days earlier.
Ginger our cat had lain over the top step allowing no one past as if protecting us and as I lay in bed she jumped up and positioned herself to watch the bedroom door.
Blackness overwhelmed me; so dense I could taste it. A feeling like being in a cocoon you could not see but it dulled every emotion. I would come to know the feeling well and welcome it but for the moment it swamped me.
Ron had come home and I was waiting. I knew he would and I'd be here.
I wore his t-shirt to bed, smelt his odour that lingered on it and let the blackness take me.

The morning began with the sound of chatter from the girls. They rushed into my bedroom and onto my bed and snuggled under the duvet, one on either side of me.
I hugged them close, breathed deeply and quietly explained Daddy had been involved in an accident. He was now in Heaven and he would always look after them and watch over them while they grew up. Tonight we would search the night sky to find him twinkling down on them.

I became aware of the sound of our sobbing echoing throughout the house.
That most heart wrenching noise is still with me today.
They sobbed and clung to me and I answered all their questions as honestly as I could. Ginger remained on my bed protecting us.
Once our sobs subsided my dad knocked on the bedroom door and brought in a tray of scrambled eggs, toast and tea.
He smiled and left.
He didn't know what to say. No words from him were needed. His usual dish served on a tray emitted his feelings.
I made the girls eat, then after a short nap we went downstairs to face the world that waited.
Once downstairs, last nights event swamped me. I poured myself a large whisky.

My dad and Colin were to go once again to formally identify Ron's body. No one ever told me why I couldn't.
I was going to the Young Offenders Prison where my brother was on remand to break the news of Ron's death to him personally. My brother had carried out his criminal act to benefit me and this journey to see him, although difficult, was my responsibility.
Shona, Colin's wife, drove Caroline and myself and although it was a kind offer somehow I didn't think she was

happy about doing so.
The prison staff were wonderful. A small room had been set aside and a doctor was on standby.
My news made his being locked up worse, he felt so helpless. His questions came rapidly and my answers didn't make much sense.
As we sat alone in that small room with the prison officers outside, the world took time off and a special quiet moment descended on us.
After I left he had to be sedated, his small cell became a medicated cocoon.

As we approached home, Shona ran into the back of a car at a roundabout. Not knowing what to do or say I jumped out the car and spoke to the other driver and exchanged all the relevant details. I felt so sorry for Shona and I did my best to alleviate her feelings.
On our return, the house was full with visitors so I decided to dart upstairs and hide. The sound of the two cars colliding began to echo and become louder in my mind.
Had Ron heard the same sound? Our bump had been a small one so Ron's must have been much bigger for him to die.
What was the last thing he heard?
What was the last thing he saw?

What was the last thing he felt?
My mind was filled with questions but the answers escaped me.
My dad sought me out and I explained I needed a stiff drink to get me through the next few hours, he obliged.

The girls had been taken to Biff's house to spend the day with her children.
The drinking friends of Ron's all arrived together, shuffling in to stand in a row like naughty schoolboys. I asked at what time he had left them the night before. They all mumbled words of sorts and never raised their eyes from the carpet while they oozed discomfort from every pore. I thanked them for coming and dismissed them. In record time they had gone.
Colin had got angry with Shona about the bump with the car so he took her to her parent's house and returned to my house. I could understand why she didn't want to remain at my house.
My in-laws were present but their actions and words from the previous night made me angry with them so I didn't want to speak to them.

Father Devany arrived; he was so kind his words gave me tremendous comfort.

I explained Ron's words and actions over many recent nights. I was so sure he was trying to explain something to me but I couldn't understand.

Father Devany explained Ron's actions were the actions of a man who deeply loved me and had wanted me to understand that he was having a feeling of something happening that he couldn't fully comprehend. Many people suffer feelings of something they don't or can't explain is going to happen to them.

When he finished speaking to me, Ron's words from those nights came into my mind and at that moment his words made sense.

Minister Barrie arrived a short time after Father Devany had bid me farewell.

Arrangements were detailed and planned. A short service in our home, while Ron rested outside in the hearse and then onto the new cemetery at High Blantyre on the outskirts of his hometown. The minister was new to the parish and he was visibly excited at the prospect of a big funeral so new into his arrival.

When he left I was relieved to see him go.

My dad became very protective. I wasn't allowed to answer the door, the phone or to drive and when I left the house I always had someone with me. Dad and Colin became my

protectors.
Before he left for home, I stood alone with Colin in the hall. I held his hand and asked what really happened to Ron. He didn't have the answers to help. He looked lost as he left and I thought you have lost more with your brother's death than you will ever know.

Aggie washed dishes continually. My parents moved back into my spare room and made sure every visitor to the house was well looked after and Caroline spent time with the girls.
I spoke to the undertakers, who would uplift Ron from the morgue. As I had not been allowed to see him I asked if they could make him nice so I could kiss him goodbye. They reassured me they would do their best.
The meal after the funeral was to be held at the house. Homemade soup, homemade steak pie with the trimmings and a good dram would suffice.
To cater for at least fifty meant a huge undertaking but my parents and Aggie set to it.
I ordered all the food and they cooked. Friends and neighbours handed in plates and cutlery. A nearby pub supplied the glasses.
My dad and my father-in-law, Joe, went to the cash n' carry to buy the drink needed for the funeral. I had given my dad

£75 and the total bill came to £100. So he had to ask Joe to give him the shortfall, promising he would give it to him when they returned to my house. Later, before Joe left my home, he asked my dad for the money back. I was out, so my mother repaid Joe!

The undertaker phoned to explain I couldn't have a dark wooden coffin as I had requested. They only had a lightwood available. Why? I asked.

Ron was so tall he wouldn't fit the dark coloured one.

"Easy" I said, "break his legs."

A sharp intake of breath on the end of the line plus everyone in the kitchen took a sharp intake of breath too. Aggie dropped cups in the sink and my dad eased the phone from my grip.

Ron would have laughed at my statement because that was his type of humour.

I went to see Ron's car, it was under a tarpaulin on a break down loader. My dad asked the garage owner to remove the tarpaulin to allow me to see it; he obliged and left us alone. The driver's side of the car was perfect, the other side was a mass of tangled metal. I thought that by viewing the car it would help me understand what happened, it didn't.

I was surviving on hot chocolate, sandwiches and large

whiskies. One to get me out of bed, one to get me out of the house and another when I returned.
The smell of food made me want to vomit.

I went with my dad to view Ron in the chapel of rest, or that is what I thought we were going to do.
They gently explained his injuries were so severe that to view him was impossible.
I was ushered into a small room where his coffin lay. The lid was positioned in such a way that he was only visible from his lower chest to his feet and I asked to be left alone.
I spoke words of my love to Ron. I held his hand, kissed it knowing this would be the last time I would ever be close to him physically and placed a letter with a photograph of our little family and a single red rose on his chest. I also held his feet knowing he would never walk beside me again.
I had to look upon his handsome face once more and kiss him goodbye and as I put my hands on the lid ready to lift it off my dad and the undertaker walked in.
"Somehow I thought you would try to do this," my dad said.
The undertaker screwed down the lid of the coffin as we watched then handed me the small gold tops of the said screws explaining that the coffin was now impossible to

reopen.
As I now inspected the coffin I noticed the age on the brass nameplate was wrong, maybe if I prayed hard enough I could have him back till he reached the age inscribed.
On leaving the undertakers what was left of my heart had been blown to pieces, the chance to see him visibly again was now gone.

Tuesday the 25th September was my brother's birthday.
A prison warder walked into his cell that morning and asked him what would be the best present he could receive.
"To go home to my sister as she needs me" was his reply.
"Get your gear, that's where you're going," he told my brother.
Outside the prison gate my brother ran all the way to the nearest main road and flagged down the first heavy goods vehicle that came along.
Ron's C.B. radio handle was Rubber Duck and many, many drivers knew him. The driver of the lorry he stopped knew Ron and had heard about his accident. Once in the cab, Tom explained where he was going and why. The driver left his route and dropped him off outside our house – a true knight of the road.
When he walked into my house my mother thought he had escaped, Caroline burst into tears and he asked Dad where I

was.
He knocked gently on my bedroom door, eased it open and blew a soft whistle in my direction.
I had been sitting on the bed staring out of the window, when I turned around at the sound of the noise I was shocked to see him, it wasn't until he sat down beside me that I knew he was real.
I had wanted him to be home so much and here he was.
Why hadn't that worked with Ron?

On Thursday morning of the funeral I went to have my hair done. The same girl had done it the Saturday Ron was killed; she now asked what special occasion it was for this time. "My husband's funeral" I said. She froze in shock; I then spent time being my usual smiley chatty self to put her at her ease.

Paul was a small boy the same age as my Louise who was deaf and dumb and wore a special box to help him with his disability. He lived opposite the side gate to our house.
Louise and Paul spent many hours playing, she was always gentle and firm with him and in someone who wasn't yet three years old, it was a delight to watch.
His mum had silver service waitress skills so she offered her services to help us with the funeral meal.

Marjorie's mother in law was also a sliver service waitress and she arrived to help too.

As the morning gave way to the afternoon, we now had a total of 84 wreaths and sprays of flowers lined up in our large hall, down both sides of the drive and covering the full floor of the garage. The smell was overwhelming.
Dad had phoned the undertakers earlier to arrange another car to carry the flowers. Many people had paid good money for these beautiful tributes so they had to be treated with care.
The hearse arrived and I made my way out towards where my darling now lay bedecked with flowers.
The service in the house was simple and short.
During the service a tremendous warm feeling engulfed me that was so overwhelming that I whispered to my dad something special was happening. He patted my hand and said quietly "you're fine."
The house was so full with people it took some time for everyone to file out into their appropriate mode of transport.
At the end of our road, Tam, who owned the video hire shop, stood on the pavement with his right hand placed over his heart and his head bowed. I was touched by his act of kindness.

The policemen appointed at certain roads made sure the funeral cortege moved through the town centre with ease. As we approached the cemetery, the scene was full of buses, cars and a sea of black dressed people massed together like a flock of black birds. I said to my dad "what a huge gathering of people, someone's getting a good send off."
"They're all here to pay their last respects to your Ron" he said.
The people and the flowers became a blur but the sound of the rain battering off the lid of Ron's coffin became deafening. The minister's words went unheard, as the raindrops were relentless.

Ashes to ashes, dust to dust, I picked up a small handful of dirt to throw into Ron's open grave and as the rain hit off my hand the dirt quickly turned to a muddy trickle through my fingers.
I wiped my hand down my skirt.
The pile of sodden earth lying nearby would soon fill in this hole that was to bear Ron's remains. This would be the last thing we would share. The small amount on my hand belonged to me.

My knees felt weak and I grabbed for my dad. With the help of him and my Uncle Sonny, they soon had me seated in the funeral car.

As Ron's parents and brother filed into the seats in front of me, I heard my mother-in-law complain about the rain and how wet she was.

"Ron couldn't do anything right when he was alive and he can't even get the weather fucking right now he's dead" I said.

"You're fine," said my dad as he continued to pat my hand he said, "If it rains on the day of a funeral, the corpse is happy."

"Well he must be fucking delirious if this rain is anything to go by" I replied.

Once again, he patted my hand and said "You're fine."

The smell of home cooking filled the house and as each person arrived they received a drink and were shown to a seat.

My friend Biff had the girls, so I had only myself to cope with.

I felt so alone; I escaped to my bedroom with a large drink to ease my inner turmoil. Soon I would have to go downstairs and mingle with the family, friends and colleagues who had returned to the house.

As all the dishes were being cleared away I was taken aback by the clockwork precision that had come into play to allow a few people to feed so many so quick.
Drinks flowed and soon everyone had a story to tell about Ron or the ‘Big Yin’, as he was known. The house was filled with kind words and the sound of laughter.
I couldn’t have asked for a better send off for Ron.

Biff returned with the girls before everyone had left. The girls clung to me as everyone who left pressed money into their hands.
As my in-laws left by the back door, they explained they needed milk; they hadn’t had time to buy it earlier due to the funeral. The funeral had been at 2pm! “Give them milk,” I told Aggie.

I wanted to be alone tonight, the girls and me alone in our home. So I sent off Tom and Caroline to their flat nearby. My parents took Aggie home before returning to Wellington House.
I bathed with the girls, lay on my bed and answered their many questions, read them a short story then tucked them snugly into their beds. I sat and watched them fall asleep before I tiptoed downstairs. With only the small lamps giving off a warm glow, I sat on the sofa and sank into the

cushions.
A large pile of letters and cards; 84 to be exact, lay on the coffee table alongside the cards from the flowers that now bedecked a huge area surrounding Ron's grave. Earlier my dad had went to the cemetery to collect them.
The house was silent; I felt we were in a protective cocoon.
As I poured myself a large drink the phone rang.
"I don't want to disturb you, I only want to know you're all okay," my dad said.
I reassured him everything was fine and hung up the phone.

I sat down and began to read the cards from the wreaths.
Kind words of sympathy, comfort and love leapt out of every card and letter. So many from people who cared, yet I felt truly alone.
The screaming was still as loud. Over the last few days I had had to make an effort to ignore the constant screaming.
Someone knocking gently on the inner glass door brought me back to present time.
As I approached the door I recognised the shape as my dad.
I opened the door and smiled. "What's up?" I asked.
"Promise me you won't do anything silly" he replied.
"I can see your pain and I know how much Ron meant to you but please, reassure me that you're okay on your own tonight" he continued.

"Dad I'm fine, you've kept the world away from me the last few days now let reality come to rest with me. I'm fine, the girls are sound asleep and I'm going through the cards and letters, so go home and try to get a good nights sleep. I'll see you in the morning" I said gently.

I locked the outside storm door when he left and returned to my cards.

As I walked through to the kitchen to pour myself another drink, I got as far as the huge arch that separated the sitting room from the dining room, when I felt myself being hugged very tight and close to something I couldn't see. My heart began beating faster and I felt frightened for a few moments when I realised who was holding me.

"I'll be here but I won't be here." I remembered his words and I said out loud "Ron I know you're here, you've never left but please, don't frighten me."

His grip became gentle and I stood there until his grip on me melted away. He had crossed the great divide to show me love. I couldn't see or hear him but I knew within my heart he was close.

Next morning was the first day of our back to normal routine.

I didn't know what normal was or what normal was expected so we did our best.

After bath time the girls ran into the sitting room and flung open the curtains and began to squeal loudly that daddy had come to say goodnight.

Aggie, Caroline, my dad and myself walked towards the window. Above the house opposite hung a huge bright twinkling star. The girls jumped up and down excitedly waving and blowing kisses towards their star.

I had previously explained Daddy was now the brightest star in the night sky and he would always appear to say goodnight and as on cue, he had appeared.

As I stood taking in the scene I recognised this bright object, it was the same one that had come to visit me since I was 10 years old. I turned to my dad and said "Venus, dad." He smiled and said "a Heavenly Angel only doing her job." Our Heavenly Angel appeared every night and when it was cloudy or overcast the girls still blew their goodnight kisses skywards.

I had been invited to a meeting with the procurator fiscal to discuss Ron's accident. As the gent who sat before me eyed me over his half glasses that were perched on the end of his nose he reminded me of a turkey. A look of distaste was etched on his face.

He began by stating time, date and place of the accident. Next was Ron's full name, date of birth, address and date of death. Next he listed Ron's injuries from his neck down to his feet. Broken bones I could understand, other medical terms went over my head.

He was most perturbed when I was unable to agree that Ron had hardening arteries of the heart. I explained as I wasn't a doctor, how could I know. He also explained the alcohol level in his blood and could I accept this. I simply nodded. Shortly after this, I was dismissed.

I left and as I walked along the pavement my dad arrived in his car. He had been driving past for the last half hour hoping to bump into me. He took me for a drink and I ranted and raved about the most awful time I had just encountered. It had been a waste of time, when was someone going to tell me the bloody truth about Ron's accident? I felt very down and the screaming was at a crescendo. It took many drinks to dull the pain but the drink didn't block out the screaming.

The visit to our lawyers wasn't much better. Grant listed all our assets first and it looked healthy. Next he listed all our debts and I laughed and said, "You're joking, your sense of humour is improving."

He didn't smile, reality kicked in immediately and I knew it was serious. Next was a list of our insurance policies. Two were up to date the others had lapsed and due to the arrears on them being more than three months they could not be reinstated.

One policy paid off fully Wellington House in Windmill Road. The other paid out a few thousand pounds. I was now facing payments on two mortgages on our own home.

The bank account held less than twenty pounds and the Halifax account held only twenty-seven pounds.

I was in a state of total shock.

Where was our money?

Why so many lapsed policies and why so much mortgage arrears?

To take my mind away from the questions Grant filled in all the forms that were required to claim my Widow's Mother's Allowance. Our weekly income had been in excess of £180 to £200, now I was to receive less than sixty pounds per week to live on.

Somehow I had to find money to pay off all the debts.

Debts do not die with the deceased so my whole life was going to change and change for the worse.

Credit cards were cut in half and an arrangement was agreed to repay them. The only credit card I insisted and I mean insisted to the point of throwing a tantrum was my Marks & Spencer one. As long as I could continue to dress the girls as I had always done, I would not have to skimp on their clothes. Grant agreed.

I swore Grant to let no one know about my situation.
I needed time to think, time to get my head around all I had to take in. When I left his office I went up to the cemetery, to sit and talk over with Ron what the hell was going on.
How?
Why?
When?
Where was all our money?
As I drove out of the cemetery gates my mask went on and I became an actress.
No one and I mean not one person was going to know of my present financial situation.
No one was going to think badly of Ron for leaving me with no money and a pile of debts.

Ron's work jacket had a few hundred pounds in the top pocket and a bit of paper with a long list of numbers on it. His wallet also contained a large sum of money plus more numbers, none of which matched the first list.
Ron was going to be arrested on Monday he had told me. So now I would have to be a detective and try to find out what he was involved in.
I sat alone into the early hours pouring over facts and figures. I lifted the phone several times to phone Colin but was unable to dial his number.

Who could I tell?
Who could or would help me?
I needed time, time to think.

The cemetery was to become my bolt hole when I couldn't cope with acting as though everything was fine. I would go there more and more, to sit listening to Ron's music tapes or to scream out loud to the moon or plead to the body lying beneath the grave, whom everyone said was Ron, to give me answers.
Ron had been involved in something serious and criminal, maybe he had taken all our money and was hiding out somewhere and soon he would send for us to join him. There had been a lot of blood so maybe the person in the car had been someone else who was wearing Ron's clothes? Or maybe…
Many scenarios ran through my mind. I had to find answers. How or where I didn't know.
All this extra worry on top of losing Ron in a horrific car accident at times became too much so I shut people out. It was the only way I could keep it all together.
The girls were so precious to me. From the moment of each birth they made me feel whole, I loved them so much so I had to keep their young lives as normal, safe and secure now and always.

They made me smile, their hugs made time stand still for a few moments and a calm would embrace me.

With my brother I went back to see the car however this time I took it to bits. I explained to the garage owner I was looking for a gold chain Ron had been wearing but hadn't been in his personal belongings returned to me by the police.
My brother stood looking at me as though I was possessed. I sat in the drivers seat and it was fully intact. I gripped the steering wheel and said out loud "well Ron, show me how it happened."
He hadn't been wearing his seatbelt, if he had he would have suffered whiplash and walked away.
The passenger seat was stained with blood and I followed the stains up the door, over the inner roof down towards the back passenger door and onto the seat behind the drivers. Two bottles of perfume lay in the glove compartment.
I opened the back door and took in the dark green stains. As I knelt on the seat blood oozed into my tights like a sponge. The boot contained the shattered remains of the windscreen. Four bottles of perfume, numerous bits of paper, which I took. Who was all the perfume for? It wasn't for me as I only ever wore one type. Ron's bomber jacket that was wrapped in a ball of hardened blood, again with dark green

stains.

Under the seats, beside the spare tyre, every wee nook and cranny, I examined best I could. I never found the chain.

By the time I left the garage my legs were all bloodied, my tights all ripped and my hands and nails ingrained a deep red with Ron's blood.

Ron was mine and only mine. I had to find a way out of this mess.

Woodside Walk Part 3

The upstairs part of the house had three very large bedrooms and I now had to generate an income to pay the mortgages.

So…

The largest bedroom became my new sitting room. My brother moved my beautiful stone built fireplace from our sitting room and re-built it upstairs. The carpet was also lifted and re-laid upstairs. Papered and painted, it looked lovely and cosy.

The girls shared the next bedroom and a play area was made from the spacious upstairs landing.

I then sold my wall unit, stereo unit, my dining room cabinet plus any other unwanted items. The money from these paid for cheap carpet to be laid downstairs.

An idea had sprung to mind. Ron had been in haulage. A large main car park in town at night was used as a haulage park up. Eating in town wasn't cheap so I could offer home cooked meals.

Leaflets were printed and distributed in the car park and a small toilet was added onto the back of the house, so our own bathroom upstairs would remain private. With two large tables and ten chairs I could do two sittings if it was a success.

Aggie and Caroline agreed to help. No one else knew of my plan. The first night arrived, I had made food for six people if more was required the freezer was full.

I told Aggie and Caroline I would do the first night alone. Caroline and Tom were having the girls for an overnight stay.

Was it a success?

I'll never know.

I sat on a dining chair with the lights out, listened to the knocks on the back door and heard the questioning mumbles. Then silence.

Hours later I got up from the chair, cold and stiff, then went and lazed in a hot bath and wept.

Why had I taken cold feet?

Simple… I was scared, so scared it wouldn't work. I had always believed in myself. Now my belief was shaken and I was scared.

Ron may have had his faults; everyone has but one sure thing he cared for me.

Now, I had no one who cared, so I was shaken and scared. The situation needed a solution.

The Sunday Post newspaper had printed details of Ron's accident and death before he had been dead twelve hours so our telephone had been constant with friends and people who knew us calling to confirm what they had read. This added to my distress and when I contacted them to complain the only explanation I was given "Well it is news," how sensitive from a family newspaper!
The small piece didn't go unnoticed by a local young man who began to watch our house late at night.
I thought my best course of action was to ignore him.

Pat was a business friend of Ron's. He was never brought to the house as Ron described him as dodgy.
Ron had known him for many years. He would appear without warning, stay around for several weeks then disappear without warning or explanation. He had shown up three weeks before Ron died and I knew he had something to do with the lists of numbers I had found in Ron's car and jacket. However a few days before Ron's death he went AWOL.
Mike was a good friend of Ron's and he phoned asking to come and see me. I agreed. He explained Pat was back and he wanted to see me. Pat had parked near the house on several occasions but hadn't the courage to come to the door and introduce himself. Mike had told him about my

actions on trying to track down information relating to the lists of numbers.

I thought over his request for a few moments and agreed to meet him a couple of days later at Mike's house.

Pat came across as friendly and likeable. I could see why Ron had liked him. He appeared truly shaken by the loss of Ron. He asked about the numbers on the lists and I told him what I had done.

On knowing Ron hadn't been given his share of the scam that he and others had been involved in I made it my business to track down those involved.

Ron's death made everyone awkward whenever they were around me so it didn't take long to get names and addresses. I then paid them all a visit and asked awkward questions. Soon I had the place where the goods had been taken.

I walked into a large shop that sold everything you could think of that was situated between the town centre and a local housing estate in a nearby town. I asked for the manager and introduced myself. His face went deep red and he suggested we spoke in private in the back shop.

"No, here will do" I said.

"I know where the goods are and I want Ron's share," I continued.

"I've nothing to say. I can see you're upset but I can't help you. I'm sorry" he said

"I know how much the load was worth," I bluffed as I took out the lists and held them in my fist.

"I want Ron's share or I shall report you to the police. Ron's dead and they can't prosecute a dead man but they can prosecute you." I said firmly.

"Sorry, I can't help" he said in an arrogant manner.

"So be it," I replied and I left the shop.

Outside I reached under my car seat and picked up the heavy metal wrench I kept there. Within a few moments I had broken four large panes of glass that accounted for most of the shops display windows.

As I was about to break the next window Sandy the manager came running out, he stopped dead as he saw me.

"I want Ron's share or else" I said.

"It had been a waste of time, we made no money from it" he shouted.

"You're such a liar," I said.

"Ron is dead and you stand there and call yourself a mate of his. I don't think so," I shouted back.

With the lists in one hand and the wrench in my other I walked towards my car and stopped. I turned and said in a raised voice "you can have this as I don't need it."

The wrench flew towards the window, hit its target and landed in among his display.

I drove off not stopping my shaking until I reached the sanctuary of the cemetery.

Pat appeared shocked by my actions. “Ron always said you were so special but he could never fully explain how or in what way. I think I understand what he meant by that,” he said.
He told me about himself, his wife and his young daughter. He came across as okay. “Do you want me to visit Sandy?” He asked. “No need” I replied. “Two days later a large envelope was delivered to the house containing money. Not Ron’s entire share but I didn’t care it satisfied my actions.” I explained.
“Anyway he did have windows to replace.” I laughed.
Pat said, “You’re a crazy woman.”
I replied “grief does that to a person.”
Over the next few weeks him and his family dropped in to see me a couple of times per week.

On the 11th of December my brother was sentenced at Edinburgh High Court to 4 years for his part in the robbery he and his friend had committed. I felt numb throughout the whole time it took the judge to deal with the case and I had to fight the urge not to be physically sick. I had lost Ron now my brother who had done so much for me was about to be taken from me. We were all allowed a few minutes to say our good-byes and I knew my words and actions were inadequate but it was all I could muster. The screams were washing over me in waves I needed to be alone.

Later that night Caroline and I went to the cinema. Why? To do something normal but still be with each other yet alone. As the film progressed we became lost in our own worlds.

Colin continued to drop in almost every day at some point and I was always glad to see him, as were the girls. He had a way of making me feel at ease and I was sure he enjoyed his visits. I always felt safe when he was around and on several occasions I was very close to confiding in him but I couldn't be sure he would understand. Innumerable times during our marriage Ron had always insisted his brother would be the one to do right by me. He also insisted Colin had feelings for me and that made Ron feel comfortable because he was adamant he would definitely stand by me whatever.

The run up to Christmas was awful but I decided the girls would have many presents and lots of fun. I also decided to invite both sets of parents as usual for Christmas dinner. Bad mistake.

While I prepared dinner downstairs I could hear the girls

having great fun upstairs, however, their fun was abruptly stopped and as they came running downstairs to me, their cries became louder. As they spilled out their tale of woe I became slightly annoyed. Papa had told them off for being too noisy and my dad then said they both needed a good smack for being too excited.

I marched upstairs and informed everyone sitting glued to the television that this was a difficult day for everyone so a little patience was not too much to ask then I about turned and headed for the bathroom with the girls in tow. Behind the locked door we sat huddled together on the carpet and cried while everyone continued watching television. The meal passed quickly and I was so glad to see everyone leave.

Colin and Shona invited their parents, my parents, Caroline, my friends and myself to their house for Hogmanay. We all sat making pleasant and useless conversation while trying to hear the radio to announce the New Year bells. As everyone wished each other awkward best wishes I escaped out of the back door with a drink in my hand and sped off in the car to the cemetery.

For a short time alone with my memories and my shattered heart I prayed for my love to return and carry me off to some distant shore to bring me inner peace. I waited but my love didn't come.

On my return my dad met me outside the back door.
"Did they leave the gates open for you?" He asked. "You are getting another chance to start again so think hard about what you want," he continued. "Be who you are meant to be."
"Don't lecture me on what to do as you've no idea about what is going on," I hissed.
"Confide in someone, any bloody one to get whatever is on your mind out in the open" he said through clenched teeth.
"Get lost dad Ron's dead and you've no right to moan and go on at me" I replied.
He smiled and replied, "I only want what is best for you. A happy New Year pet."
Everyone was showing impatience to leave so when Shona's parents said they were leaving it was a mad dash for all the parents to leave. When they left Shona was upset that Caroline, Marjorie and myself weren't making any move. Colin went to pore out drinks for us all and she dashed upstairs furious. I suggested we left but he insisted we remained. "Now that the oldies have left let's party" he went on.
"I don't think we are welcome maybe we should go. I don't want to cause any upset between you both" I said.

“This is my house too and I want you all to stay” he replied. So we stayed for a short time and as we were about to leave Shona stormed downstairs and flew out the back door. I brought her rapid departure to Colin’s attention but he wasn’t interested. I knew it was time to leave.

As we all sat in the car I asked Caroline where my handbag was and as she had forgotten to pick it up it was still lying beside the armchair. Whenever we were out Caroline always looked after my handbag so I jumped out of the car and was about to knock on the front door when Colin opened it and I went in.

“I knew you would come back,” he said.

“I’ve only come back to uplift my handbag” I replied.

As I reached the chair I felt warm arms sweep me into a loving embrace. I felt giddy and next warm and moist lips met mine. My head began doing somersaults and my emotions soared as did Colin’s who was holding me so close. His tongue found my mouth and I was lost.

Ron didn’t kiss me like this?

Who was kissing me?

Colin’s arousal brought me to my senses and I had to get away as this wasn’t right but it felt right so my confusion intensified so I found it difficult to leave his embrace.

“Please, stay I need you” he said.

“No I have to go” I replied. The sound of my car horn

brought reality wham into place. He continued to beg me to stay until I reached the front door then I didn't look back but I knew he was watching me as I left.

In silence we drove home I was totally shocked. A kiss with such passion and feelings cannot be written off lightly or ignored. A kiss with such emotional content is truly given and intensely felt. On returning home after dropping off the girls Aggie asked what was wrong. I could not explain, I did not have the words. When she left to go home I sat alone in the darkness and I allowed my feelings to emerge and I sobbed until the dawn.

The following day I telephoned him and asked him to come and see me, as I needed to confirm what had taken place had in fact taken place. At first he declined but eventually he agreed and duly arrived. He stood several feet away from me yet the true feelings we both had felt the previous night vibrated around us. We chatted away most mundanely and he left. The subject would return to haunt me.

One night a few weeks later when I was tipsy, I told Pat about Colin and what had happened at Hogmanay. "I know all about Colin" he said.

"How did you know?" I asked.

"Ron confided in me on many occasions" he said.

"I also know how much he loved his daughters and you,"

he continued.
Colin was a treasure, helpful, kind and thoughtful but he kept his distance. When I did encounter him, his eyes always gave his true feelings away.

The young man who was watching the house now became a problem. He began moving the girls' outdoor toys around the back garden during the night and on one occasion when Caroline and I returned from a night out in the wee small hours he rung my doorbell. I flew to answer the door in a rage, no one rang the doorbell at least no one who knew us. There before me stood a slight small young man who smiled up at me and said, "Can you tell me where I can get dancing lessons."
"Dancing lessons! It is 3am and you ask me about fucking dancing lessons. Are you totally insane? I growled and spat.
"So sorry don't be alarmed I only wanted to know if I could help you" he replied. He then smiled turned and walked off towards town.
Next morning I contacted the police who came to see me and noted all the bazaar things this young man was doing. As they left he was stood in his usual position looking towards the house. They picked him up and took him to the police station where he was cautioned and told to keep away from my home.

A few days later a polite middle-aged couple called to explain they were the parents of the young man who had alarmed me. They apologized and insisted he had meant no harm. Somehow I believed them and their calmness soothed me.

Maybe I had been a bit harsh in reporting him to the police so I decided to walk around to where he lived with his parents to confirm I had truly accepted their apology. The house appeared empty and a sale sign was in the garden. Maybe I had taken their house number down wrong so I decided to ask the next-door neighbour. She was most helpful and informed me the house had lain empty for some time. The previous occupants had been a lovely middle-aged couple with a young son in his twenties.

"Had been?" I enquired.

"Why yes, they moved when he died" she replied. "When was that?" I asked.

"About six months ago. He was involved in an accident and he couldn't' walk anymore which in turn meant he couldn't dance again. He never recovered and they moved shortly afterwards." She explained.

The screaming that plagued me swamped me and I bid a very hasty retreat and bolted to the cemetery.

Sometime later back home I explained the events to Aggie who seemed to accept the whole situation as real and meant. I insisted she went to see the house and speak to the neighbour to confirm I wasn't going insane. She went. She returned and confirmed all details and told me to take from it what I was being given. As she was the one now making no sense I decided to drop the whole subject to allow me to retain my sanity.

Lucy was a very big lady in weight and mouth. She was a good laugh and we enjoyed many social nights out with a group of acquaintances from the mother and toddler group. She had married a man older than her and they had a young daughter ages with my Louise who was a little sweetie. Lucy had a reputation of being unfaithful on numerous occasions and her long suffering husband Rob was so quiet and gentle he always turned a blind eye. It was not my place to judge her about her behaviour but I must be honest and admit she was never unfaithful whenever I was around. Her forever-jovial mood made her good company and at times she helped chase away my inner turmoil.

On one of our nights out together, Caroline and I ended up at the house of a friends of Lucy's to celebrate their house warming. Pat and Ann his wife accompanied us.
We arrived at the house in a jovial mood and soon after all the introductions we settled into a pleasant evening. A

young stud had arrived and Lucy and her close pal Sharon had decided he was to be their catch for the evening. Rob was pouring drink down his throat at an alarming rate to dull his feelings over Lucy's indecent behaviour.

I turned to Caroline and said, "Let's go I don't want to be here."

"I'm going to the loo, you get our coats and I'll meet you at the door" I continued.

Rob was walking behind me up the stairs.

"You'll have to wait. I'll only be a few moments," I said to him.

He nudged me in the small of my back as I walked into the loo. As I straightened myself up I turned to see Rob close the loo door, lean against it and slip the bolt.

"What are you doing?" I said stammering.

"She's not the only one who can play away," he slurred.

He began to unbutton his shirt and I felt a panic rising in the pit of my stomach. I climbed into the bath and stood stalk still trying to put space between us and kept talking in as calm a voice as I could muster.

As he began to undo his trousers I heard voices outside the door.

Thank God I thought.

The first thud on the door startled me. The angry words being shouted told me Lucy was on the opposite side of the door and I knew I'd soon be safe. How wrong was I? Soon her thuds were replaced by kicks to the door.

"Please, open the door Rob, this is stupid," I begged.

The more she shouted the more he retaliated. With the next kick her foot appeared through the door. The lock burst as the door flew open and Rob landed in a heap on top of the toilet.

Pat who had been outside the door beside Lucy trying to get her to calm down reached in grabbed my hand and pulled me out of the bathroom and down the stairs. I was shaking from top to toe.

Lucy was punching Rob so hard we could hear them hitting home as we gathered in the entrance hall.

Lucy towered at the top of the stair and screamed "you'll pay for this I'll name you in our divorce."

I stood still and as I looked up at her I replied, "I'm fully clothed in case you haven't noticed and he's such a poor sole to put up with you."

Pat put Caroline and I into a taxi and on the way home I began to laugh.

The whole situation was unbelievable; laughing was once again my safety net.

Aggie was concerned and fussed about me trying to calm me down. She knew my behaviour was not my norm. I had to latch onto the amusing aspect of the incident, if I didn't

I'd lose the plot. After a few drinks, I began to visibly calm down.

Pat and Ann arrived. Lucy was furious because the young stud that she had been chasing most of the night had left after the rumpus.

Rob was so drunk he denied seeing me in the bathroom!

Pat asked to speak to me alone. As he sat beside me and hugged me he asked, "Do you want me to get your dad or Colin?"

"No I'll be fine," I said wearily.

The blackness consumed me as soon as I lay down in bed.

I was awoken next morning with Lucy doing an impersonation of an army invading Poland.

She shouted and snarled at Aggie. The girls ran into my room and hid under my duvet. I told them to stay cuddled together while I spoke to Lucy.

She stomped back and forth and her huge form wobbled like a mountain of jelly while making threatening comments.

I said, "Good morning or maybe good is not a word you like?"

"Don't be fucking smart" she replied.

"Please don't use fowl language in my home. My girls are upstairs so don't shout as I don't want them distressed" I said.

"I'm going to sue you for adultery. You have ruined my marriage and I hold you fully responsible" she said with a sneer.

"Okay, I'll see you in court, now please, leave" I said.

As she stood looking stunned, I asked Aggie to see her out.

For the next two weeks she bombarded me with threatening phone calls, while Rob telephoned continually to apologise. BT put a special service on my line and all calls were monitored and recorded. Her last few telephone calls had been demanding money to keep my name clean. I had chosen to ignore them and this incensed her even more so she arranged for her lawyer to send me a letter to scare me.

I took her letter to my lawyer and explained the situation to him.

"Were you fully clothed at all times?" he asked.

"Yes" I replied.

"It is a known fact, the sexual act cannot take place if you are fully clothed" he said.

"How long were you locked in the bathroom?" he asked.

"It felt like forever but it was probably only a few minutes" I replied.

"Is the husband admitting to having sex with you" he asked.

"He said I wasn't in the bathroom" I replied.

Once he stopped laughing he said "we'll see them in court."

"This should be fun," he continued.

It never reached court and I received a letter of apology. Lucy met Aggie by chance in the bus station a few weeks later and she explained that the extension on their cottage had run into financial problems and she thought up this plot to find money to pay off her escalating debts. Before walking away from her Aggie said "did you not think to simply ask her for the money?"

"Tell her I'm sorry. Maybe one day she'll have a drink with me?"

"I don't think so," replied Aggie.

I spent many days being quiet to allow my mind to calm down. The blackness was now engulfing my days and nights.

I wanted to find comfort being held by Colin but this was impossible.

I couldn't find any comfort anywhere and I found myself sitting in the cemetery more and more.

Oh to be in a cocoon, somewhere safe.

Pat and Ann began to spend more time at my house. Listening to Pat's stories about Ron and their antics brought me a sense of comfort in an unexpected way. Everyone around me appeared frightened to mention Ron. They all acted as though he didn't exist, he was dead but the memory of him was all around.

Early one morning Pat arrived looking worried. He explained money was tight and their brand new house was going to be repossessed and he needed somewhere to move his furniture to until it was sold and he also needed to find lodgings for them to stay.

I knew how he felt but I didn't let on about my situation so, their furniture was brought to my downstairs room and stored. Within one week it was all sold so it wasn't too much of an inconvenience.

I had an empty double bed sit in Windmill Road so I decided to let them rent it. As my parents felt comfortable with this arrangement they didn't moan.

Pat then asked if I could arrange a unit and trailer for him so he could earn some cash.

Once organized he spent at least four days away overnight hauling loads up and down the country. Sometimes Ann and their daughter would accompany him and on other occasions my dad would tag along with him to help. I had no reason not to trust him.

One night Colin, Shona, Pat, Ann, Caroline and I went out for a meal at the restaurant Ron and I always dined at. The evening was fun. Colin appeared and flirted like mad with me.

After the meal we all ended up at the local nightspot and

although Shona didn't look too happy she smiled through gritted teeth. On the dance floor we were all having fun, however Shona was sitting with her jacket still on wanting to leave. Colin's teasing and flirting began to infiltrate my senses and I decided two could play at his game. Once he acknowledged I was in retaliation mode he changed his tune, he held onto both my wrists and fired harsh words at me as Caroline popped out of nowhere and said, "Smile" the flash from her camera brought me into reality.

"Fuck off back to your little wife and leave me alone" I snarled.

We all left after this and as Pat, Ann, Caroline and I walked back to my house I decided to make light of the whole episode. On our arrival Aggie's owl like eyes descended on me and I knew she could tell something was amiss. In the kitchen she asked Pat and he told her of the nights events. He then sought me out in my bedroom and asked if I was okay.

"I'll go and see him. I'll explain he must stop doing this to you and I'll tell him what Ron would have thought about all this. He can't have his cake and eat it. I'll sort it out, don't worry." He said.

"No leave it. I mean nothing to no-one so save your breath" I replied wearily.

When everyone had gone I roamed the house trying to shut

out the screaming and find a quiet spot within. I didn't succeed and by the time Aggie arrived the following morning I looked drawn and pale. With the girls away to school and playgroup I decided to go to bed as the events and the drink from the previous night had caught up with me. By lunchtime I was still in bed and suffering a huge hangover and Aggie's constant moaning at me was beginning to grate on my nerves. I asked her to go a few errands to get peace.

"By the time I come back you better be out of that bed showered and dressed or else" she boomed.

"Get lost. Who pays your wages" I replied.

"You do but I care so get up" she replied.

On her way out I heard her speak to someone then I heard the loud slam of the outer storm door.

Hooray I thought now I have peace to sleep.

The bedroom door slowly opened and in walked Colin. He sat on the edge of the bed while I tried really hard to raise my head off the pillow. He began by apologising for his behaviour the previous night. I remained silent.

He then said, "I would have an affair with you in a minute but it is who you are that is stopping me."

"Who am I?" I asked.

"Your Ron's wife and that is what is stopping me" he replied.

"Correction I'm Ron's widow so fuck off and leave me alone. I can't bear to have my emotions messed around by someone who does it so easily," I said.

He got up and left and a part of me went with him.

On Aggie's return I was still in bed as she walked into my bedroom ready to give me another tongue lashing however when she saw the state I was in she hugged me close and I wept until I could cry no more.

Colin stayed away.

Pat was angry at the way I handled it and wanted so much to put the situation right for Ron's sake.

However I was adamant and as my emotions were so raw everything was beginning to take its toll.

I had lost a drastic amount of weight, I still wasn't eating proper meals and every day was an effort. The only thing that made me smile was the hugs from my girls.

With my brother incarcerated the girls had taken more to Colin and with his non-appearance now noticeable their questions on where he was always made my heart heavy. I explained he was so busy with his police work that he didn't have as much time as he used to have.

It never fails to amaze me how resilient children can be. They had lost their Daddy, Tom had went far away to work in a prison and now Colin wasn't visiting them either so after a short time they stopped asking on a daily basis as to why, and their childhood continued as safe and secure emotionally as I could make it.

Pat now became more demanding regarding money or diesel to keep the unit and trailer on the road. I had inspected all his delivery notes and I knew that soon a good and reliable source of income would be generated. I hadn't seen or spoken to him for several days when a gent from the docks in Hull telephoned me about a delivery that Pat was hauling that was now overdue and causing them some concern.

The conversation's tone was now concerning me and I had to admit I had no idea what was going on.

Later that same afternoon Pat telephoned and his tone was menacing. He agreed he had on a load of steal worth roughly about £25K and as he had no insurance for it should anything happen to it I would be held responsible. He reminded me that the unit and trailer were in my name so I would carry the can. In order to ensure he delivered it safely I was to agree to give him a certain amount of money that would enable him to begin a new start somewhere. He then hung up after he stated he would be in touch soon.

I was physically sick and threw up all over my bed and carpet, crawled on my hands and knees to the bedroom door and out onto the landing and summoned up the strength from somewhere to call on Aggie.

I was terrified. The more I tried to remain calm the more I threw up so I decided to take the car out and drive to my bolt hole at the cemetery. Maybe just maybe when I returned it would all be a nightmare and normality would have returned.
For the next four days he phoned to make threats and demands for money. Each time the amount increased. The gent from Hull was now frantic about his load and I truthfully explained the whole situation. He contacted the police and soon my phone was tapped to enable them to trace him. Something inside me told me he was close by so I contacted all Ron's known haulage contacts and told them I was looking for a stolen load and I made sure they all knew who was responsible.
Two days later an old work colleague of Ron's who now ran his own taxi company telephoned me.
"Hi that load you're looking for, remind me of the number plate?" he asked. I told him and he replied.
"As we speak I'm looking directly at the unit but it has no trailer with it. I'll keep an eye on it till you get here."
"Bill I can't thank you enough I'm on my way." I replied.
My dad insisted Colin went to pick it up with us as it meant my dad could drive my car home. I agreed but it was very difficult as I felt he was made to help when he didn't really want to.

The next morning my dad phoned and said "I've just returned from taking Shep the dog his morning walk and you'll never guess what is dumped around the corner from here on that derelict site."

"I can't guess just tell me" I said wearily.

"25K worth of steel on a trailer" he said.

I didn't reply I hung up the phone, flew down to Windmill Road ran around the corner and there stood the most glorious sight to my eyes.

I had to make arrangements and fast so I left my dad watching over it. A gent who owned a haulage yard in Airdrie offered to help and I very gratefully accepted. He would supply the diesel and driver who would deliver it to Hull a.s.a.p. Then pick up a return load for Glasgow. Once that return load was delivered the unit and trailer would be returned to the hiring company with no costs being landed on me.

The return load would be his payment for this kind act. I arranged to meet him at the trailer as Colin had agreed once again to drive the unit that was now parked at the side entrance to my home.

With everyone discussing how to back up the unit to the trailer that was sitting at a very awkward angle I knew I had to rely on a miracle.

Colin and I climbed into the cabin of the unit and I spoke

calmly as I explained what we needed to achieve. The first attempt was awful. To stop the whole load from toppling over we had one and only one chance to get it right. With the unit now realigned ready to be reversed onto the coupling bracket this was a difficult manoeuvre and we needed a miracle. Inside my heart I knew the one person who could achieve this task and I whispered his name and asked for him to help. As I glanced over at Colin's arms I instantly recognised those strong muscular limbs that I knew so well.

"Go for it" I said to Colin.

With lots of engine noise and metal meeting metal the bracket and coupling became one.

Warmth embraced me and I thanked Ron from my heart. I also thanked Colin.

That night I slept like a baby and I prayed this would be the last I would hear from Pat.

Whoever I was praying to he or she definitely wasn't listening because my nightmare was about to go epic.

Next day the phone went and the soft tones of Pat's charming voice on the other end of the line made me begin to visibly shake so much I had difficulty keeping a hold on the receiver.

"Nice work with the load. I knew you could do it, so my

next little request won't be a problem either." He cooed.
"What do you want?" I demanded.
"Now, now don't get all worked up. I've been a bad boy and I need some pennies to help Ann and I start a new life far away. If you promise not to get angry and do exactly as I say I will promise to leave your precious girls alone. If you choose to involve the boys in blue or don't do as I ask you; you can say bye bye to your daughters." He softly said before he hung up.
My mind flew into a panic, where were the girls? Who were they with?
I ran out of the house in a blind panic. Aggie and Caroline had mentioned taking them to the park. Which park? After checking the nearest one to the house and not finding them I ran back to the house to get the car. I had a better chance of finding them by going off around all their usual play parks. I drove around like someone demented and with each park drawing a blank my fears of him taking them increased. The screaming inside my head was at such a crescendo I was beginning to find it difficult to appear sane. As I approached the one-way system near the road that was the one way to our house I spotted them all walking hand in hand along a nearby pavement. I slammed on my brakes got out of the car and ran through the traffic towards them. Meanwhile other car owners in the traffic were sounding

their horns, shouting abuse and doing their best to avoid hitting me.

Aggie saw me first and her reaction to my appearance didn't need too many words.

"Aggie as you are very near to the house run please, run and lock yourselves in, Pat's after the girls for money."

Caroline hadn't heard everything but with Aggie's look and my appearance Caroline took off like a gazelle holding firmly onto the girls' hands. Aggie and I followed them. The car would have to wait until I knew they were safe indoors.

With doors and windows locked I went to retrieve my car. Over the next few days he telephoned and continued his threats. On one occasion I decided to tell him the truth about my true financial status. He didn't believe me and my so-called lies made him angry.

Bill was a policeman who rented a bed-sit from me at the Wellington and he knew the situation Pat had caused with the load of steel, so on one occasion when I had called in to see my parents and uplift the rents he approached me and said if I ever wanted advice or help I was only to ask. Anything I asked would be treated with confidence. He appeared pleasant and as he worked in the control room of the local police station I assumed he would be helpful if he

could.
I decided to confide in him about Pat's phone calls and about my fears of my girls being harmed. He also knew that Colin wasn't on speaking terms with me and explained I was better off without his help. This statement confused me and I asked him to explain. When Pat and Ann had stayed in the bed-sit Bill had gone out of his way to make them feel settled but Pat was always a little wary of him. However Pat was more than willing to share the upset Colin had caused me. I later found out Pat had bragged he had warned off Colin and he was going to make sure nobody would cause me any upset.
Bill suggested getting my phone lines tapped plus having him and another uniformed officer to drop in to my house on a regular basis so if Pat was watching the house a police presence would make him think twice. As I had never given it a thought to him watching my house this thought now made me more scared so I agreed to accept Bill's offer of help.
During a very long lonely night I found myself again picking up the phone to dial Colin's number but once again I held back. Ron's words about Colin helping echoed round my head until a few drinks dulled my senses and allowed the blackness to swamp me.
Each telephone threat was becoming more harrowing than

the last and I decided on Pat's request to meet him in a car park situated within the local Strathclyde Park. I felt it was time to try all I could to make him understand that I had no money and ask him, as a friend of Ron's to leave us in peace.

I swore Aggie and Caroline to secrecy about my meeting and after a few stiff drinks for courage I drove off for our meeting.

The night was cold and frosty and the agreed car park was empty when I arrived. The sky was jet black and the stars shone like beacons as I walked up and down the shoreline of the man made loch in Strathcylde Park. My thoughts were interrupted by the arrival of a couple of cars that sat only a few moments before leaving. Time was ticking by with as yet no sign of Pat however the cars that were coming and going on a regular basis began to take on a similarity and I decided that something was amiss and I left.

Before I had left the park a dark coloured car tailed me slowly ignoring my attempts for the car to overtake me. Someone was playing a game with me so I decided to play my own game where only I knew the rules.

I sped off and they kept pace with me all the way through Bothwell and into Uddingston, then back again before heading to Blantyre then onto High Blantyre past the cemetery then through Hamilton towards home. I parked the car at the side entrance and as I walked into the rear of our large hall I heard Aggie say “I have no idea when she will be home.”

“It’s okay Aggie I’m here” I said to her and the two men standing in my front entrance hall.

“Can I help you?” I asked.

“Have you seen Mr.Pat McMachon anytime this evening” one asked.

“You’ll know better than me. Did you enjoy your little drive about? See any nice scenery,” I asked in a very sarcastic tone.

“If he has been watching you have really botched things up more than you will ever know,” I continued.

“Can we talk to you?” the other asked.

“Go to hell” I replied as I walked away and headed to my upstairs sitting room. I heard Aggie suggesting maybe it would be better to call again in the morning once I had settled down. They agreed.

I asked Aggie how they knew and she timidly admitted that she had phoned Colin and asked for his help. She was so scared something serious might befall me and the idea of having to explain to my parents terrified her so Colin was her only option.

I couldn’t remain angry with her, as she never failed to show me her understanding and loyalty.

The telephone ringing made us jump.
"Wrong move. I said no boys in blue so the price has just gone up. I'll be in touch," Pat snarled. He hung up before I could reply.
The blackness overtook me before I had reached my bedroom. I needed outside help to resolve this harrowing situation. My granddad's words came to rest on me that night. I needed to find my solution.
Next morning the C.I.D. arrived and I sat down and began at the beginning. My whole attitude was calm with an under lying determination to be rid of this pest. Their words echoed mine and I knew I was on the right track. They reorganised the phone taps and agreed to let Bill and his partner remain inside my home to assist in our in house security and extra police patrols were put on to help with outside surveillance. It was also agreed every night two plain clothed officers called at the house via the back door to check out the premises for the night.
I explained the situation to my parents but they appeared uninterested so I decided to keep the whole upset to myself. As long as Aggie and Caroline remained loyal to protecting my girls I would see this through. I couldn't even bring myself to confide in Colin and as he still kept his distance my senses withdrew deep within my being.
Almost a week had gone by with no results when I had an

alarming personal visit. The two officers had offered Aggie a lift home promising to return to do their check. Caroline was on a night out with a couple of friends and I was alone in the upstairs sitting room. With the girls tucked up in bed the house was silent and I was enjoying the calm when my sitting room door opened and in walked Pat!
“All alone? You’re lucky I’m in a good mood I’m only after a little advance” he said. He looked around and his eyes fell upon the pile of notes from my rent collection lying on top of the television unit.
“I’ll have this. You don’t mind?” he said.
Through tears I begged him to leave and explained I needed the money to survive. He didn’t linger long enough to reply and before I could gather myself together he was gone. The noise of the two officers downstairs in my kitchen sprung me into moving. I screamed at them what had just happened. Over the next several hours the whole of Lanarkshire was put on alert to his callous action.

Next morning my constant overnight pacing had exhausted me and I knew this whole situation had to come to an end. Two new officers called to see me and their whole manner and appearance gave me an inner uplift. They explained they were from the Glasgow squad and they were now taking control of the matter with the help of the Hamilton

lot.
With this knowledge I asked for someone to explain fully what and who Pat was. They duly did and I was taken aback at the criminal form Pat had. He certainly wasn't a stupid wide boy but they were holding something back and I wanted to know. So I threw a tantrum and they agreed to bring the big boss from Glasgow out to see me.
Aggie and Caroline were so supportive. The police offered and put into place protection for the girls.
Lyn was shadowed on her way to and from school plus while she was in the playground. The headmistress and her staff were informed and they were excellent and very vigilant.
Louise was also shadowed on her way to and from playgroup. Her routine never changed, into the local sweet shop with two burly plain clothes police in tow also buying sweeties.
I insisted the girls' routine was kept as normal as possible as not to cause them any upset. I also agreed to allow them to keep tabs on me.
The big boss was a delight, in a class of his own.
He explained fully and I mean fully all the details he held on Pat. He had 22 outstanding warrants, so he was no petty criminal. He then listened to my full albeit short association with Pat. He asked about Ron's involvement with Pat but I

wasn't able to give him much information because Ron had always insisted on keeping him separate from his home life. I now knew why.

The police needed bait to catch him and they were so determined to hook him. Every fish needs bait to enable it to take the bite. So I suggested myself.

My situation. My solution.

He was aghast at my suggestion but my determined attitude won him over into thinking about it. The bigger boss in Glasgow would have to agree so I sent him off to sweet-talk his boss.

Next day he returned with a full set of plans for my approval. Over several cups of coffee and tea we agreed on most of the plans and I kept my inner senses deep within. My Eleanor Rigby mask was firmly fixed in place.

When they left I sat with Aggie and slowly went over the details of me being used as bait. On cue she went hysterical and I laughed till I cried at her antics.

My lawyer helped put my will in order and I explained what I was about to do and why. He was most helpful and he took time to insist on every small detail of my involvement with Pat being written down. He shook my hand and offered very kind words that made my emotions rise.

The afternoon was taken up with the girls and I enjoying a

picnic at the park together. I was aware of the unmarked police car parked nearby but the girls were oblivious. To onlookers we looked like any other family having fun at the park. Inside I felt like someone awaiting an unseen fate. Teatime was fun and Aggie and Caroline both put in a tremendous effort to make it smiles all the way. Bath time was a more than usual wet affair however by the time it came to story time the girls had settled and were sleepy. I hugged then tightly and kissed them till I thought they would blend into me.

I sat upon my bed and asked for help and strength to carry out the task I was about to do. The only person who could stop this nightmare was me. I had foolishly invited this monster into our lives, why?

He always talked about Ron with kind words and described him as a brother he had never had. How could he do these awful deeds towards my darling babies and myself? The big bad monster had to go.

Doesn't it say that in all the good storybooks?

Composed and with a bright smile I reassured Aggie and Caroline things would be fine. Earlier I had had a heart to heart with Aggie giving her advice on what to do if I was hurt or worst. Her tears that flowed washed a determination into my heart.

As I drove out of the drive she stood looking terrified and

bewildered and I knew within my heart her feelings were being taken to their furthest outpost on the wings of loyalty.

The drive to Cambuslang via the cemetery didn't take too long in time but it felt like eternity within. On the outskirts of the town I stopped the car, turned off the engine and sat at one, alone within my heart and mind. I spoke aloud and said "Ron this friend of yours in no friend of our children or myself. I know you will love me always, so bring a cloak of protection and place it upon my shoulders as I do battle to be rid of this monster who dares to call you friend."
Warmth embraced me and my car found its way to my allocated spot situated alongside a taxi rank to await whatever was about to descend on me.
I had been told I would be closely watched and an army of officers were positioned and prepared for any eventuality however my main priority was that under no circumstances was I to allow him to enter my vehicle or move my car off the appointed position. Should I become a moving target a new ball game would come into play as the situation would be more serious and life threatening and everyone on the team had had it spelt out in big bold letters that I was not to be hurt under any circumstances. Any injury to me would result in heads rolling.
I sat and looked around, everything appeared totally

normal. The taxi ranks on either side of the road were full of empty taxis with only two appearing to be taken up with the drivers all talking. At the bus stop a couple stood arm in arm. Two men in workmen's overalls stood one appearing slightly under the influence of drink while a third workman stood at the side of the bus shelter trying very hard to keep his drunken being in an upright position.

I was beginning to think I had got the wrong location when a bright and I mean bright fluorescent green car sped past me going in the other direction, abruptly stopped turned on two wheels and shot up and stopped directly behind me. As the car shot off past me speeding down the main street a gentle knock on my passenger window startled me.

"Don't let him in my mind screamed" repeatedly, before I was aware of how he was sitting in the passenger seat with his arm draped across the back on my seat.

"Good girl. Relax just do as you're told and everything will be fine" he said in an underlying tone. He looked around then continued by saying "I'm not too happy about sitting here so let's go for a little spin."

I opened my mouth to reply but the feeling on an object being forced into my rib cage silenced me. "I'll use this if I have to, so move," he growled.

My mind was racing; I knew it wasn't a knife he was pushing into my ribs and the only other possibility was the barrel of a gun. The screaming within was now at fever pitch and I began to shake however I knew I had to appear as calm and in control as I could.

I was now on the battlefield and my enemy was now showing his true colours.

"How can you do this? How can you call yourself a friend of someone you looked upon as a brother?" I asked

"Easy, needs must and anyway Ron's not here" he replied.

"Now move this fucking car on else," he growled.

I turned the key in the ignition and the car stalled. Why? I have no idea. Second go and it stalled again.

The gun was now causing me great discomfort and I prayed "If it goes off inside me please, make it quick."

My attention was drawn to my rear view mirror and in slow motion the big boss was running towards my car with each vein in his face showing great strain while his mouth appeared open and mouthing unheard words. The silence that had cocooned me while watching his approach was shattered by the onslaught of numerous bodies hurling themselves onto and over my car. The passenger door was yanked open and many hands grabbed him and dragged him out. The gun was snatched out of his hand and he was flung against the car and handcuffed. I gripped the steering wheel and terrifying screams filled the scene.

"Who the hell is screaming?" I thought.

A gentle tap on my driver's window brought the sound to an abrupt halt.
"You shower of lying bastards, you promised not to touch him while I was here. You all lied." I roared.
"This woman officer will drive you home and we'll be around to see you later. Well done" he said.
"I drove myself here so I'll drive myself back thanks" I said through clenched teeth.
The policewoman sitting beside me was the one who was part of the couple at the bus stop. In fact all the people I had seen in and around the scene were all police in some form of disguise. Stammering and shaking uncontrollably she was attempting to light a cigarette she was having great difficulty holding onto. "Are you okay?" I asked her.
"I've never been involved in anything like this before. I feel shattered and in much need of a strong cup of coffee to settle my nerves. I really do need to lie down," she informed me.
On and on she went about how awful she felt and the whole situation would haunt her. I drove on in silence while she ranted and raved. This woman was supposed to be there for me, to offer me support and her constant twittering was beginning to stir up my emotions and not my gentle ones so I drove to the police station and dropped her off then drove home alone.

I parked at the side entrance and stood for a few moments and said a silent and heartfelt Thank you to Ron and whomever else he had enlisted to ensure I was safe.

In the kitchen Aggie broke into a flood of tears as I appeared, not one word was said as she poured me a very large drink. No words were needed.

After his shift was over Colin called in to see how things had gone and he joined us in a drink. Sometime later the main officers handling the case also joined us and with excited chatter the evenings events were poured over. I was in the same room with everyone but my inner self was off to a quiet spot. Eventually all their voices penetrated into my mind. I looked around at them all so jubilant. I spoke very softly and got all their attention.

“I am so glad you are all so happy, now please, each and every one of you fuck off and be jubilant elsewhere.” They all very sheepishly left murmuring apologies.

I was informed the next day that the gun was loaded and that he would have had no hesitation in using it. He was convinced it had been Colin who had set him up and Colin had agreed to let this be the case.

It was also explained why the hoard had descended on my car as they did. I had to be protected and to become a moving target would have been disastrous so I accepted the apology in the true intention it was given.

For the next few weeks time moved at an easy pace with only minor hick ups.
I drove several times to England to visit numerous haulage outfits that owed me money for the deliveries Pat had made. My dad and Bill nearly always went with me. Always dressed in my black business suit I may have appeared fragile but when the words "no we don't pay out in cash," or "we'll send you a cheque," was uttered the fragile little being became a roaring and snarling lioness.
We never returned home empty handed!

My parents were becoming more demanding with their request for a weekly wage over and above the living conditions that they had so I tried to avoid them as much as possible. I also took the advice of a friend and decided to get the money together so the girls and I could go away on holiday.
Bill began calling in more while pounding his beat and as he was okay I didn't mind. He had been demoted from the control room but as it was none of my business I wasn't interested. In truth I thought he had the hots for Aggie. My mum worshiped him. After his night shift he would take home early morning freshly baked rolls and a wee bag of her favourite sweeties and in return she made sure his whole uniform and his boots were always spotless. My dad

used to moan that she showed more attention to him than anyone but she always denied it.

One day Bill invited me out for a drink with the other residents of the Wellington. I refused and Aggie talked me into it. Caroline went with us and in fact it turned out not too bad a night.

The girls were missing Colin popping in so in a way Bill filled the gap. He made a fuss of them and he began to join us as often as he could when we went on our nightly jaunts to the various parks we visited before bedtime. He had a very low opinion of Colin and was more than willing to tell me what remarks Colin was making about me to other police officers.

As I was now alone, no longer part of a couple most of my friends gave me the wide berth, as I may have been a threat to their marriages! And family had chosen to also give me the wide berth because I was a constant reminder of the tragedy that had befallen all of us.

I couldn't please anyone and I was worn done trying to keep my facemask on.

Time to escape.

I drove into Glasgow one day on impulse and for some reason I ended up outside a travel agent's that only handled flights, holidays and emigration to Australia. I stood for some time staring at the big model aeroplane that hung in the window.

Oh to fly away and begin a new start somewhere far from all my troubles.

I went in and stood staring at the large posters that lined the walls. Maybe this was my answer. The girls were young enough to adapt to change and with only the girls to worry about I could pick myself up and go on. A gent speaking to me interrupted my thoughts.

"Can I be of any help Mam?" he asked.

"How much does it cost to fly to Australia?" I asked.

We spoke for a short time and his manner and soothing tones captivated me in a way I couldn't explain.

"Can I be so bold to ask you a personal question Mam?" he said.

I nodded in reply.

"Has Mam been recently bereaved?" he asked.

Again I nodded.

"To run is to hide to stay is to conquer. May I suggest that one takes time to think this through? Should you feel the same a year from now I will gladly arrange it. Take time it will become easier to live with. Now let me give you some brochures for you to take home for your children," he said.

Here was a complete stranger who could see my pain as much as I could taste it. I thanked him and left feeling calmer within.

Aggie would look after the house during the day and Bill would stay over to keep an eye on things during the night. Downstairs I had turned the two very large public rooms into two shared bed-sit units. The front room housed three girls including Caroline who had given up the flat she had shared with my brother. The other I decided to wait until I returned before letting it out. Our house had all girls while the Wellington became all male.

Bill and his beat partner took us to the airport. We were off somewhere special. No jumbo jet or fancy airplane just a small twelve seater.
The destination? Barra.
Home. Home to a special place to heal my heart.

I had arranged a hired car so it was waiting for us on our arrival. The short drive to the north of the island took only a few moments. A man in his thirties with a very rough and weather beaten appearance welcomed us and gave us the caravan keys, pointed to where it stood and took off like a bullet shouting he would call later to pick up the balance of the rental. As I wrestled with the stiff lock the girls ran around the machair playing. When the door finally burst open the smell hit me first then the flies descended like vultures. My inspection didn't take long; if this was luxury I hated to think what squalor was!

As we drove into Castlebay my heart was heavy. We couldn't stay there so I would have to find somewhere fast. I asked the lady in the post office if she knew whom our weather beaten man was and where I could find him. She directed me to the mini market where the man's sister worked. She listened while I explained my plight.

"He's a bloody rogue. I'll kill him when I get my hands on him" she roared.

"How much money has he taken from you?" She went on.

I told her the amount of the deposit I had sent to him by post.

"So that's how the swine had money," she continued.

She continually apologised as she counted the money into my hand she had just taken from the cash register. She also made up a small collection of sweets for the girls. I thanked her and wandered outside trying to get my mind to calm down to enable me to find somewhere to stay.

My eyes wandered to the spot opposite on the waterfront where my old man had sat last year. His usual seat was vacant and my mind wandered back to my meeting with him. My mind was brought back to the present with someone saying

"Hello it is Mrs. Pearson? Am I right in saying you were

guests at my hotel last year. Your children played with mine? Are you alright my dear?" she continued as she took hold of my arm.

In a dazed state I heard myself spill out words to explain to myself and to her.

"Let's get you all settled. Make your way to my house I'll be there shortly," she said kindly.

Like a robot I did as she said and over a pot of tea she explained. Her hotel had an empty double room for three days. We could have it then she would move us into the staff quarters in the attic and meals would be included.

"Pay me what you can now and send me the balance on your return home. Under the circumstances I can give you a very good discount. So don't worry everything will be fine. Now cheer up, you're on holiday" she continued.

Her kindness touched me so much and I thanked her warmly although my words seemed inadequate. Before we left for our new holiday accommodation she looked out of her huge picture window and stared towards the sea and said "I am sorry about your loss, he was a good man, but you're home now safe so allow the island to heal your heart."

As she snapped me back to the present she laughed and said "Oh come on move you're on holiday."

She stood and waved until we rounded the bend at the foot

of her road. The staff at the hotel were awaiting our arrival, they were so sweet and helpful and soon we were settled. The beach was a stone throw away from the hotel's rear entrance and soon we were walking along the sand in our bare feet with the gentle waves lapping the shore. The scenery touched my heart and calmness descended into my inner sole. I was home.

Every day was sunny and we explored every nook and cranny to our immense enjoyment and delight. Many locals invited us in for cups of tea and home baking and we always accepted their heart-warming hospitality.

The beach opposite the one used as a landing strip was reached by hiking across a large field and down through a vast area of sand dunes. Then the sight and sound of the mighty Atlantic rollers breaking against the shore was breath-taking.

Playing on the sand chasing the huge waves were three children whose squeals of delight captured my girls attention and off they sped in their direction. The happiness etched on all their faces was pure joy to behold.

Sitting snugly together huddled in a sand dune were two adults who I presumed were the children's parents.

"Hello what a lovely day" I said.

"The scene is truly one of God's glorious," the man said.

The woman then said "Take it into your heart and on a day

of despair it will lift you up."
"Thank-you I will" I replied.
Their accents told me they weren't local but I couldn't take a guess on its origin, however it didn't matter they appeared nice people.
My eyes were drawn to the far end of the beach where a large rocky area ended the vast expanse of beach. The rocks led to an inaccessible part of the shore by land.
A lone figure stood not looking out to sea but to where the children and I were standing. He appeared extremely tall yet with the distance from us he should have looked small!
I was captivated and I began to walk slowly towards the figure and my mind began to race. It was Ron. Here he was waiting for us to come and join him. My prayers had been answered. Here he was and my emotions soared with each quickening pace and my heart began to beat faster.
I stopped several feet from the figure and my heart sank and so did my knees into the sand.
There before me stood a very tall dark haired and bearded gentleman who was handsome with fine porcelain features. Silence… no waves crashing onto the shore… no wind and as I turned to look towards the children their squeals of fun and delight were silent. The silence was so great you could taste it. He helped me to my feet without touching me. Thoughts screamed through my mind. What was

happening?
As though he could read my thoughts he said, “Do not worry, you’re fine and your children are safe. I am sorry I am not who you want me to be but I only want to reassure you.”
“Your heart is heavy but one day you shall sing. Find your voice,” he continued.
His words filled my whole being. I turned to reassure myself the girls were fine and as I turned back to make my reply he was gone.
He had vanished.
No way could he have climbed over the huge rocks so quickly and anyway it led to cliffs.
He was gone but he had left me something precious… words.
After a few moments I began my walk back towards the children who were still playing. Half way along the beach the wind, waves and the children’s excited tones assaulted my ears and the returning sounds of the events startled me. Something strange and unusual had just taken place yet I felt a true sense of calmness surround me.
I called to the girls we had to go as I had arranged to have afternoon tea with Father James and I didn’t want us to be late.
I walked ahead as I wanted to speak to the two adults who

were still sitting huddled together. I smiled as I approached them and as they returned my smile I asked. “Can you please, help me? I would like to ask you both a question.”
“Ask away” said the man in a jovial manner.
“Did you see me talking to someone at the far end of the beach?” I asked.
They both nodded they had.
“Do you or did you see where he went?” I asked. “He was there then he was gone. It’s crazy he just vanished and I know no-one can do that,” I continued.
“Do not fret, on occasions unexplainable events take place that are truly beautiful. You are so fortunate blessings come in many shapes and forms so treasure this moment.” The woman replied.
To a practical mind the whole trip to the beach could make some go crazy trying to figure it out, but deep within my whole being I knew I had encountered something I could find no words for.

Tea with Father James was pleasant and I discussed my encounter on the beach. He listened intently then said “Very spiritual and magical events happen on this island that no-one can explain. Maybe you have been given a sign that one day shall make sense.”
“A sign? What kind of sign?” I asked.

"Only time will tell," he replied smiling.
He went on to invite us to his first B.B.C. live radio service taking place a few days later, suggesting as every local and visitor would be attending my beach family would be present enabling me to talk to them again. I accepted his invitation and made a promise to myself to try and track them down before then. Next day the girls and myself set out on an adventure to speak to everyone about our beach family. As Barra is very small island I was sure I would find them.
With so many locals on the lookout for the family it was disappointing that no one found them or could recall seeing a family of five lodging anywhere. As the Sunday service approached I had to admit to being unsuccessful in the search.
Father James used my encounter during his sermon. The afternoon was most enjoyable.

Mary who ran the local taxi invited us for tea as her aging mother was insisting we called on her. The old lady had been bed ridden and house bound for many years and she always spoke about wanting to see a certain visitor at her home before she died. It was as though she was waiting.
Old Maw, Mary's mother clasped my hands to her heart and her tired eyes grew bright and sparkled as she spoke to

me in her mother tongue. Her words my mind couldn't understand but my heart felt each one-drop from her lips. The old lady's words sent a tingling through my whole being; a knowledge deep inside me and a voice telling me to accept them made me nod my head.

Mary and her husband were childless, so to watch him entertain my girls out in the garden as they were his own made his kind and gentle manner touch my heart.

When Ron was alive we travelled abroad extensively and on each of our jaunts I always met someone I knew or someone local who would treat me as though I was a long lost friend or a distant relative. Ron was always flabbergasted and at times emotional because he knew he was witnessing something no one could explain. To this day whenever I am out and about with friends or family people are drawn towards me and I always take a few moments to speak to them. They always appear happy and content when I say bye.

When we left the picturesque cottage of old Maw I knew that soon she would be gone. The sparkle that had radiated from her tired eyes shone on me like a beacon. I had brought her something she was waiting for but she had given me so much more.

Bill began phoning me at the hotel every night always the worse for drink. Endless words that meant nothing however the underlying tone was ugly.
He suggested we should get married on one occasion! After I picked up the receiver I had dropped through shock I laughed his remark off by saying “Don’t be silly we’re only friends.”
“Yeah but you’d marry that bastard Colin without a second thought” he spat down the phone. His words unnerved me, maybe I had been wrong to look upon him as a friend.

The morning before we prepared to fly home was very emotional, once again I was leaving my safe cocoon. For the duration of our ten-day stay time had stood still and I was now nervous at the idea of going back to normal living in Hamilton. Or was it normal?
Each step towards the small plane waiting on the beach was a nightmare. I wanted to stay so much it hurt.
As the plane sped along the sandy airstrip to soar into the bright blue sky an overwhelming feeling of loss hit me. A gent in the next seat touched my hand and softly said “Leaving your home is always difficult but you always take a part of it with you. Don’t you agree?”
“No. I’ve left a big part of me there but one day I shall return and claim it” I answered.

Bill, Sam his police buddy and Shirley from the bedsit were waiting at the airport to meet us. Bill and Shirley came across as over friendly with each other while Sam was acting awkward although he was very helpful with the baggage while I kept my eyes firmly on the girls.

Aggie, Caroline and Chris were all waiting for us in the kitchen when we arrived home. Everyone's squeals of delight at seeing the girls echoed around the house.

Aggie and I went upstairs and left everyone to catch up with the girls' stories about their holiday adventures. As she sat perched on the edge of the sofa her manner was telling me something was wrong.

She went on to explain most of the rent money from the bed sits had gone missing. Bill was blaming Caroline for stealing it but him and Shirley had been consuming large amounts of booze and the evidence was outside in the bucket to prove it. When she had tried to discuss it with Bill he had been rude and abusive. She had wanted to phone Colin and tell him but she was frightened to do so because Bill had warned her not to involve him or else!

I counted what was left and a sudden anger surged through me.

"Will I phone Colin?" Aggie asked.

"No. Bill has told me what he has been saying about me to

other cops, so don't bother" I replied.
A knock on the sitting room door surprised me, it was Sam.
"I am going now," he said. He then stood once again looking awkward.
"What's up?" I asked.
"Please, be careful and don't trust Bill," he said.
"Why?" I asked.
"Just something he said a couple of times" he answered.
Before I could say anything else Bill walked in and Sam took off like a bullet. Aggie mumbled some excuse and she also took off downstairs.
"Has she told you about Caroline stealing your money?" He sneered.
"With hand on my heart I know it wasn't Caroline" I said softly.
"So who was it?" he snarled.
"You know and I know so let's not play mind games. Make arrangements to repay it and I'll leave it at that." I said.
"Now can you please, leave as I need time to think all of this over?" I continued.
He snarled some reply that I didn't fully hear but as he was leaving it wasn't important. The last ten days had been bliss now reality of the horror I had went on holiday to recover from was beginning to rear its ugly head. Was the nightmare over?

I decided to have a bath. Warm soapy bubbles would perhaps wash away my fears and troubles. With both taps running the noise from the falling water was hopefully going to drown out my thoughts. A fierce grip on my shoulder startled me. I swung around to be faced with Bill snarling at me as he pushed the bathroom door shut and slid the bolt across. The look on his face was frightening and fear gripped my senses.

He began to undo and remove his belt. The buckle was big square and made of shiny metal. Gripping me tight I couldn't move. The slaps, punches and groping froze my mind. His hot evil breath swarming over me and his crude and vile words made me realise I couldn't escape.

"Don't resist or I'll call your precious girls to see what I'm doing to you" he spat.

As he thrust and pounded into me I focused on his belt. With each thrust he tore at my body. The sound of the others downstairs in the kitchen seemed to echo around the whole house so I decided to focus on their smiling faces.

A hard slap brought me back to reality.

"Don't hide away in your fucking mind I want you to see how much pleasure this is. Thee Mrs. Fucking Pearson being beaten in mind and body by me. Pat or Colin couldn't beat you but I have and am" he growled.

When it was over he kneeled over me and kissed my cheek. "Thanks now I can say you were fucking great. Get it?" He snarled. He laughed as he kicked me aside and walked out. I lay curled up tight as pain shot through my body and mind. I eventually struggled to lock the door, as I couldn't chance him coming back or the girls running in to join me. My whole body was trembling and I had to fight against the spasms that were washing over me. After several attempts I managed to ease myself into the bath. If I could wash away the blood from my scratches and cuts I might not look so bad.

The hot water, soap and sponge may have washed away the blood but what would wash away my thoughts and feelings. I crawled up to my bedroom wrapped in a bath towel all the time praying for the girls to remain downstairs. I sought out one of Ron's large tartan work shirts and eased it on. I then raked around to find a pair of old jogging bottoms I wore when I was pregnant and I gently pulled them on though my tears then lay exhausted on my bed.

The girls came running in and jumped upon my bed with Aggie following them into my room.

"Mum's tired, go and ask Caroline to help you make fairy cakes for the tea party we are going to have later" she said and off they went.

"Are you o.k.?" she asked.

"I have to go to St.Francis, can you stay till I come back? I might be late." I asked.

"Sure no problem. What's wrong has something happened? She asked.

"I'll explain later. I really need to get to St.Francis" I replied.

I kissed the girls and tried not to wince as they gave me a loving bear hug. Easing myself into the drivers seat was difficult as I was so sore and the drive was slow and laborious.

I rung the bell and Sister Joseph opened the door and gasped at my appearance and tried to hold onto me as I slid in a heap on the doorstep.

"Oh dear God. Come my child," she said as she led me like a dazed animal into their day room.

"I will phone for Dr.O'Rielly to come immediately and I'll organise some tea," she said.

His welcoming smile vanished when he looked at me.

"What in God's name has happened to you?" He asked.

Through blinding tears I stammered out my ordeal. I was ashamed. I felt dirty and I wanted to howl like a wounded animal.

"Right first things first. I will have to examine you," he said.

I winced at the thought but I knew he was right. He was

very gentle as he examined my injuries and tended them and his kind words soothed my mind. I still find it difficult to come to terms with the rape. He was like an animal, yet do animals act like that?

“Oh my dear child how much more can you endure” he said softly as he took my hand.

“Whom from your family can we phone as you can’t possibly drive home in this state?” he asked.

“What family. I have no one. They would only say I deserved it, as they all seem to think that bastard and I were together. I only trusted him because he appeared to understand what the whole Pat episode had done to me. How wrong was I?” I stammered.

“I drove myself here so I’ll drive myself home after I spend some time alone in the chapel” I continued.

“I’ll tell the sisters. Come back and see me next week to remove the stitches and for an overall check up. Also think over my advice on going to the police as I can provide my medical opinion. Take care and God Bless,” he said.

The calmness of the chapel soothed and prepared me for the drive home and I stopped off at the cemetery to weep, expecting Ron to be able to make things right.

For the next few days Aggie’s enquiring looks asked many unspoken questions and my nights were filled with nightmares always focusing on that belt buckle. I decided to

tell her I had hurt my back! It didn't work but at least I tried to appease her.
The police inspector at the local cop shop was only interested in him (Bill the Bastard) returning the money I had lost! He also suggested it would be best for him to remain at his bed sit at the Wellington until all the monies had been fully repaid!
As far as the accusation of rape was concerned I had no witnesses and Dr.O'Reilly's examination and statement weren't enough evidence, however he would speak to Bill and he would be disciplined if he thought fit!
The boys in blue were closing ranks!

I began to feel unwell in a familiar way.
The first specimen came back negative and the second specimen confirmed my worst nightmare. The yellow confirmation slip lay beside the clock on the mantelpiece awaiting Aggie's arrival.
In she walked looking exasperated as she said, "I demand to know what is going as on my nerves are shot to hell because I know something is wrong with you."
I handed her the yellow slip and she read out her own name then gave an almighty scream and slumped onto the sofa then her questions came fast and furious. I explained by using her name I could keep my secret for as long as

possible and she nodded in agreement. I also began to relate to her the events of the day we came home from holiday.
"What are we going to do?" she sobbed.
"You are going to make a pot of tea and I am going to disappear up my own arse" I replied.
"Don't joke, not now. What are we going to do?" she yelled.
"Truthfully Aggie I don't know but a cup of tea always helps" I smiled as I replied.

I drank the tea then promptly threw up. I took on board the full reality of my situation, I was definitely pregnant. Whenever I had been pregnant I couldn't drink tea as it always made me nauseous, now I had my second confirmation.
On arrival at St.Francis Dr.O'Reilly was waiting and as usual he was patient and supportive as he listened quietly as I informed him I was pregnant. I paced the room as I explained the monster inside me had to go and I needed time to get my inner self on track. I was pacing like a caged tiger and the fear and panic and utter hatred for this inside me was making me feel unreal. I had to escape.
To give me some time alone I was admitted into St Francis. As I had reoccurring woman's health problems from time to time no one would think it odd.

A visit from the then Archbishop Winning gave me two options of help.

Option 1: Stay with a family in America who would look after the girls and myself until the baby was born then I could decide whether to keep it or have it adopted.
Option 2: A convent in France would house the girls and myself and once again the offer of adoption would be offered.
All our needs would be provided and I would have no financial worry, he tendered a Blessing to us both before he left. Was this a chance to escape?
I was taken to a nearby hospital for an ultra sound scan and as I was anxious the lady doctor performing the procedure was gentle and reassuring.
"Let me show you the heart beat of your baby" she said as she turned the monitor in my direction. Screams, ear shattering screams then blackness.
I awoke in my own bed at St.Francis not knowing how I got there. On waking fully all I could hear was the word heartbeat.
I returned home a few days later taking another demon to haunt my blackness and with the knowledge time was ticking against me.

On telling my parents they reacted just as I thought.
“How could you be so bloody stupid?” they both yelled. As they continued to rant and rave at me I decided not to confide in them about the rape. What was the point? They wouldn’t listen so I left. They told Bill and he arrived at my home the following morning requesting to see me. Aggie stood dumbfounded as I snarled and spat words in his direction and he quickly left.
The monster inside me had to go and go now.
I telephoned a friend who was a midwife and asked for details on how to carry out a personal attempt at an abortion. I explained I was frantic and time was slowly ebbing away.
My parents, Aggie and Caroline sat in my sitting room having a chat over a drink while I was in the bathroom trying to end a life!
Did I succeed?
I only succeeded in giving myself a pelvic floor infection that caused me a great deal of pain. Dr.Sandilands called to see me and we had a serious discussion.
Mentally, physically and emotionally I was not in a condition to continue with the pregnancy. An appointment with a consultant at a nearby hospital was arranged for the next day and Franco drove me there and waited for me.
During my previous pregnancies I was always unwell but

now I was feeling horrendous and hiding my shape was taking its toll. In my mind's eye my belly was huge when in fact it was totally unnoticeable.

The consultant was rude abrupt and had hands like shovels. He was also very brutish while carrying out his internal examination and my silent sobs startled him.

"I was raped by a bastard of a brute, are you trying to outdo him?" I sobbed.

He was so apologetic and admitted he had not fully read my notes however arrangements were made for the following morning.

Soon this nightmare would be over.

Once again Franco drove me to hospital and waited while I was settled. My parents came to visit early evening. My in-laws had no idea and I wanted it kept that way.

By 11am next morning it was all over and by 2pm I was on my way to St.Francis to lick my wounds and convalesce.

Tucked safely in my usual bed clutching a hot water bottle I was administered a strong sedative and I was out till next morning.

Archbishop Winning arrived to see me and we spoke at great length. He was non judgemental and blessed me before he bid me farewell.

(Today as I write this I weep for an innocent little one I keep within my heart not a monster).

During my five-day stay the girls were brought daily and my in-laws came twice. Colin and Shona came to visit the day I was an emotional and mental wreck and the expressions on their faces spoke volumes, so I was glad they didn't linger long.

I felt I was the freak show that everyone had to come and see.

The Sisters of St. Francis cared for me tenderly and warmly while my time spent sitting in their small chapel brought a comfort and an inner feeling of being whole and at one with a great being who eased my weary and broken heart.

On the day I returned home I truly prayed the time had come to return to normal.

Ron's first anniversary was looming and in the ten months since he had been killed I had been on a roller coaster ride of immense emotional turmoil, maybe, just maybe.

Bill stayed on at the Wellington until the monies he had stolen while I was in Barra were repaid, then he was suspended and he moved out. I felt safe knowing he wasn't around and not having the fear of bumping into him in town was reassuring. A few weeks later my friend Marjorie phoned me to tell me she had just seen Bill on the beat in the shopping centre. I decided to march into the Gold Hat's office at the police station and told him very politely he had

24 hours to remove him from the streets of Hamilton or I would permanently. This monster had been shielded by the boys in blue however I would not tolerate him being anywhere within my vicinity, so I was not willing to enter into any discussion. Move him or else!
I'm glad to say I did not ask twice.

The debt letters from unpaid bills from before and after Ron's death became a nightmare and I began to dread the postman and the telephone ringing announcing another company after money. Franco was a true friend because he was always willing to help out as often as he could. I had to find a way to settle the most important ones and get them off my back. A gent from Ron's teenage years had helped him once before, maybe he would be willing to offer some kind of help. I went to see him and he was a delight but he had a healthy appetite for betting on the horses and of late they were winning more than he was. He was disappointed he couldn't help but he did suggest speaking to his brother Ernie.
"No time like present" he said as he lifted the phone. When he replaced the receiver he informed me I was to call into see Ernie next morning about 11am. I felt my words of thanks were inadequate but his kind comments about Ron made me on impulse reach up and kiss his weather beaten

cheek. Here was a man who knew Ron, really knew him as he truly had been as a young lad.

Next morning I called into see Ernie as suggested. Before me sat a man the clone of my grandad. His soft tones on speaking, his gentle mannerisms, his kind eyes, and his ability to understand without great details captivated me and held me spell bound.

"I didn't know your husband as well as my brother but his word will do me," he said.

"How much do you need on a weekly basis?" he asked.

"I've delivered your milk for numerous years so send your Aggie down here every Friday morning and I'll give her a brown envelope with the cash inside" he continued.

"Do you want me to sign an i.o.u. every week?" I asked.

"No lass. I may not know you but I can trust you as you're only doing this for your children. I can't understand why Ron's family don't help," he said.

"They would never do so when he was alive so I know they won't now. How can I ever thank you?" I said.

Every Friday Aggie walked down and picked up the envelope that contained the funds to help me begin to clear my debts.

Very slowly my inner strength was ebbing away and all my

inner demons and phantoms were invading my waking moments.

I took to spending many hours late into the night sitting in the cemetery. I was lost. Ron had been my anchor and now I was being emotionally buffeted against unseen mountainous seas.

The house, our home, had become a place of no refuge. Each corner hid a nightmare of all the incidents that had taken place since I had moved in. At night, instead of the house being my safe sanctuary, it now filled me with dread. I began to stay awake all night and only sleep when Aggie arrived in the morning.

Franco tried his best to reach the place I had locked myself away within. He never once faltered at trying to lift my mood. One day he arrived with a great idea.

Him and Marco plus the girls and I move into Windmill Road and live as one big family. With the sale of Woodside Walk and all our monies combined the pile of debts could be settled and he would take care of all the weekly financial outlays in return for me being a mother to everyone.

I refused. Why?

Because I thought he wanted the whole family set up including the physical side. He was a good friend and as my whole being was so fragile I was now petrified of being hurt mentally, emotionally and physically. He was very upset but I'm sure he understood. It was a very kind and sincere offer but I couldn't allow myself to go down any road that may cause me pain.

Christmas came and went and Hogmanay loomed. I decided to throw a party and both sets of parents turned up with Colin in tow.

Aggie knew my reasoning behind the party. I wouldn't have the time to dwell on that kiss from the previous Hogmanay. I could lie to everyone to stop them knowing or finding out the truth but Aggie had a knack of being able to tell me what I was feeling and thinking. I am ashamed to say I got totally drunk as a skunk but it only eased my upset a little.

Into the New Year I reshuffled the downstairs rooms and let the back one out to a lady who was as bubbly as she was big and with her infectious laugh she soon won me over. Her personal life was a total mess but after what I had been through she was like a breath of fresh air. Everyone enjoyed her company and she doted on the girls. Lynda had an unexplainable way of making me feel safe.

Franco was doing business with a young Iranian guy who was interested in setting up in business on his own. Franco knew I had brains and a good eye for business so he introduced us. Massood was married with a young baby, he was a good laugh and he knew I didn't like unknown men as I regarded them all as bastards. He dropped in anytime he was passing and I soon began to stop looking at him as the enemy. He offered to take me out to dinner so he could discuss a business plan he wanted a second opinion on. Lynda talked me into going.

"It's not a date silly its only dinner" she laughed.

She was right he was happily married and with my brain lying dormant it would give me a chance to get the little grey cells moving again.

The night was a success and he made me laugh so much at times I had to pinch myself to make sure it was real. He told me all about his childhood and why he had to escape Iran while I told him only parts I wanted to share about my life.

He became a good friend and I saw him on a daily basis. His business plan of opening an estate agents and insurance company began to grow on me and he offered me the chance to become his business partner. His wife accepted me and was more than willing for our partnership to go ahead.

I found us a property at the end of my street and with people in the right business I raised a mortgage to allow us to move in. There was a large amount of renovation work needed but Ernie was prepared to pitch in. The week before

I picked up the keys my brother was paroled and home once again beside me.
The visits to see him had been awful but when I went in I was always Mrs. Happy. I still have the large pile of letters, poems and drawings he sent me and one day I shall write about him in full, along with all my other family who were a part of my early years.
Tom got on with Massood and their antics when together were priceless. Although Massood found it difficult to cope with my brother and myself together when we were in high spirits.
With Franco and Shirley now an item they moved into one of the bed sit's in Windmill Road and Tom and Caroline taking up another in Woodside Walk, I decided it was time to move out. I needed a place to call home for the girls and I. I sat down and laid out all my financial ins and outs and decided; on the outcome of the new business venture being a success, putting more effort into the running of Windmill Road and turning my upstairs three rooms in Woodside Walk into double bed sits, I could afford it.
I ran it by Ernie who agreed it looked as though I could manage it. As Ernie had been such a huge help I needed his approval, as I didn't want him to think I was forgetting his continual financial support.
It only took me a few weeks to find a new house. My

parents ranted and raved but as that was their normal behaviour now I was getting used to it.

With my belongings packed I was ready to leave behind the house that had at one time been a home.

Fergus Gardens

Fergus Gardens was a modern semi detached villa with three public rooms and three large bedrooms situated in a private cul-de-sac in an exclusive part of town. As the cul-de-sac had only one entrance of a road leading to a private estate I felt it was a very safe location. After a few small renovations it was soon comfortable.

With money from the bed sit rents and the office income things were slowly looking up. The money side of life wasn't perfect but I felt I could cope.

Windmill Road was running as smoothly as it could. My parents were conscientious and the rents were always paid on time. The residents were all like one large happy family. They all enjoyed social nights out and the communal kitchen was always buzzing with their group recipe cook in. Anytime I was present they all treated me with great respect and they were always so caring towards the girls.

Renting out bed-sits opened my eyes to how many people in our community lived without family support.

The office was a challenge now the renovations were completed and as it was up and running smoothly I gave it my full support when the girls were at school.

I decided I was never going to be pregnant again. The events leading up to the termination continually flashed into my mind and invaded my dreams. I wanted to be sterilized a.s.a.p. The NHS had a very long waiting list and I couldn't wait. I felt it was imperative to have it carried out immediately. The only route open was to have it carried out privately. Arrangements were soon made and I booked myself into a private hospital in Glasgow. One overnight stay and my past nightmare would be a closed chapter. During the routine sterilization operation I woke up. I can still remember the anaesthetist words. "Bloody hell she's awake." Muffled sounds and soon I was engulfed by darkness.

Three days later I awoke. Dr O'Reilly had been sent for from St.Francis to enlighten them to my plight. I had been very diligent in informing them of my reaction to anaesthetic, so something or someone had made an error but everyone was being very coy about answering my questions.

On my return home I felt so ill and the blood loss was alarming. The hospital had prescribed antibiotics for any infection I may have plus small white pills to stop the bleeding. The white pills were useless!

Ten days later the consultant made a home visit, not his usual practice his secretary snootily informed me. I was very weak and I explained I was concerned something serious was wrong. Another batch of tablets were prescribed and eventually I returned to normal. However the incident had taken its toll on my overall health.
The hospital sent in their account and I was staggered by the charges. The accounts department were not interested in my complaint only in their account being settled.
Money worries were back to haunt me. Income into the office I had invested with Massoud wasn't living up to expectations so my share dropped dramatically.
My parents had an idea of making extra money for themselves. They offered the residents of the bed-sits full laundry service plus breakfasts and packed lunches. It appeared to be a huge success however I was not offered any share of the profit.
Even though it was my electricity, washing machine, iron and cooking facilities being used I was accused of being greedy!
Since Ron's death I felt I had been invaded by something I couldn't see or hear but somehow I knew it was real. The feeling of being inside looking out at times was claustrophobic. To be totally honest I felt overwhelmed by the thought of each new day. The events of the past years,

before and since Ron's death were taking its toll, big time.

Lynda suggested a crowd of us went away for a long weekend on three pleasure boats sailing on Loch Ness. Pleasant, relaxing and fun. (As I am writing this my girls informed me they were scared stiff the whole time we were away. They were convinced we were all going to drown!) Massood was a prat that weekend and I had to continually verbally assault him each time. He was a friend but at times he could drive the calmest person to distraction.
His wife was tall, slender and thick at times. Her marriage was a sham but it had to work no matter what. He played on her something awful and whenever he did I would always speak out. She admired this because he always listened to me.
On our return home I had cross words with my dad, which led to me experiencing a full-blown panic attack. I thought I was having a heart attack and it was not a pretty sight.
The urge to become a recluse was growing on me daily.
I decided to sell Windmill Road. Ernie and Franco had helped me financially but it was time to get off the merry go round as I was rapidly going around in circles and the more I tried to find a way out the worse the situation became. I was in the middle of a financial minefield. The money from the sale would solve most if not all of the

debts.
I also decided to put Woodside Walk up for sale. Since the rape it didn't feel like my home anymore, that was why I had moved to this house.
My parents didn't take the news very well and demanded I bought them a house. As they had gave up so much I owed them. I explained I wasn't in a position financially to do so. After angry words and threats they stormed out only to storm back a few days later while Lynda and myself were going over my plans.
Lynda was insisting I contact Colin. She suggested he would offer a fresh input and he would be only too pleased to help.
I explained I couldn't. I couldn't because I didn't know how to speak to him anymore and anyway he wouldn't be interested.

As my parents car pulled up outside I asked Lynda to go upstairs and wait. My mum terrified her so I didn't have to ask her twice.
They sat side by side on the sofa. They had been to Edinburgh to see about obtaining a council house. As they had given up a long-term tenancy to come to Hamilton rehousing them wouldn't be a problem. Only one obstacle marred the solution, they couldn't choose which area of

Edinburgh they wanted. Whatever was offered would have to be accepted. I thought it was good news however they obviously didn't. On and on they moaned. I felt I was being bullied relentlessly.

My mum's next move surprised and shocked my dad and myself.

She stood up and lurched towards me. As I was standing in front of a roaring open fire I quickly side stepped. Too late. Her grip on my neck knocked the wind from me and she began to push me backwards. With her two hands in a throttlehold around my neck I was beginning to feel great discomfort. Pushing me backwards through the sitting room and into the dining room, her hold intensifying, my back hit off one of the dining room chairs and I couldn't stop myself from becoming sprawled over the table. Out spat her words of hate. The pain was now excruciating and visions flew through my mind. I had been on the receiving end of her fists for most of my childhood as she always beat me and blamed me for her marrying my dad. Memories from then mingled with what was happening now, blending so smoothly my mind was in total confusion as I felt skin lifting from my throat and I could hear the most terrible groaning noises.

Oh to sleep, to close my eyes and go beyond this pain, to awaken in the light. As my head continued to be pounded off the table her manic eyes and her evil harsh words kept me from the light.

Poor Lynda unknown to me was having a hellish time upstairs, pacing the bedroom in a panic not knowing what course of action to take.

Come downstairs and help? No. She might attack.

Phone the police? No, the phone downstairs would ting and she'll know I am upstairs and she'll come and get me!

With all these thoughts running through her mind she continued to pace.

Dad finely realised I was in serious trouble. My lips were black and my face deep purple when he prized her off me. He held on to her tightly as he lifted her bodily towards the front door. While doing so he shouted it was my entire fault.

I was so happy to hear the front door slam if I had had the energy I would have danced for joy. However as I stumbled to the fireplace I heard Lynda coming downstairs. As she walked into the sitting room I was standing holding onto the fireplace.

"Oh my God what has she done?" Lynda said as she burst into tears.

"It must have been something I said," I croaked with a faint smile.

"Why do you always find a morsel of fun in every

horrendous situation?" Lynda exploded.

"I have to, it's my survival" I replied before I passed out and hit the floor.

When the doctor arrived he tried not to look shocked. After his examination he informed me I needed urgent medical treatment at hospital. He began to phone for an ambulance but I stopped him.

"I'll drive myself to hospital" I said.

"I don't think that's wise "he replied.

"She has damaged my throat not my hands," I said painfully.

He agreed, wrote me a letter to take to the hospital and left. Aggie walked in as the doctor was leaving. With Aggie and Lynda both crying as Lynda went over the morning's events I reminded them that I had to be out of the house before the girls came home. I insisted not a word was to be said to the girls.

At the hospital the doctor thought I had been savagely attacked.

"She has, by her mother" Lynda shouted.

A full examination of my throat plus x-rays followed all the while the doctor was having a problem taking in that my own mother had inflicted these terrible injuries.

He wanted to admit me for observation and depending on

the swelling examine the inner throat tissues under anaesthetic.
I explained I couldn't stay and after a long frustrating and painful conversation he agreed I could go home but I had to follow his orders to the letter. Armed with tablets and a throat spray plus an appointment for a few days later we set off for home.
"Make sure you lock all your doors," he said as he bid me goodbye.
Did he know something I didn't?
The scratches and the bruising were unsightly and the pain was washing over me in waves. The drive home seemed endless. Lynda couldn't drive so she decided to relate to me her thoughts of when she was trapped upstairs. Tears rolled down my face as she said "Oh I didn't mean to upset you."
"You're not it's just too bloody sore to laugh" I spluttered.
Poor Lynda was mentally and emotionally done in. I explained to the girls I had a very sore throat and they hugged and kissed me gently and skipped off to their playroom. Normality had returned.

After teatime my brother arrived looking shaken. "What's up?" Aggie asked him.
"Mum is out prowling about looking for you. She has a huge bread knife in her bag and she is going to wait until

you're alone then finish you off" he stammered out.
"Dad's in bed and as he's taken his tablets he'll be asleep till morning" he said. "She means business and she's snarling like a mad animal and she's warned me not to say a word," he continued. "Do you want me to stay?" he offered.
"No" I replied.
I decided to send Aggie home by taxi. Lynda insisted on staying.

With all the doors and windows double locked plus safety catches in place and the fire stoked with full coal buckets stored in the kitchen I sat down to await my fate.
The girls were safely tucked up in bed unaware that a mad woman who was their gran and my mother was stalking the house.
"Phone the police they'll help" Lynda said.
"No they were useless after the rape and the Pat's episode was a pure farce" I said.
"Phone Colin he'll help" she said.
"No he will not" I replied.
"Yes he will please let me phone him. I'm sure he wouldn't want anything terrible to happen," she pleaded.
"I know you mean well but please, he will not help, no one can. I don't want to discuss it" I hissed.

We sat on the carpet in front of the roaring fire and told each other our funny little stories, our fears and our inner most secrets throughout the night till first light. In the morning with the girls safely in school I drove Lynda home to bed then I headed to my lawyers.

Very slowly I asked him to read over the statement I had written detailing all the events of the previous day. Talking was now so painful so I decided to write my words down. He asked many questions and I wrote down my answers. So a very slow and laborious meeting followed. We agreed an injunction was to be served on my mother to keep her away from my family, my properties and myself, except the one she resided in.

The injunction was not to include dad. Why? Because I knew in the cold light of day his sanity would kick in and he would understand my actions.

I wore polo neck jumpers and scarves for many weeks. After numerous hospital visits and unpleasant treatment my throat recovered. However some long lasting damage was done and to this day whenever I take a sore throat the damaged tissue makes the symptoms worse.

Before this incident I wanted to become a recluse, now I

felt I had to.

I went to view a flat in a country house in the middle of a huge wooded area, which made it very secluded. Remote? Yes. Safe? Yes.

Lynda talked me out of it.

Next I went to view a run down old manse in a small village situated deep within wild secluded hills. Remote? Yes. Safe? Yes.

Once again Lynda explained the girls would be isolated from other children and all their friends. Once again she won over my sensible head.

I needed to escape.

Massood's brother was stuck in Turkey on the border with Iran. His wife and child were with him and he had to escape because he had gone AWOL from the Iranian air force and his life was in danger.

To cut a long story short Massood and I went out to join them to offer our support. This trip would allow me time to escape and as a British passport holder no one would give me hassle so I would have time to chill out.

Lynda and Aggie along with Caroline and my brother looked after the girls and I felt totally comfortable with the arrangements.

The trip was bloody awful! The local people were unpleasant to say the least.
The accommodation was not fit for my cats and the food was tolerable just!
After visiting many agencies to find a possible passage I agreed to fly to Dublin on my own to try to set up a legal entry route. I spent four days on my own and as I strolled along the streets and visited the sights I recalled my past visit with Ron and the girls. I was alone but I knew someone was closely walking with me. The trip was unsuccessful to those in Turkey but not for me as I found a sense of peace being on my own.

On my return to a backwater area of Turkey my luggage was lost. We then missed an internal flight or so the armed soldier informed us, even although we could see the plane on the tarmac still loading.
The armed soldier was insisting we were late. I became outspoken, Massood raised his voice to me and I verbally retaliated. The soldier hit me and I lost a tooth.
Did I shut up?
Only when a pilot who was standing nearby rushed forward hugged me close, smothered me in kisses uttering soothing words in his native French tongue and ushered me to a quiet spot did I shut up. Massood stood open mouthed as he

looked on. For several hours the pilot Jay tried to get us another flight and a phone line to inform those back home what was going on.

My dad answered the phone but the noise in the background was making it difficult to hear each other. I quickly explained my plight and asked to speak to the girls. Lyn explained they were having a party and it was great fun. Lynda had invited all the children from their classes and by the sounds it was mayhem. She giggled a good-bye then went to find Louise.

Louise said “Mummy we’re having great fun phone back later,” click the line went dead.

I was devastated and as my tears fell Jay organised another phone line and somewhere to rest. I phoned home again and this time I spoke to my Dad. Over the next three days I poured my heart out to my French saviour. A true saviour out of the blue. Massood and his family were now very coy every time they were around me.

Once back in Istanbul we all had to attend the British embassy. The consulate was from Edinburgh, my home city, so over real tea and scones I explained in private to him the real reason for my visit. I was trying to help others in trouble because I knew how it felt to have no-one. He already knew everything because my dad had contacted the proper channels and all the information had been passed on.

The night before our flight home I feigned a headache and once in our bedroom I very carefully searched through the bags of Massood and his family. I found multiple copies of documents that were obviously forged. I helped myself to a couple of each. These people were dangerous so for once I was going to have to play dumb.
Massood and his family were elated they had been granted a visa for twelve weeks. On the flight home Massood questioned my sombre mood. I explained I fully understood why I had been invited and being used was not something I felt happy with. I also pointed out that his relatives did not only speak in their mother tongue, in fact they could speak fluent English. He then went off to explain I knew everything. They pleaded with me and I felt uncomfortable so I remained silent for the rest of our flight home.
On our arrival at Heathrow airport I slowly strolled through customs and passport control and while they had to queue in what was then called the 'alien entry' department I idled up to a policeman. He smiled and asked if he could be of help.
"Yes" I replied. "I've been in a place where time stood still and I was treated like a second class citizen, so I would be very pleased if you could relate to me what has been happening in the news while I have been gone. He duly did

as requested.
As the others walked towards me their faces became ashen.
I thanked the policeman and stepped forward to meet them.
Passport control had been waiting for them and their visa had been reduced to three weeks as the consulate in Istanbul had contacted London direct. What action was to be taken after then I did not wish to know. I only had one task firmly set in my mind. I was going home.
Home to my girls with a promise never to leave them again.
The drive from London to Hamilton seems to take forever.
I crept into the house at 5 am. Lynda awoke at my touch and whispered the girls had been as good as gold. The plans for the party had excited them and kept their spirits up. As she inspected my dishevelled state she asked, "How was it"?
"Don't ask, I'm home safe and sound so go back to sleep we'll talk later" I replied.
I crept into Lyn's room, her eyes opened and she launched herself into my arms.
Louise, who had always slept deeply took only a few seconds to respond to my gentle touch on her cheek.
As we all fell into my bed our tears melted away and their familiar smell eased my senses. I was home and it was oh so sweet.

Windmill Road was now sold and an agreed entry date was set. Soon my parents would be back in Edinburgh and I could relax.
It was at this time my relationship with Massood became sexual. Why?

One night when I was feeling very low, insecure and lost it just happened. It was bloody awful. I squirmed and cried and flashbacks of Bill flooded my mind, this wasn't making love it was sex and it was awful. Our relationship had crossed the line between business and pleasure, so I put a stop to our intimate relationship immediately. It didn't happen again.
I still do not know why it went sexual. Ron had cheated on me on several occasions now I was doing the same to Massood's wife. I felt truly ashamed.

Windmill Road was packed up for my parents move and the surplus furniture and soft furnishing were sold although my mum left with more boxes than she had arrived with.
All the residents found new accommodation and each one was kind and generous to the girls. With two weeks left before my parents moved every day was filled with dread of them maybe causing trouble. I managed to have a short polite conversation with my dad and he wished me well. He

would miss the girls but in time things would come right. On the day they left for Edinburgh a huge weight was lifted from my shoulders.

The money from Windmill Road repaid Ernie, Franco and other debts.

Ernie did not know me personally but on trust he helped me financially to the sum of a very generous amount without interest or any paperwork signed by myself. He was a true gentleman who never judged or condemned me, he only wanted to help, and he did so without falter. I will always hold his kindness close to my heart. A true Good Samaritan.

I also repaid Franco a large amount and again he wouldn't accept any interest. He knew how I felt about keeping myself financially secure to enable me to provide for my girls.

A thought sprung to mind. If I sold all the properties except Woodside Walk and renovated and decorated the whole house to make it look like new we could move back in.

I had given my lawyer full permission to sell Woodside Walk for the best price however unknown to me an offer had been made and as it was well over the asking price he was in the process of accepting. I was devastated so I went to see the people who had made the offer, would they

consider withdrawing their offer?
I opened up my heart and pleaded and they explained their house had been up for sale for several months and they had just legally accepted the offer. Their answer had to be no.
Gone, lost forever so I couldn't go back.
The blackness devoured me for days.

The office was becoming unbearable and Massood's whole attitude had changed. Since his family had arrived he had become arrogant, rude and cocky. He also couldn't understand why I had no interest in him sexually. In fact this drove him nuts as he thought of himself as a stud as he had numerous sexual encounters with anyone at the drop of a hat. His wife was finding him difficult also. I asked him to buy me out but he refused. We continued to have angry words and I just wanted all the hassle over.
Oh to be free.
Returning from a day trip to visit friends in Livingston I called into the office. The brass nameplate was missing from the outside door and as I walked into the front reception a vacant room welcomed me. As I walked from room to room I noted each was totally empty. All the expensive office furniture and fittings gone not even a paper clip was left. Everything had been stolen. The back door had been forced to make it look as if it had been

burgled. I smelt a rat and that rat was Massoud.

The girls ran around playing in the empty rooms while I tried to get my head to accept what my eyes were seeing. I called the police, they weren't interested and they insisted it was a civil matter. I was totally shocked once again I felt so alone.

Next day I called at the bank. The two tellers looked at me then at each other, I had seen that look before. The manager invited me into his office.

"How are you feeling?" he enquired.

"I'm fine" I replied.

Massood had told him I was in hospital very ill.

"Can I see the accounts?" I asked. "The accounts have been closed" he replied.

My mind raced and I felt a panic attack coming on. The manager became alarmed as I paced his office floor like a caged tiger demanding answers. He slowly explained as I fought to bring every fibre of my being into focus.

Massood had requested the accounts closed. His request had been supported by a hand written letter from myself asking for the appropriate forms to be given to him to enable me to sign them during my hospital stay. As the appropriate forms had been signed by myself and witnessed all the rules had been followed to the letter so the accounts had been closed and the monies uplifted by him.

The bottom fell out of my slowly never-ending crumbling world once again.

For several days I tried to contact him at home but he always evaded me. His poor wife was devastated and could offer no help. I contacted his last employers and was soon reeling at my findings. He was a serial fraudster. I was not his first victim. The police did know about him but no action was ever taken against him. He was a crook. He had broken into my property, stolen goods, committed fraud and yet it was a civil matter. I can understand why many people question the role of the police.

I became even more reclusive and Aggie and Lynda tried their best to cheer me up.
I was having panic attacks daily and one severe attack made me pass out. They put me to bed and insisted on phoning the doctor who duly arrived.
Dr.Graham wasn't my usual doctor but as he was on call he'd have to do. He was austere and abrupt and he obviously thought he knew my circumstances by his attitude. He was so far off the mark and as I tried to explain he interrupted saying "Everyone has problems. Sort out your mess and your symptoms will improve. Should you ignore my advice you will have a heart attack or a stoke

depending on your stress levels. Take these tablets and rest, if you don't you'll only have yourself to blame."
He then picked up his bag and went downstairs to impart the same words to Aggie and Lynda before he left.
I was already feeling awful so his words and attitude didn't help.

Tablets to calm me down during the day and pills to make me sleep at night. The answer is never found at the bottom of a bottle and spending my days and nights doped up to the eyeballs was not the solution to my situation so I refused to take them after the first day.
Maybe it was time to move on.

I drove into the Australia House travel centre in Glasgow I had visited after Ron's death. I asked the staff for the gent who had been so kind on my earlier visit. The manager asked me to describe the gent I had spoken to." Are you sure it was early 1985?" he asked. "Yes" I replied as I went on to explain the full conversation I had with him.
"I believe you and I don't wish to appear rude or to upset you but you must be mistaken" he said.
"No I am not" I replied feeling slightly annoyed.
"Please, forgive me as I don't wish to upset you" he continued.

"Is it his day off?" I asked.
"Please, allow me to get us a cup of tea and I shall explain" he said as he escorted me into his office.
The gent had been a greatly respected company owner and he was very dedicated to his duties. He had arranged for many people to begin new lives in his beloved homeland and his death had been a great loss, however he had died a happy man overlooking his beautiful and beloved estate in his native Australia.
"Oh I'm so sorry, when did he die?" I stammered.
"1973" he replied.
Goosebumps came out all over me as I asked "When in 1973?"
From somewhere I heard a voice say "March."
I continued "No don't tell me. Was it March?"
"Yes how did you know" he replied looking bewildered.
"Yes that's the month and year I was married" I replied.
Once I regained my composure I thanked him for his time and left. I drove home in a trance.
Was I being given a sign?
What was I going to do?
Could I go on? Did I want to?
Later that night I spent a short time at the cemetery looking towards my stars. On my return home as the girls slept peacefully I sat in the back garden and looked out into the

blackness to find Ron's star.

I had no one. Family had written me off and friends had their own lives and worries. Daily life was a constant struggle against so many knocks. With each knock down the struggle to stand up and continue was taking its toll. Maybe it was time to stop trying. A plan began to form in my mind.

There was a way out. The girls and I were going on a journey that would only require a one-way ticket.

Would we be missed? No.

As no one truly cared the outcome of my plan would be a nine-day wonder. I kept quiet about my plan as I slowly collected the things I would need.

With everything in place I told Aggie to take the following day off. When she asked why, I made a plausible excuse and told her I would see her on Friday. She wasn't happy but she eventually agreed.

Next day I made sure the whole house was spick and span from one end to the other. The girls and I went out for tea and on our return we all bathed together and sang our hearts out.

As they lay asleep my mind wandered back to each of their births. They were bundles of pure joy and love and I could never leave them as they belonged to me.

I took pen and paper and began to write a letter to each of the following.
My parents. My in laws. Tom and Caroline. Colin and lastly Aggie. I then laid them out in an orderly fashion on the coffee table.
(As I write this I have looked out those letters and re read them. I was going to include them, however, maybe one day).
On the cooker in the kitchen a pan of milk was simmering and as I crushed each tablet and mixed it into the liquid I was becoming aware that the pan now contained a very lethal mixture. Soon the pain would be gone.
Louise loved warm milk and with hot chocolate mixed through it she would drink it without any problems.
Lyn didn't like warm milk too much so I would have to coax her.
I would wait until I was sure the girls were with Ron then I would join all of them.
No one would shed any tears, they would only sigh with relief.
As I laid the spoon on the work surface the milk on it spread to form a small pool on the work surface.
WHAM! A full-blown panic attack kicked in. My mind began screaming. "What are you doing?"
I crawled to the phone as pain racked my whole body.

(Similar to a ball inside a pinball machine).
Grasping for breath I clutched the phone. Who could I call? Who would help me?
I dialled a number and a familiar voice said "Hello."
"I need you here now please, come and help me. Oh please, come, as I need help now" I cried.
"We are on our way, sit quiet my child and we'll be with you shortly," the voice said.
"Please, don't let us down. I need you. God help me" I continued to sob.
"Hush my child I am with you. We will be there shortly so sit quiet," She said.
Time stood still. What felt like a few minutes was in fact a full half hour when a light knock on the front door heralded my saviours.
As the two St.Francis nuns walked in one led me slowly into the sitting room while the other went into the kitchen. I heard her busying herself with the pan of milk and I knew we were safe. She then came into the sitting room with cups of tea and said "It's all gone, washed away no need to worry."
They sat with me as I poured my heart out and I let them read the pile of letters. As they listened they poured love onto my emotional wounds, spoke words of comfort and renewed my spirit for living, their words are locked away in

my heart.
As the milkman laid his delivery on our doorstep the sisters left promising to phone me later in the day to arrange a visit to St. Francis for me.
The girls had just left for school with their friends when Lynda arrived.
"Are you alright?" she asked.
"Yes. Why?" I said.
"You've been in my mind all night" She said.
"I'm fine just a bit tired" I replied.
As I went into the kitchen to make tea she went into the sitting room to stoke the fire.
"What are these?" she asked. Holding in her hand the letters I had forgotten to pick up from the coffee table. I didn't have to reply as she read each name on the envelopes her face and eyes told me she understood. I related the previous night's events and over the next seven days she never left my side. Not once did she judge me or condemn my actions she only gave brilliant emotional support. Ronnie her boyfriend didn't complain about not seeing her.
Aggie was upset but not shocked when I told her. She suggested I invited all the family on both sides and explain what I had nearly committed, when they knew the full facts they would all become more supportive and caring.
"No fucking way. They have all chosen to condemn me," I

shouted.

I wanted to live and my beautiful girls needed to live to grow up into brilliant adults. So my journey went on and with each hug and kiss from them I slowly picked myself up.

The house went on the market and Lynda took control of the viewings for me. The office was lying empty and it was big enough to provide me with a safe sanctuary to help me find time to find a quiet spot within my being.
The house sold quickly and with our belongings packed I arranged our move. Lynda planned a fun packed day out with the girls to allow me to move without the worry of them getting under my feet.
The girls were always a wonder to me and as long as they were close for me to give out big Mummy hugs for reassurance they always adapted to wherever we were or whatever we were doing.
As usual I did my tour of the house to say good-bye but as I drove off I didn't look back.
Into myself I thought, "I can and will go on."

Gateside Street

Gateside Street was a ground floor residential flat I had renovated and used as an office suite along with Massood as "Golden Wealth Insurance and Estate Agents," which was now defunct.

Fergus Gardens sold quickly, so I moved into the office to live with the girls.

The main office that was mahogany wood lined became our sitting room. The rear staff / combined training room with a tiny kitchen leading off, the kitchen being a small sink with one cupboard, became our dining room and playroom. The bathroom had no bath, only a toilet sufficed. The front office became my bedroom; the back office made a cosy bedroom for the girls. With no bathing facilities it was basic. The windows at the rear had iron bars on them, they overlooked a large cobble stoned enclosed private car parking area. In the tiny kitchen I had an electric kettle, toaster microwave oven and a two ring camping gas stove.

With the help of an old man who owned a removal business and a young lad, the three of us soon had everything

moved. When the old man first arrived at Fergus Gardens he was surprised I had no one else to help. However by the time he and his young lad left the flat had taken shape. Which meant by the time I picked the girls up from school our new home awaited their delightful chatter.
Being on the main road, close to the town centre at times it could be noisy when the night's revellers wound their way home. However the girl's bedroom at the rear was quiet, so they settled in quickly.

Massood had busted the back door and as I couldn't afford to repair it, I heaved the two very large and heavy old storage heaters behind it. Should anyone wish to break-in they would have had to be King Kong to move the heaters, also the noise it would make would alert me. I also kept a very large old-fashioned soup pot on the top of the storage heaters, should it fall it was a back up alarm. Plus a large wooden Irish shillelagh on the small table next to my bed. Sounds good, well it did in theory anyway. I also know I would have used them if I had to do so.

With proceeds from the sale of Fergus Gardens I paid three months mortgage in advance. The balance from the sale, which was not very much, went towards outstanding debts, so money was still tight.

I couldn't find a job, as I had no one to take care of the girls. I could no longer employ Aggie due to my money situation however she would drop by as often as she wanted to see the girls. I only had my widow's pension and family allowance, money was again a problem.
Old friends knew where I had moved to, but they did not drop by. I felt like a small island, alone, surrounded by an ocean of intolerance.
When the girls were tucked up in bed, nights dragged by and I found myself alone with my thoughts and fears.

We did not have a bath but we made bath nights fun. I filled the girls baby bath and placed it in front of the fire with lots of bubbles, I made it fun, however it's not the same as splashing and playing around in a big bath.

Marjorie invited us round to her home one night for dinner then offered the girls a bubbly bath. It was nice of her but it did not feel right. I felt awkward although I am sure Marjorie would have been upset if she knew.
My In-laws invited us up one afternoon after school to have a bite to eat and to allow the girls to bathe. It turned out a nightmare, the girls made too much noise and they splashed around too much. My father in-law was not happy about this and he couldn't hide it.

Dinner was hot soup and cold meat sandwiches. On thc drive home the girls both said, "We don't want to do that again, it was Yuk," So "yuk" made me find another solution.

An idea filled my mind... Next morning, with the girls safe in school I went along to the local swimming baths. The place had a separate part that housed large cubicles, each which consisted of a huge cast iron bathtub, a chair and a wooden slatted standing board. The place was warm and big bath towels were supplied. I sought out the supervisor; I explained my situation and the Supervisor looked at me with a glare. Could the girls and myself come along to swim in the pool then without any problems, could we go straight through to the hot tubs? His face lit up as he smiled broadly and nodded in agreement, he thought it was a fine idea. I shook his big strong hand and kissed him on the cheek. It was arranged, I would return when I picked the girls up from school.
I went home and prepared soup and crusty bread for later. Opposite was an excellent Italian Restaurant that was owned by a friend of Franco's so I arranged to pick up a pizza for after our soup.

The swimming baths were empty when we arrived; it was

to be like this most days we attended. The staff were so pleasant, one pool attendant called me over to the side of the pool and said "we will watch the girls in the pool while you transfer your clothes and run your bath." I agreed. "Use cubicle number seven that can always be yours," my eyes filled with tears at their kindness. I gathered up our clothes and went through the connecting door and ahead of me was cubicle seven.

The Supervisor had placed a bottle of kiddies' bubble bath in our cubicle. I was so touched by his kindness I wept as the hot water flowed into the iron tub.

The tub was so big we all fitted into it, we giggled, we splashed and we sung our hearts out. Monday's, Wednesdays and Fridays, our bath days were brilliant!!

Another problem I had to overcome was washing our clothes; I couldn't plumb in our washing machine, as there was no room in our tiny kitchen. The local Laundrette had closed down so the nearest one was in Motherwell, a town near Hamilton. I could only afford to go once a week, so I made inquiries.

Marjorie again offered to do my washing but I felt it wasn't fair to impose on her, although when money was really scarce she insisted.

Once washed, I couldn't always afford to use the tumble

dryers, so I had to find somewhere to hang it out to dry. My in-laws agreed I could use their back garden, but once again it was a problem so I only used it twice.

One sunny afternoon as I looked out through the bars onto the cobbled back yard it came to me how sunny and warm it was, a suntrap.

I searched through my unpacked boxes and found my clothes rope and pegs. I heaved the two brick filled storage heaters and opened the back door. Using the bars on the window and hooks on the facing wall of the shutdown factory I crisscrossed my rope and I had an instant drying area. Once again I felt I had achieved something wonderful. Slowly my confidence was rising; I had to firmly believe I was capable, yes capable, of achieving anything!

We still went to visit Auntie Lynda who had now moved into a mobile home. Then in turn myself and my girls with Auntie Lynda would go along to visit her friend Scottie, who herself had three children, two girls and one boy… Louise and Lyn both enjoyed all the visits, mixing with children outside of school was very good for the girls. I could relax and act myself with these friends while at the same time spending time, although indirectly, with the girls close by!

On Lynda's mobile home site was a gypsy called Sindy who was a complete nutter but nice with it. She made me laugh with stories about her antics with men. Another was an older woman who claimed to be a witch. She lived alone with her big black cat called Lucifer. She had been widowed three times and each husband had left her money. I could never understand why she lived there.

She was always lovely to the girls and me. Gypsy Sindy was petrified of her and was always edging around on eggshells whenever the witch invited us to take tea.

All these people accepted me for who I was, and they made us feel welcome. The girls as always snuggled happily with the lovely people who were around us feeling safe.

I was paranoid about their safety. I always had to be around them. During school days I would sometimes walk down to the playground and watch them at playtime. I was always discreet.

The girls were my life, I felt we had no one who cared, friends yes, and family no. However one problem remained at times. After deducting money for the launderette and the baths plus daily living expenses left me skint. Friends inviting us to tea were so lovely and a beautiful gesture of kindness, but to always accept would have been wrong.

One night I went across to the Italian Restaurant to pick up a pasta dish take-away. As I counted out my money I realised I was short. I became flustered and I thought I would die of embarrassment when the receptionist took me aside, took my hand and quietly said "We remember what you did for Cathy, have this meal on us, and anytime you're short let us know, your kids will never go hungry." As I stumbled out the door and across the road I felt a warmth race through my body. Later that night as I sat alone in my darkened sitting room I wept at the kindness, I was deeply moved.

The following afternoon, just after lunchtime the doorbell rung and there stood the receptionist, I invited her in. I thanked her kindly for the previous night.

"I have come to help," she said, "order what you want and at the end of each week pay whatever you can pay." I couldn't answer; the lone tear rolling down my cheek was my gratitude. This was a huge relief to me and I accepted it with the kindness it deserved.

Later that same afternoon the doorbell rang again, there stood Colin. He was delivering Lyn's birthday present. I invited him in and he sat in our office/sitting room with an odd look on his face, I'm sure he was thinking - What is she doing here? Why is she living here? I could almost hear his thoughts racing around in his head. He made polite conversation and tried to appear calm but I knew he wasn't.

Why couldn't he come to see the girls?

Why was he shunning us?

Questions swam around in my head. I so wanted it to be like how it used to be between us, to be able to just talk, and I know he wanted it to be the same, however the gulf was huge.

In my head something said "Huge yes, but not out of reach."

He didn't wait to see the girls; I knew they would be disappointed so I didn't mention his visit.

Time moved on and I kept our spirits raised as much as I could. I never allowed myself to wallow in self-pity in front of the girls or anyone.

When the girls slumbered I would run things over in my mind, feel lonely and occasionally allow tears to flow. On those nights I knew the blackness would engulf me when I went to bed. Would Ron come to me in my sleep?

On the nights he did I would always awake feeling loved yet lost. I knew we couldn't remain living in the office, even though I had made it so homely. The girls couldn't be let out to play and with no other children close by I had to think about moving.

When we first married Ron had put our name down on the Local Housing List. As we had never taken it off maybe I could get a Council House. I decided to go and ask. I made an appointment and was as nervous as a kitten as I explained my situation.

The Housing Officer kept on and on about the fact I had originally lived in Edinburgh. He asked why didn't I go back there? Why did I want to stay in Hamilton?

Did I have family in Hamilton? He knew my in-laws. Not in-laws, real family he pointed out.

Trying not to get annoyed I explained I had lived in Hamilton for fourteen years. His reply was "What difference does that make you're still an Outsider. You've had all these bought houses, why should we help? He went on… I slowly stood up, stretched out my hand and thanked him for his time. I walked out with my head held high.

"Stuff him," I thought.

That was no solution, so I would have to re-think my situation.

My Granddad told me when I was young "every situation has a solution, you don't always have to think too hard to find it." His words now echoed around in my head. With all my previous situations I had always found my solutions, albeit some were very painful to find, however I had survived this far so I had to go on.

The blackness consumed me for several nights and the days were filled with terrifying flashbacks, but I managed to exist as normally as I could.

By this point all the hangers on had departed. My parents had returned to Edinburgh. My in-laws were avoiding me like the plague, and old friends were on the fringe watching and waiting to see how my life was going to unfold.

The girls lifted my spirits, and when I was with them I always smiled, sung and reassured them we would be fine. "One for all" I would sing and "And all for one" they'd sing back.

But when their bedtime came the hours till daylight seemed to take twice as long to go round. I spent most of my time alone. Alone in body, but never truly alone. It was a feeling I could never explain. So much had gone on since Ron was killed; sometimes I felt it was a crazy dream. When reality kicked in, I knew the dream was real.

The office was no permanent home for the girls, so I had to seek out my thinking hat.

A three bedroom semi-detached house came up for sale on the same road where Marjorie lived. Her house was number 11 and this house was number 41, so I went to view it.

An elderly couple that were delightful owned no 41. The house felt homely and welcoming. As a mortgage wasn't a problem, with friends still in the business, when there's a will there's a way.
I sold the flat to a Solicitor who was very impressed by the high standard of renovation I had achieved. He still practices from the premises as I write this.

Once again I packed my boxes, not as many due to the fact many had never been opened during our short stay. I phoned the old man with the young lad, and arranged a date and time for our departure from here to there. He and his lad arrived, smiled and said "We will be finished in time for our elevenses," and we were.

Laburnum Lea

Laburnum Lea was a three bedroom semi-detached. The garden was well stocked and through the small gate at the bottom of the garden there was a small stream.

Soon it was cosy and we settled in quickly.

Marjorie my first neighbour from Low Waters Road, now stayed at number 11, her two girls were ages with mine.

Caroline, another neighbour from Low Waters Road now lived at number 56; she also had two girls ages with mine.

So the six of them had great fun together.

This was a time when I relaxed into a sense of security around old friends, we all spent time talking. I held so many traumas within, so I found it difficult to confide in them, which was silly; we had known each other for so long, yet, I held back.

I had paid four months mortgage in advance, so as I wasn't working I had to enhance my weekly pension to survive.

I still had boxes and boxes of goods from all the houses.

I had a Ford Sierra 2.01 black car, so I sold it and bought an old an old Triumph Dolomite car, an old banger with class, and it had a beautiful walnut dashboard, which was probably worth more than the car.

Caroline, my brother's girlfriend gave birth to my first nephew at St. Francis Nursing Home in Govan, the same Nursing home where the girls had been born. He was a beautiful baby. At the time of the birth they were living in a caravan on a site owned by a man called 'Andrew Baird.' Ron had delivered milk for him when he was a schoolboy. He was a character who loved horse racing; unfortunately, the Bookies did most of the winning. The caravan was damp and not healthy for the baby so Caroline and Tom decided to move back to Edinburgh.

I found an indoor market in Wishaw that had a car boot section, so on a Sunday with the girls well wrapped up against the elements and our old banger 'Betsy' packed full of all sorts of our unwanted goods, off we would set every week.

When our first item was sold, we would go and buy our filled rolls. During those Sunday's the girls found lots of new friends to play with and I had my faith renewed in the fact that not all people were bad. Most of the stallholders looked out for me. In fact a couple of them bought things I'm sure they didn't need.

That time also taught me to have a conversation with

people who were not out to judge me.

'Auntie' Lynda was still enjoying living in her mobile home and we kept in touch. In fact she worried about me so we had to have mutual visits at least twice a week. She made me laugh, and she genuinely cared for us, with no family of my own around friends became paramount. Aggie still popped in but only to visit or baby-sit, however when she came she always helped out.

Most times within myself I still felt odd. Alone. The deep blackness still remained, waiting to engulf me whenever I felt down or when the screaming returned to plague me. However it was the first time since Ron's death I felt I could survive. I could win the war raging within me and emerge victorious.

Lynda talked me into joining an up market Dating Club. A friend of hers had divorced, joined up, then met and married a very rich man and lived very happily.

So Lynda guessed if it worked for her friend then it could work for me.

The following has given me so much laughter, that it is now part of my party piece when I'm around friends.

1st Date: On the telephone he sounded like velvet chocolate, a lovely voice. He was divorced with three girls.

He came home one day and found his wife in bed with her girl friend!
For weeks he phoned once a week and he came across as a nice guy. I arranged to meet him at the Dating club. Ginger was nice but not my type. He phoned and invited me to his brother's house warming party in Renfrew. My friend in Livingston watched the girls, and she let me borrow her car for the visit, as 'Betsy' wasn't up to the journey.
On arrival in Renfrew I noted all his family were present, as were friends, neighbours and pets! They were all avid Rangers Football Team supporters. As our family supported the opposition, my thought was "Oh joy."
As I was driving; I had a glass of every soft drink known to man and with every sip the rest of the family got very drunk. I was smiling through clenched teeth as my mind was frantically searching for a feasible excuse to leave.
When his sister touched my arm and said, "You will wear ivory as this will be your second wedding and it would be lovely for all five girls to be Bridesmaids."
With a sharp intake of breath, mind racing in circles, thinking Ivory – Girls – Bridesmaid. The look on my face must have spoke volumes, only her volumes were not the same as mine.
Oh Boy! I had to go, and go now. She apologised for letting the cat out of the bag, as she put it, she thought he had

already proposed to me.
I smiled like an idiot, excused myself and once in the hall was about to open the front door when Ginger appeared. I stood in the now open door and smiled as I blurted out some feeble excuse to leave.
He followed me to the car and by the time I reached the car door I was running, into the car, shut door, he kisses the window and not me, I speed off like a bullet.
I drive home shaken but somewhere along the M8 my humour kicks in.

2nd Date: Again another one with a voice like velvet on the telephone, he was a farmer from Fife, single, and his parents were dead. He shared his life with two collies. He compared himself to Don Johnston from Miami Vice.
Don Johnston is not my type but as I only wanted friendship, what was the problem? We spoke a lot on the telephone and he was lonely and missed a good homemade meal.
Lynda suggested I invite him for lunch on a school day, that way he would be gone before the girls came home from school. She also suggested that she telephone me every half-hour from when he arrived just to check things were O.K.
The day was arranged. Homemade soup, mince, vegetables

and potatoes finished off with rice pudding.

The garden sloped down to the sitting room window, so when his car drew up I could only see its roof. Lynda was on the other end of the phone calming me down; she was saying "it's only lunch and friendship so calm down and breathe."

Next thing pure hysteria broke out within my head. There, beside his car he stood, flowers and a bottle of wine in his hands. He straightened his tie and walked down the drive. I was now lying on the floor like a commando, hissing down the phone. He had on a flat cap, Burberry raincoat, round weather beaten plump face with metal frame glasses. Don Johnston! Don Johnston! I hissed at Lynda, more like Benny fucking Hill. Now it was Lynda's turn for hysterics, laughing hysterics.

I breathed deeply and opened the front door. He spoke nervously as he walked in but all I could hear was "Benny Hill, Benny fucking Hill," loud in my head.

Then I thought right let's focus, breathe, and get lunch over as soon as possible.

Food went down well, then we moved into the sitting room, as it was a cold day I had a roaring coal fire on. He made himself comfy in the chair and fell fast asleep. He slept like the dead, forty minutes later he woke. He explained he always napped in his tractor after lunch!

Lynda phoned twice, we laughed all through our conversation.
I had to get him out before the girls came home from school. Lynda agreed to pick them up.
Would he move? No. On and on he talked, next thing the front door burst open and in ran the girls and a smiling Lynda.
Oh no! No! He had to leave. I heard myself explaining we had to rush due to the girls dancing lessons. Only to hear Lyn saying "Oh Mummy, that's not till tomorrow."
I felt everything slow down; I didn't like the feeling. I knew it so well. I knew the blackness would come. He made his goodbye and left.
He wasn't as far as the end of the street, when the girls rushed upstairs to play, the funny man forgotten and slowly Lynda coaxed my humour out.
Over a bottle of wine later that night, we, Lynda and I both agreed the girls wouldn't remember today, however I would!
You would have thought by now, I would have given up.

Date No.3: A schoolteacher, his Father was a retired police officer, his Mum was dead, and he also said he was a look-alike Don Johnston.
Oh Boy, I sure was dumb. He only wanted a friend to go to

the cinema with, which sounded simple, straightforward. We agreed to go and see the film 'Fatal Attraction' at a local cinema. He would pick me up at the house, Aggie agreed to baby-sit.

I was upstairs when the doorbell rang. I heard excited chatter. The girls rushed into my room, fell on my bed, and giggled about the funny man downstairs.

I explained I was going to the cinema, they both agreed it was O.K.

As I came downstairs I could hear Aggie talking and laughing; her eyes caught mine as I entered the room.

With his back to me, my eyes caught his white socks, black shoes, half-mast trousers and waist hugging red leather jacket.

He as about 5ft tall and when he turned around, Oh no! Don Johnston my ass. Freddie Starr Oh yes!

Oh God, what had I agreed to? In the kitchen Aggie was trying to stuff the dishtowel into her mouth.

Okay! It was only the cinema I kept telling myself. Focus and breathe I could do this. Off we set.

We were early so we went into the local Italian Hotel for a drink. The owner, who knew me, came over to say hello and he asked me if the gent was causing me concern. I heard myself say "No I'm fine!"

Inside my head, I can't print my thoughts.

In the cinema, it was a sell out and I prayed I wouldn't meet anyone I knew.
We sat in the last two seats in the row beside the wall.
In front of us sat a middle-aged woman with her daughters on either side of her.
Someone must have told her earlier about the rabbit in the pot scene because all she kept saying was "Where's the rabbit?"
I wanted to scream at her "When you see the fucking pot you will know that's where the rabbit is."
The film is good and everyone knows the ending.
Before the end when it came to the part where she is lying under the water in the bath everyone assuming she is dead; she suddenly she springs out of the water and at that moment the whole cinema seemed to take a sharp intake of breath in fright, then the film ends.
Everyone gets up to leave. Friend Don Johnston leans over and says "What happened? I was scared, so I had my eyes shut tight for the last ten minutes!"
Oh boy, home at last. As he dropped me off, he said he had had a great time. Oh yeah! He tooted his musical horn as he sped off.
Giggles from Aggie and Lynda welcomed me. No more, not again.
Later, when I was alone, I sat outside on the back step and

wept. I had to come to terms with all that had happened. Why was it so difficult?

I wanted a hug so much, but Ron wasn't here, the blackness returned.

I now knew I wasn't ready for any relationship. No matter what my friends thought or said within my heart I knew.

I cancelled my membership with the Dating Club.

Across the stream at the bottom of the garden stood a large detached bungalow with a huge garden that was now owned by a divorced man and his kids.

He kept two very large, huge longhaired Alsatian dogs that were kept on long chains as guard dogs. They had their own dog house at the entrance gate.

One sunny afternoon the two dogs barked and barked on and on. I could hear a lawn mower, so I assumed they didn't like the machine's noise.

Then the screaming began.

I told the girls to go along to Marjorie's house and stay there. I telephoned and told her to expect the girls. I explained about the noise coming from the garden over the back. She advised me to call the police; I said I'd think about it. The screams went on, the dogs kept barking louder and louder.

Off I set down the garden, over the stream, through the

hedge and there stood the Alsatians, drooling at the mouth.
I heard a voice command "Lie down now."
I realized it was my voice but down they lay down whimpering at me at me with beautiful eyes. I bent down, patted them and told them to be good boys. They didn't move.
The side of the garden sloped gently; at the bottom of the slope lay a lawn mower still whirring away. At the top of the slope lay a young boy, terror beaming from his eyes, screams of pain filling the sunny afternoon. There was blood everywhere. Deep red blood staining the grass, his clothes, his legs, my hands, and my trousers, seeping through the material onto my skin.
I had felt this before, blood seeping through my tights onto my legs when I had gone to see Ron's car after he was killed. I fought to bring my feelings under control.
Three toes lay mutilated on the grass. I sprung into action. I unplugged the mower at the extension cable. I used the mower to make a footrest, higher than his heart, then I ran into the house through the open French windows.
There was music playing so loud the house was pulsing to the music's beat. I burst into the sitting room, there stood a young girl ironing, she jumped back in terror when she saw me and a terrified cat shot through my legs.
"Who the hell are you?" she yelled as she held up the hot

iron as a weapon.

I walked over, pulled out all the plugs I could find and a silence bathed the scene.

I explained the situation, "I need ice plus a tea towel now" I commanded.

Off she went to get the things and I dialled 999.

With his foot encased in the cold iced tea towel, I held him close. I soothed his fears, his tears stopped and he talked about his parents divorce.

His sister stood like a statue. Far off, I could hear the sirens heralding the ambulance's arrival. The dogs leapt into action barking and growling. The ambulance crew stood rooted to the spot.

I let the boy go, walked towards the dogs and without a word they lay down. The ambulance crew sprang into action.

I stayed with the dogs. I was talking to them gently and patting them, when the terrified wee cat came towards and lay close to me. I spoke to her softly.

A car screeched to a halt and a middle-aged man with a look of fierce rage flung himself out of his car.

He ignored me, walked past and shouted at his daughter and then he went to slap his son but was prevented from doing so by the ambulance crew.

Once he knew what had happened I heard him say he would

follow the ambulance in his car. As the ambulance drove off he went to get into his car, he stopped, he looked across to me and said, "Who are you?"

I explained the afternoon's events. He thanked me for my help then said, "How did you do that?" "What?" I said, "These dogs are wild, I can't control them and yet you're sitting beside them and they love it. You must be special, thank you."

The next day flowers arrived from the family to say thank you.

The following day I arranged to visit the young boy in hospital. He had lost his toes, however my actions had helped control his blood loss.

Soon he would be home. His Mum sat holding his hand when I visited him and somehow I knew this terrible accident would get his family back together again.

The wee cat began to visit our house on a daily basis and our cat Ginger made her welcome.

One day a few weeks later the young boy was on his way home from school when he knocked on our door. He said, "Our cat's name is Smokey, I think she would like to stay at your house because our dogs scare her too much."

As he walked away at the top of our drive he turned and shouted "Thanks Missus, you're the best."

This young boy's words touched my heart. That night

Smokey came to stay for good.

I was down to the last of our unwanted goods and on our last visit to the car boot sale I was overwhelmed at the generous gift's given to the girls.
These people accepted me for who I was. As we drove out most of them stood and applauded, tears flowed, people could be kind. That day lifted my spirits.

Lynda's neighbour Sindy introduced me to a Gent who sold stock to all the markets. James was his name and he had taken over the business when his father died unexpectedly. He was a Barra Boy with a touch of class. I set out a Business Plan to do 'Party Plan'. Lynda, Aggie and myself would take cut-price linen goods into people's homes and sell them.
James agreed to give me credit on goods I wanted to sell, so 'Romance by Henrietta' was born. As Lynda and Aggie couldn't drive, I organized a driver to take them to the parties, his name was Jamie. He was the son of Tam who owned the video shop; he was young and full of fun. Sales weren't brilliant but I made enough to keep me going.
The girls were a source of inspiration to me. Always giggling. Days filled with School, Brownies and Gymnastics and visits to friends.

Never shy to throw their arms around me at anytime for a loving hug.

Colin and Shona lived quite close now and they passed the main road often. The girls used to wave when they saw them pass but they never waved back.
Continually the girls asked Gran and Papa to take them up to Colin's when they went to visit him, but as usual the answer was "No" and always the same excuses.
Why they wouldn't take them I never really knew. Their excuses sounded feeble, however they hurt more than words can say.
My children were continually shunned and ignored. My in-laws only came to visit to check up with what was happening. Always the look of disdain, sighs of intolerance, plain and idle chat, at no time warmth or care.
Ron always thought he was the black sheep of the family. I lived with his feelings all the time we were together. Now I knew how he felt, I was the wart on their unblemished life.
My brother kept in touch and came to visit every three weeks. He made me smile, because he knew most of the truth. He always lifted my spirits.

My friends Ronnie and Joe moved to Livingston with their four kids from Cumbernauld. We began to visit them more

and more.
Ronnie didn't know anyone in Livingston; I knew how that felt, memories about myself moving from Edinburgh to Hamilton made me offer support.
We would drive through on a Friday after school and stay over; sometimes we didn't come home till Sunday evening.
While at Ronnie's I cooked for everyone. I always arrived with shopping and soon had the pots on the cooker.
Their house was in a cul-de-sac, lots of kids and very nice people.
The houses were originally built for Police and Fire Brigade Officers. Many had been sold on, but many remained.
My opinion of the police made me awkward, however I soon realised not every officer was a Bastard.
Ronnie's house was a busy household. There was always someone popping in and she found her four kids a handful, so I helped her lots and by doing so I didn't have time to dwell on my own feelings.
Days blended into weeks, school, visits to friends, and running' Romance'.
Time ran on, the circle of life was spinning round me, but deep within I felt I was standing still.
Time to reflect? No, it was too painful, too soon and Christmas was approaching. I wanted it to be cosy.
Colin came down with Louise's birthday present while the

girls were at school. He looked relaxed, yet awkward as he sat looking around. His eyes spoke volumes.

He didn't stay long and when he left the blackness consumed me before he drove off. Lynda was great, she arrived before close of school and I fled to my calm spot, the cemetery, while Lynda looked after the girls.

The pain I could feel within my heart, consumed all of me. Numbness stopped time; I was still living with Ron within my own mind and trying so hard to come to terms with everything.

I had won my fight over panic attacks, however some moments of panic arose and they could fill me with terror and dread.

I had a beautiful family. Friends could see that, so why couldn't Ron's or my family see that?

Now it was time to pick myself up again.

Christmas presents all bought and wrapped. Christmas tree and decorations all displayed.

The week before Christmas my purse was taken from by bag in the supermarket. Terror engulfed me, how would I buy in food to last over the festive season? At my wits end, I asked my in-laws to watch the girls.

I was going to go cap in hand to James to ask for money. My in-laws wouldn't oblige, so there was no point in asking. They only accused me of being stupid for losing my purse.

James had been called away unexpectedly, his Mum had taken ill. I waited an hour, then drove home not knowing where to turn.

On my arrival home I wasn't ready to face anyone, so I was taken aback at the girls crying as I walked in the front door. Papa had given them a row for making too much noise upstairs. I felt the irritation rise within me.

I calmed the girls down and thanked my in-laws for looking after them.

As I walked into the kitchen to put on the kettle, my father in-law walked into the kitchen behind me. Since the rape I couldn't bear anyone walking behind me, it scared me immensely.

I spun round just as he said with such a tone "You are such a liar," my mother in-law spoke "No, Joe leave it."

I now faced him squarely across the table.

He was a quiet spoken Geordie. All the time I knew him he was always the same, very quiet. Now he roared like a lion. "You are a liar, always have been, and always will be. All the family hate you and always have."

He said I had been responsible for his son's death and he would never forgive me. I would always be to blame.

I heard myself saying "It may have escaped your attention, but I wasn't in the car."

On and on his verbal onslaught went. My mother in-law held on to his arm, as it looked as though he was about to hit me.

This family really hated me. My in-laws, Colin, Shona and all the others hated me.

Survival kicked in out of sheer shock and anger. I could hear the words and it took some time to realise it was my words.

"My fault?! You need someone to blame, sure, blame me if it makes you feel better. Yes I've lied, I've lied to everyone, even myself. Why? To save your son's memory. He was having a renewed affair, piles of debt, no insurance money and on the Monday following his death he was to be arrested. He was drunk on the Friday night plus the booze on the Saturday afternoon - that's what slowed down his re-actions. So yes that made it my bloody fault."

I spat out the words through tears. I then yelled at them to leave and not come back.

The girls, unknown to us all, had come downstairs. They were crying at their Grandparents to leave me alone.

As soon as I heard Lyn say "Leave Mummy alone, you're bad," I came to my senses and walked past them to hug and console the girls. I told them again in a hushed tone to leave my house.

As the front door slammed shut, the girls and I sat entwined on the sofa. The fire was nearly out when I eventually let them go.

To lift their spirits I suggested we have a carpet picnic. I laid the tartan blanket out in front of the newly stoked fire. Rich tea biscuits with butter and jam on them, hot tea, plus a treat of coconut delight cakes I had been keeping for Christmas.

Early evening after their bath, I tucked them up in bed and took time to answer their questions about the day's events. I explained Papa was upset with me not with them. Lyn said "But he said everyone hated us." I kissed her fears and tears away.

When they were tucked up for the night, I sat on the sofa, no lights on, only the glow of the fire lighting the room, crying and feeling so low I don't know how long I sat there. The phone ringing made me jump.

Marjorie was phoning to invite the girls and I to a mince pie and hot chocolate party the next afternoon with herself, Caroline, Biff, and our eight kids. I accepted. She asked if I was "All right?" "Sure" I said, "I'm just tired."

Before I went up to bed, I spent some time out in the back garden gazing up at the stars trying to clear my thoughts. Suddenly I heard the words clearly "It's time to move on."

Next afternoon while all the kids played upstairs in

Marjorie's she opened a bottle of wine.

When Caroline left, Biff and Marjorie asked me what was wrong. My mind was blank and my guard was down as I heard myself relating all the previous day's mess. They knew it was serious; I had never spoken so openly since Ron died.

I also told them I was moving, leaving Hamilton forever. They didn't have to do anything but what they did, still now as I write moves me to tears.

The very next day Marjorie phoned and invited us to tea. Her and Biff then gave me two large bags of shopping. A full Christmas day and Boxing Day meal, plus lots of extra goodies.

We always exchanged a wee gift at Christmas for each of the kids. As I had bought mine earlier I was pleased to pass on ours to the kids. My girls received two each from all my friends and a special one from Santa.

My mother-in-law had phoned Biff to ask if I would allow them to visit the kids on Christmas day. I said, "No, no way, they all hate me, why should I let them see my girls?" However Biff continued to wear me down until on Christmas Eve I agreed. I said they could visit for an hour and I would stay in the kitchen.

The girls and I had planned to spend three days and nights in front of the fire over the festive season. Plenty of coal for the fire, plenty to eat thanks to my friends and lots of presents to open and time together to shut out the world, perfect bliss.

Christmas morning snuggled together singing Christmas carols with wrapping paper strewn all over the carpet. We sat sipping hot chocolate with marshmallows, the girls were so happy.

The doorbell broke through our bliss. Before I opened the door, I reminded the girls I would be in the kitchen and that it was alright, no-one was going to shout or hurt me.

As I let my in-laws in numbness cocooned me. I said, "Hi, the girls are in the sitting room I'll be in the kitchen."

I made tea and coffee and took it through then I returned to the kitchen and listened to the girls excited chatter in the next room.

The kitchen door opened and my Father in-law walked in, my whole body tensed, "Please, God not to-day" I was pleading in my head.

What he said was "Thank you for letting us see the girls."

"It's alright" I replied.

He then said, "Biff tells us you are moving away?"

"Yes," I said "It's time to move on" I replied in a whisper.

"Why?" he asked. I raised my head and looked straight into his eyes and said very softly "There's nothing to stay for and I won't be hated, but more important I won't let my children be hated, so I have no choice."

He didn't reply as he left the kitchen.

As they left I thought "They're off to have Christmas dinner at Colin and Shona's, that should be interesting."

They can all celebrate our departure.

As they were leaving, my Father in-law took my hand and squeezed a bit of paper into it. My fist clenched tight, my thoughts raced around in my head. "Now he's put his abuse of me on paper, was it not enough the last time?"

I put it into my dressing gown pocket; it would keep till later, today belonged to the girls.

Many friends phoned to wish us a Merry Christmas.

Christmas dinner was super and too soon the girls were tucked up in bed, exhausted but very happy.

A little later I tiptoed into each room and gazed down upon them, contented, happily snuggled beside their teddies.

I was now ready to face the note in my pocket. I sat gazing into the firelight and unravelled the letter. I was confused, it wasn't a letter it was a fifty-pound note.

Was this a way of apologising or was this to make sure I did leave?

I sat and wept, I would return it, and Biff would take it back for me. The blackness engulfed me that night and I welcomed it.

Three days later the girls and I emerged from our cocoon.

At Biff's house I asked her to return the money. She refused and explained it wasn't for me it was for the girls, and I needed it badly to survive until my next widow's pension day.

Deep down I knew that was true, but I felt to keep it would only sully me more.

Biff yelled "Let them all think what they like, we know you, you care too much for those girls to let them suffer. For their sake swallow your pride."

She was right, the money would see me through, so I sent a plain and simple thank-you card from the girls.

Over the next few days I was a hermit, everyone was preparing for Hogmanay. The girls and I toasted in the New Year with a very weak shandy and the girls thought this was ace. Then we watched TV for a short time before I tucked them into bed to head to slumberland.

Alone in the darkness my mind wandered to that New Year kiss and Colin.

Why did it plague me so?! I curled up in bed and welcomed the black cocoon.

I awoke from the blackness with a start.

Why had it all gone so wrong?

Why did Ron die?

Why did he go away and leave us?

Why did his family hate me?

Why had my parents turned so nasty?
Why did Colin and Shona shun my kids?
The questions mounted in my head until I thought I would go insane.
Panic and fear began to engulf me. Where, oh where could I flee to?

The ringing of the phone startled me awake. Ronnie's excited chatter unfroze my senses. She was inviting us through to Livingston for a New Year party. Most of her neighbours were going to be there and several of them had been asking why I hadn't been to visit over Christmas.
I agreed to visit and a tingle ran over me. We were wanted by people who took us for what we were.
Next morning I flew about the house with wings, we were ready in no time. A few quick phone calls to tell Marjorie and Biff where we were going and then we set off.
The girls and I sang all the way. As I drove into Ronnie's cul-de-sac a 'House for Sale' sign caught my eye. It was a small sign but to me it was twenty foot high.
Ronnie's house was full of kids and adults filling everywhere. When we walked in they all cheered. What a welcome, a welcome that was genuine.
In the wee small hours Ronnie and I sat outside on the picnic bench, it was bloody freezing but the booze inside us

kept us warm.

Ronnie didn't get serious too often, but now she spoke with feeling.

"How are you?" She asked, "Fine" I said. "Bloody liar" she replied.

The word liar triggered in my head; soon she knew all the events over Christmas and Hogmanay. I was now exhausted.

Then she said, "How long has it been since Colin's kiss?

"How are you really?"

"Kick me when I'm down" I sighed as I replied.

"Never" she said, "But maybe you'll let your true thoughts out?" She continued softly.

Suddenly out came all the pain, turmoil, hate, and love.

Also feelings I had never experienced with Ron.

Ron had always said it existed within Colin for me, but I always ignored his words. Now his words kept running around in my head.

Colin had put the blame on me, why?

He had made the move on me! Now I was hated.

Quickly I realised my barrier was truly down. "Never mind, I've got broad shoulders, I can take it" I laughed.

Susan came outside to find us. Party on, it's time to forget.

Next day I strolled down the cul-de-sac to talk to Isabell

and John who were selling the house. The sitting room at the rear of the house and the very large extension looked out on to a multitude of trees; it was bliss.
The three bedrooms were all facing the trees. I made up my mind to go for it. The house felt warm and welcoming.
I wouldn't say anything to anyone until final arrangements were in place.
We enjoyed our few days and we set off for home relaxed and happy.
As soon as the girls returned to school, I set my plans in motion. I sold the house privately with the help of Lynda and it sold quickly.

My brother Tom came to visit and offer me support and help with the move. I spent time with all my friends separately and fully explained why I was going.
They all understood and each one gave me kind words that I carry within my heart.

'Romance by Henrietta's' stock was returned to James and I was paid the balance.
His figures didn't work out the same as mine, but he insisted the money was mine. To this day I'm grateful.
Early on James asked repeatedly for the girls and myself to move into his Glasgow home. He said he would look after

us, no strings attached. I always declined as gently as I could. We hadn't even been on a date yet his offer was genuine.
He was a lovely man, but I didn't have any feelings for him, if I had accepted I would have ended up hating him. He had shown me such kindness, most of all he had shown me trust. He was a true Gent, with never a hint of a kiss or a touch, he was willing to help heal my soul by the offer of caring for us.
In his own way he did help me heal. He will always have my unconditional love.

The move was arranged for the last day of school before the summer holidays.
My Mother in-law phoned Biff a couple of times asking her to try and change my mind, but Biff knew I wouldn't.
I arrived in Hamilton knowing no one; I was leaving with a mountain of genuine good luck wishes and blessings, from an abundance of friends and acquaintances.

The night before our move I got my brother to bring down to the back garden a huge brown suitcase. I had lit a small fire at the bottom of the garden. Tom looked bewildered but said nothing.
I unlocked the suitcase and surveyed the contents; every

item of clothing and shoes Ron had worn on his last day lay there neatly folded.

I took out each item, kissed it and threw it on the flames.

Tom still said nothing. When the flames were roaring I threw on the suitcase.

As I watched the flames, I wept. I was leaving a town I had grown to love as home.

A town that had brought me much joy and pain lay desolate as the fire died away.

Tom couldn't cope with my tears; he sat silent on the back doorstep, drawing on his cigarette deep within his own thoughts.

Moving to Hamilton hadn't been good for him either, so we both coped with our memories together, but silently, in that small back garden.

My in-laws didn't contact us at all.

Same removal van, same old man, same but older boy plus Tom and me packed the house into the van. I packed the car and sighed deeply when it was completed.

As usual into each room, a genuine thank-you and a warm goodbye.

I left a welcome card and a nice bunch of flowers for the new owner. House locked up safe and sound for the new owners who were moving in later that day.

I phoned my in-laws to say goodbye. I handed the keys into

the Lawyer. Next stop the school. I was impatient to go, the van had already set off and I didn't want to be too far behind it.

The whole school was assembled in the small hall. As it was a small school it operated like one big family, one very big happy family.

I poked my head through the door just as the Head Mistress called out Lyn and Louise. With blurry eyes I watched them receive a small gift each while everyone cheered.

Then, I heard my name called, I was asked to step into the Staff Room. By now the kids had been dismissed for the summer holidays, laughter and squeals filled the building. With the girls by my side we headed for the staff room. The Head Mistress approached me and all the teachers in the room smiled warmly.

Her words touched my heart. She said the girls would be sorely missed and that they had a special quality that would take them far in life.

She went on to say they also had a loving and caring Mum who was also a lovely person, and that the school would like to thank me for my input. She said she knew it hadn't always been easy for me and she presented me with a large bouquet of flowers with love from them all.

Tears blinded me again, I tried to say something but the words wouldn't come.

I had one last port of call to make before leaving, High Blantyre to the cemetery.

Tom and the girls stayed in the car. I walked towards Ron's grave, I knew he was giving me his blessing. Time to move on. I kissed his headstone and left without a backward glance.

In the car everyone was giggling through tears as Louise asked "Is Daddy going with us? Are we going to plant him in our new garden?" Their humour set the mood for our journey ahead.

As we drove into our new street, most of the neighbours came out to wave us 'Hello'.

Tom said "Don't make many friends, you won't be staying long."

Munro Way

The house was a three bedroom semi-detached with a large extension at the rear which overlooked tall full-grown beautiful trees. The back garden had been well landscaped, but was now slightly overgrown.

With my boxes and furniture all put to right soon it was all as it should be.

The girls had gone off to play with the friends they had made when we came to stay with Ronnie at number 19, so it gave me time to make sure their bedrooms were ship-shape.

Our old cat Ginger had got a fright and had run off into a neighbouring garden, so I decided to leave the downstairs toilet window slightly open, to allow her to smell Smokey's scent to coax her into the house. I'm glad to say it worked.

My brother decided to sleep on the sofa with Cara his big black Labrador lying on the floor beside him on the sitting room. I had not hung any curtains, so the large patio window had a brilliant view of the garden.

With everyone settled in bed, the house took on a comfortable feel and I felt safe.

I had moved here to start afresh and take time to hide away in this den to lick my wounds.
I needed time to remove and forget the shackles that bound me and I would rise again.
I only needed time.

My cosy feeling was shattered with the shrieking of my brother as he bounded upstairs and the dog burst into my room first.
As he gasped for air, he blurted out, “Two bright eyes, no body, trees, can Louise sleep beside you and I can sleep in her bed?”
“What was it?” I asked laughing,
“I don’t know and I’m not going to bloody find out,” he said with ever growing eyes.
“Are you scared?” I said, still laughing. “No” he stated firmly.
I moved Louise into my bed and went downstairs to check for the ‘Bright Eyes’. As I sat in my darkened sitting room and stared out into the blackness, calmness descended on me. After some time the two bright eyes appeared.
I slid open the patio door and crouched down, slowly the two bright eyes took on a darkened shape. A huge black cat, friendly with a very loud purr, approached and snuggled into my knees. He was to come and visit many nights,

nobody else ever saw him, or knew whom he belonged to, out of all the neighbours I asked. He became my personal beacon of hope.

Two weeks after moving in, Ronnie, Joe and their four kids went on a fortnight's holiday to her sisters flat in Millport. The girls and myself had spent many weekends there in the past with Ronnie's family and I felt it was a safe haven to the girls and myself. Good company, good home cooking with very little money but great fun. It was very cramped, but good fun was always had by all.

Before moving to Livingston I had made plans to move to Millport. An island offered more security and I felt the girls could be protected more easily. The flat I had made an offer on was hit with a Building Renovation Order, so I changed my mind. To this day I don't really know why. It just wasn't meant to be.

On the Saturday Ronnie and Joe left on holiday other neighbours, Mark and Susan, invited me round for a drink. My brother had turned up to do my garden again, so he offered to babysit and insisted it would do me good.

Mark and Susan made me most welcome. We chatted, laughed and in general had a pleasant time. After a few drinks Mark announced he couldn't keep quiet and he had to tell me what had gone on.

As this sounded ominous, I felt myself withdrawing into my inner self. Did I want to hear? Did I want to know?

I liked Mark so I sat and listened. Ronnie had gossiped behind my back and told many of my new neighbours of my past problems.

How I was now poor.

How my in-laws shunned and hated me.

How they blamed me for Ron's death.

How I exiled my parents from the girls; on and on he spoke.

I held up my hand, "No more please," I said quietly.

Mark said, "You had to be told. You are a lovely person and you don't deserve this. You need to know what is going on. You don't need anyone's pity and by telling you, you can put this situation right."

Once home, I told Tom to sleep in my bed, and as my household slept blissfully I sat outside gazing towards my stars.

Within my stars I could let my mind find a solution and my heart could escape into the blackness.

My new home felt sullied, however not for long. The next day I took myself to every house I knew Ronnie gossiped in.

I spoke quietly, yet with such conviction my voice appeared to echo around within my head. The words I spoke did not change at each house I visited.

I began "It has come to my knowledge that Ronnie has been talking about me behind my back. Should anyone and I repeat anyone mention one thing against me or my girls, I will personally wipe this cul-de-sac from one end to the other with them. Yes, I am here to lick my wounds so accept me as I am."
Without any hesitation everyone was so caring, their words gave me upliftment.
Now to await Ronnie's return.

As I had paid 5 months mortgage in advance, I had that time to sort out employment of some description.
The girls settled in quickly and the summer that loomed before us was welcomed.

On Ronnie's return she avoided me for three whole days. How odd and most unusual I thought. After teatime I phoned her. "When the kids are in bed get yourself down to see me" I said in my usual cheerful manner.
The girls were settled in bed and the evening hours were ticking by and still no appearance of Ronnie. I was about to phone her when she knocked on my glass door. There stood someone who looked as though she was about to be led to the Gallows. Clutching her fags and lighter as though her life depended on them I told her to sit down.

"How was your holiday?" I said, "did you enjoy yourselves?" On and on I went about her holiday.
When I could see she was visibly relaxing I asked her if she had spoken to any of the neighbours yet?
"Funny you should say that, no one has spoken to me at all, in fact I get the impression they are all avoiding me" she replied.
"Any idea why?" I asked.
"No, it's quite strange" she said.
"Well allow me to enlighten you" I smiled.
In a quiet well-mannered tone out the words spilled. I fully explained what I had been told and what my actions had been. She sat staring at me wide eyed, her mouth formed words but no sound came. Her gossip had hurt me so much and I promised her I would never trust her again. I pitied her, she was a gossip bully, always had been but the buck stopped here. Every neighbour held the same opinion, but no more would anyone in the cul-de-sac allow her gossiping to continue.
From now she would be an acquaintance and not a friend. The world was full of Bastards and I had met every one. I had come to this place to lick my wounds and she had betrayed me.
She wept; she apologised and asked me to forgive her. I accepted her apology, her tears I ignored and the

forgiveness she craved was not given. I said, "My forgiveness will take time."

I found myself a good job with a Glasgow based company, driving around the Central belt of Scotland as far north as Dundee. The job provided a car, and as I could be my own boss it suited me fine.

Four days a week I drove around pubs and hotels emptying one-armed bandit gaming machines. I liked driving as I found it relaxing and the job was simple.

An older lady called Jan who was divorced with all her family grown and left home agreed to help with the girls. As I had to leave early in the morning and Jan only lived at the top of the next street, it was an ideal solution.

For a few pounds per week Jan gave the girls breakfast and walked them to school. The girls enjoyed her company, so the situation was perfect.

I was always home before the girls however if for any reason I was held up they went to Ronnie's house, so life became easy.

The job was going well, and with school life fine, plus all the usual out of school activities time ticked by pleasantly. But as usual everything was about to change, and how!

Jan took ill, so I had to find alternate arrangements and

quick. I contacted the local Job Centre and explained I needed a child minder, who was willing to come to our house, wake the girls and give them breakfast and take them to school.

I was introduced to a lovely middle-aged woman, as the Job Centre had checked her out, it was only a matter of introducing her to the girls. That done I relaxed into my employment routine.

My health had been troubling me since Fergus Gardens, but now I knew something wasn't right and I knew it was serious.

The girls had begun to waken before I left in the morning and were always weepy when I left. I was puzzled by the change in them. Repeatedly I gently asked them if something was wrong. "No" they would both say.

Then they began to cling to me when I returned from work. If I was late and they had to go to Ronnie's they would sit glued to the window watching for my car. I put it down to the new lady, as they weren't used to her, thinking it would take time.

I had never had the security of having a family to help with childcare to enable me to work. I have met many people who have their families to provide childcare for them and they take them for granted. They don't know how lucky they are!

The floods of bleeding I was now experiencing every two weeks was accompanied by violent mood swings and lots of pain. Pains like I had never had before.

Within I was scared, really scared. This was nothing like I had ever suffered in the past.

I decided to have a medical check over.

My new doctor was a woman, so I found it easy to explain to her. I asked her to listen without interrupting, any questions she wanted answered I would do so at the end.

"I know my body and I know within my heart that I am ill," I said, and went on to give her a full run down of my medical history.

It was a Monday when she took blood samples, a smear test and swabs.

Thursday at teatime the phone rang, it was the doctor asking me to come to the Surgery immediately.

I asked my neighbour Mags to look after the girls; my mind was racing as I drove up to the Surgery. The receptionist smiled awkwardly and led me through to Doctor Cowan's Surgery.

"Oh" how gaunt she looked. I sat opposite her and felt truly scared. The look on her face spoke volumes.

"I take it it's bad news," I said to break the silence. She nodded and my heart began to pound. I asked to read the

piece of yellow paper she clutched. "I've never had to do this," she said.
I took the yellow document from her hand and scanned the words. "Oh boy, Oh boy, this was serious. Cancer. My protective inner cocoon shielded me, enabling me to deal with this. Fear eased itself into every fibre of my being. This situation had no solution.
My heart felt like a lead weight within me.
I was facing death and I hadn't even began to live.
I'd existed most of my life and had only really lived a few special moments.

I was to see a Consultant at the main hospital nearby. The appointment had been arranged for Monday afternoon at 2 p.m.
This would be the longest weekend of my life. My thoughts raced into every crevice of my mind.
That night I cried to the moon, sent my fears to my stars and allowed the sky's blackness to join my mood, next day at work the hours passed in a blur.

Early in the New Year I had renewed ties with my parents. I still didn't trust my mum; her past actions still haunted me. My dad had aged and he had missed the girls so much it had affected his health.

I began by allowing the girls to visit them along with my brother on Saturday afternoons from 1p.m. to 5p.m. It was essential my brother was present.
I dropped them all off outside my parents house and I returned and sat outside waiting on them at 5p.m. exactly.
I laid down ground rules, any breach of these rules and the visits would stop. They willingly agreed and my dad apologized for my mum's behaviour when they were in Hamilton. I decided to accept the apology but I would not agree to trust them just yet, if ever.
The girls enjoyed their visits so much; I knew I had done the right thing in letting them visit.
Would they help me now I was faced with this darkness? Time would tell.
The weekend passed slowly, was time going slow because I didn't have much time left?

As I waited for the nurse to call my name I was intrigued to know why I wasn't being asked to change into a hospital gown.
Name called, ushered into a small Consulting Room, faced by a pleasant looking Doctor. I tried so much to relax, breathe and look calm.
The Doctor shook my hand, his hand felt safe. Somehow by his touch he gave me hope.

I would be admitted on Wednesday, have my operation on Thursday and be a patient for about 10 days, he explained. Days, times and arrangements swam around in my head. "Wait!" I screamed in my head. "This is too soon; I need time" I heard myself explaining to him. He reached over and took my hands in his.
He looked straight into my eyes and softly said "Mrs Pearson you don't have time. I'll give you till Sunday lunchtime, no longer."
I explained I was a widow, I had two children, and no family and I needed time to put arrangements into place. Again he explained this time with an urgent edge to his voice, I had no time, and we had to move fast.
I was scared. So scared I had difficulty in getting my thoughts straight. I had only five full days to put my house in order. Who to phone first?
I phoned Colin as he was named as Executor in my will. I explained the situation.
He said "No problem, not to worry", and if the worst happened they would take the girls. The phone call lasted only a few moments and his words held no comfort.

Then I phoned my In-laws, again no words to give me comfort to allay my fears.
Next, my parents, would they help by looking after the

girls?
The answer was yes, however it would be a problem but I wasn't to worry!
With my brother's help they would manage. As long as I signed my Widow's Pension Book and my Family Allowance Book to cover the cost of looking after the girls it would be fine. I had no other option, I had to agree.

The girls were so relieved I wasn't going back to work. This meant the bad lady would not be coming back! "What bad lady?" I asked.
The bad lady who looked after them in the mornings.
The lady I got from the Job Centre.
The lady who had been fully checked out!
I sat numb with shock as they both described in full detail how she banged on their bedroom walls, snarling, roaring and threatening them to get out of bed.
Their story continued, the details horrifically assaulting my senses.
I had always kept my girls safe, always made sure no one could ever harm them. Now my senses reeled, this explained their behaviour of late. I asked gently why hadn't they told me this before? They replied "We needed the pennies to live, so you had to go to work." I held them so close and promised that it would never happen again.

On my brother's next visit, he agreed to go with me to see the bad lady.

I knocked on her front door and her partner answered my knock. As he opened the door wider I barged past him and marched into their sitting room.

There she sat watching television; the stunned look on her face didn't affect me in any way. I grabbed her and pulled her to her feet, still holding her I spat my words into her face, my eyes never leaving hers.

I have to admit my temper flared so much, I slapped her and she fell slumped into her armchair. I could have killed her. As my girls words echoed around in my head I continued to tell her what I thought of her.

She wept, she apologised and tried to explain, she had a drink problem and she couldn't help it. The money she earned from me paid for her booze.

I promised her she would never work with or near children ever again. I'm glad to say she never did.

When we left her house we called in to the Police Station. I explained my actions to them and why. They listened and thanked me for my visit. It wasn't until I left I realised they hadn't written anything down.

Family, they were all useless. Next my close neighbours who had become friends all rallied round.

One would take them to school and bring them back, plus countless teatime invitations for the girls arrived.
At work I explained to my Boss I would have to leave. I needed at least six months off and as I had not been in the job that long they couldn't keep my position open, plus the car had to be returned.
As I was driven home from the Glasgow Office along the motorway, I became lost in the very unusual cloud formation. Clouds so strange that I felt I was being pulled towards them.
The driver made a comment about the clouds without any prompting from me. He said, "The clouds have opened to allow someone to glimpse heaven." He looked at me startled and said "Who said that? Was it really me?"
As he dropped me off outside my home he wished me luck.

I phoned 'Auntie Lynda' and for the first time I let the tears flow and I admitted to her I was truly scared.
Who would look after my girls?
Why was this happening to me?
Who would care for my beloved girls?
This question spun around in my head continually, no answer ever came, but the questions did repeatedly.

My parents arrived on Friday to go over the arrangements

for Sunday. They were going to take me into the hospital along with the girls.

On Saturday my In-laws visited. They would phone to see what was going on.

Neither side of the family gave me comfort, raised my hopes or eased my fears.

I was about to enter a battlefield where I was the only warrior against an unseen enemy.

Saturday evening I organised a special night for the girls. Picnic on the carpet, their favourite video and to round the night off we all snuggled together in Mum's king-size bed. Snuggled close together I explained why I was going into hospital. One main thought ran through my mind, "Don't frighten them."

The questions I knew they would ask came.

Would I go to heaven?

Would I be beside Daddy?

Would I die?

Who would love them?

Who would look after them?

When would I see them again?

Could they come too?

I gently answered each question painfully but truthfully.

Their tears exhausted them to sleep.

As the sun rose on Sunday morning I put the finishing words to two letters I had written to each of my girls. Should the operation not go well, I had to know within my heart my words would bring them comfort and hope for their future.

I also wrote a letter to Colin; in it I explained the girls likes and dislikes, their fears and dreams, and my request for their future.

The rest of the morning flew by.

I sat on the hospital bed while the nurse booked me in. The girls, my parents and brother waited in the visitors room. The Sister had arranged a quiet room to say goodbye to the girls.

Maybe it would be goodbye, but I knew within my heart either here or in Heaven it wouldn't be goodbye, only farewell.

As my calm exterior was about to crack the sister ushered the girls out towards my parents and the exit. I kept my tears at bay until the ward door shut.

The afternoon was a time for reflection of my life to date. Each situation I had found myself in throughout my life I had taken on board and filed away in the cabinets in the furthest recess of my mind. Throughout my life many

people, some known to me, others who were strangers, had given me many words, comments and conversations I somehow knew I had to keep somewhere safe.
I now sat enclosed in my inner cocoon and began to recall them.

My Dad came to visit me in the evening for five minutes. I wasn't to worry about my house he'd make sure he got a good price for it. The girls would be fine and he would make sure they didn't forget me. His words bounced off me. I'm glad I hadn't told him about Colin's letter. When he left, I felt relieved to see him go.

Later in the evening the Doctor who was to operate, the man with the safe hands, appeared at my bedside.
"What would most you like to do right now if I asked you?" he said.
Calmly I replied, "Go outside to see my stars."
"Right, get on your dressing gown and slippers and let's go." He said. He didn't have to say it twice.
Once outside, we walked towards the large car park at the rear of the hospital near to my ward. I viewed my stars, my sky, and thought; tomorrow I may be looking at all this from somewhere else.
"What are you thinking?" he said,"

"Should I not make it tomorrow, promise me you'll come out here and look towards my stars, find the brightest one and next to it will be a smaller one twinkling, that will be me" I said. He promised he would.

The next morning I awaited my fate. As the time drew nearer, everything around me became brighter; colours more vibrant and my senses tingled. The bright blue sky outside shone as a beacon of hope.

At the Sister's room my trolley was stopped and the wee fat dumpy nurse checked my wristband details. She was very grumpy, unhelpful and a sour faced person, not my idea of an ideal nurse.

She said "Your husband phoned," her manner got my back up and I replied "That must have been good as he's dead."

"Well it must have been your Mother" she went on. Her statement didn't warrant a reply.

The Anaesthetist, an old man who was about to retire was dictating orders while smiling at me. "I'll make sure everything at my end is fine" he reassured me.

"Can I see the Doctor?" I asked.

The doctors eyes beamed at me as he pulled down his mask. I explained what the grumpy nurse had said.

"The man upstairs gave Ron 10 pence to phone, we're going to be okay," I said. "That's good enough for me, let's go" he replied.

My first conscience moment was on Wednesday late morning. The bright blue sky beckoned to my senses through the window opposite my bed.
Drips everywhere, and a strange numbness awash all over my body. Had I survived or would it be similar to Cathy?
Did I want to know?
The Doctor and the Sister arrived at my bedside.
How was I?
Did I feel fine?
It would take time; I had to rest the Sister said.
As she walked away the Doctor pulled the curtains around my bed and sat down.
"In all my years as a Surgeon I have never operated on anyone who fought to live as you did" he said.

The growth was large and had been there for some considerable time. He also listed everything that had been removed. He had never lost a patient and he was so pleased I hadn't given up.
"Give up, no way, who would love my girls?" I said as tears rolled down my cheeks.
Arrangements had been made for the girls to visit later in the afternoon. The drips would have to come out, as I didn't

want to scare them. “No” the Doctor said, “Please, oh please” I begged.
“Fifteen minutes maximum and I mean fifteen” he said.
Two minutes after having the drips removed the girls ran in.
As in slow motion I saw them running, thinking to myself please, please don’t let them jump on the bed.
They stopped dead at the foot of the bed. Wide-eyed they inched towards the top of the bed. Oh how I hugged them.
Their smell and the touch of them made me feel alive.
My love for them took on a new meaning that day.

Over the next twelve days I had hardly any visitors. My Mother came once, my brother came three times, Lynda and Ronnie came once out of visiting hours with a huge bunch of flowers and my Dad brought the girls every second day.
My Father In-law came once and My Mother In-law came three times, once with the girls.
No one else came near and this upset me. Lying in a hospital bed with no visitor’s makes the days drag and makes one feel terribly alone.
I had numerous staples and stitches; the only person who could get me on my feet was me. So the battle to fitness began.
One day I would spend walking up and down the long ward

making movements as a skier on the snow slopes.
Next day I was John Wayne as a gunfighter, up and down I walked all day.
This amused the long-term patients at my end of the ward.
Soon I was going against the clock.
One day the doctor asked me why I was pushing myself so hard. I explained; once I went home it would be me and me all alone to cope with the girls, so I had to be fit.

On the Saturday the Hillsborough Disaster took place. As I sat and watched the scenes unfold on television, I knew their feelings of grief and I could still taste mine.
That night an Irish night nurse took me under her wing, that night and every night there after I had a warm bath, hot water bottle in my bed, hot chocolate and two sleeping pills.
Over the next few days my tears flowed like a river and deep heart wrenching sobbing. This concerned me greatly.
The Doctor explained it was all down to my hormones. A full hysterectomy plus other bits removed had upset my whole system. I had never truly wept like this since I had lost Ron, so the tears were a good sign.
As the tears continued to flow my strength began to return slowly.

Ronnie popped into the ward to see me before one of her shifts as she was a nurse on a nearby ward. She offered to take me home and I accepted. (No one else had offered).
Before I finally left the ward to go home, the Doctor had come to see me three times and he asked if I was sure I was ready to go home?
"Don't go home too early, be really sure within yourself you'll cope," he said.
A nurse had made a few comments on how the Doctor gave me special treatment. In all her time on that ward he had never been known to visit as often as he did in one day until I was admitted.
I made a complaint about her, she was reprimanded and he apologized for her behaviour.
I smiled at him as I reassured him I would be fine; he was being so kind and he was someone who would always be a great man to me.

The drive home was really scary, was I really ready?
As I walked into my home, my eyes glanced towards the stairs; I slumped against the wall and wept. I had not tried stairs; I had always walked on the flat. I didn't cry for long, up on my bum down on my bum, till I found my legs, then slowly one step at a time.

Over a cup of tea, my Mother in-law explained she had been staying to look after the girls. When she had arrived the house had had no food so she had been shopping to fill up my cupboards with the help of Ronnie, who took her to the shops in her car. I was stunned. I had put plans into place, my family had agreed.

I felt drained. I was as weak as a kitten and now felt I had been kicked while I was down. I wrapped my feelings up and filed them away, to be dealt with at a later date.

Squeals of delight announced the arrival of the girl's home from school, plus all their friends. The house was swarming with children, parents, flowers and homemade get-well cards. Many cups of tea and biscuits later the house fell calm.

Mummy had come back from heaven, and nobody believed them so they had to bring everyone to see, they giggled their explanation. I could only smile and nod in agreement.

Four days later my Mother In-law went home. My Father In-law came to collect her and looked awkward as he waited for her to get ready.

That night alone I knew I would find the strength. As I read over my get-well cards it dawned on me Colin and Shona had not sent one. How unfeeling and heartless considering I had asked him to care for my girls if I had died.

I sought out the letter I had written to him earlier before my operation. I read it carefully; I had written it with all my heart. Now I tore it up. I was meant to live. As nobody could love them or care for them like I did.

Over the next two days my neighbours popped in. "Why did you not come to visit?" I asked them all. Each time the same answer, you're Mother In-law said you weren't up to visitors and you needed plenty of rest.

Why did she say that? I didn't know, but I knew I would ask her.

I had not been home a week when Lyn took aggressive Chickenpox. I couldn't cope. Lynda phoned to say hello and all I could do was cry.

I was so tired and weak; Lyn was very sick and so demanding that I couldn't rest properly.

Lynda phoned my Mother In-law who in turn phoned me and asked why had I not phoned for her to come and help me. She arrived the next day and stayed until Lyn recovered. Louise went down with Chickenpox too, but you would never have known, she was never up nor down.

I asked my Mother In-law why Colin and Shona hadn't sent a get well card and she replied "They were too busy, as usual."

I also asked why she had told neighbours not to visit me? "It was for the best" she replied. I was grateful to her for coming to stay and help so I didn't ask anymore awkward

questions.
My parents had come to visit a few times since I had come home, however they never stayed more than an hour and I was always relieved to see them leave.
I now had my Benefit Books back. I had been given feeble excuses why they had not looked after the girls, bought in food or paid my gas and electric. I had put my trust in them when the Doctor had diagnosed me.
I honestly thought the big "C" would take me away. My trust had been misplaced I now knew it would never be the same again.

Very slowly I found my feet, each day I became a little stronger. My brother popped through to see me once a week and always stayed overnight.
On one of these visits he confessed that our Dad had gone to the hospital, sought out my Doctor and had quizzed him on what had been done to me and how would I recover. Doctor Thom explained he was in no position to discuss me and should my Father wish to know, he should ask me directly.
I was livid, so on my parent's next visit I discussed it and left them in no question of my feelings. I said I was furious at my Dad's behaviour on all levels. Once said, it was never spoken about again.

On my final trip to the hospital to agree my final discharge, Doctor Thom had a very deep and meaningful discussion with me.
Maybe if I had met this wonderful man in another place, at a different time, I could easily have fallen in love with him. However I am left with a deep gratitude and a knowledge that the spark between us was meant. That spark ignited within me a sense of life, a deep need to live, and so it was.

Money was a constant worry and soon I would have to work out how I was going to remain living in this house. One evening about 11p.m. the phone rang. A deep Welsh voice introduced himself, asked how I was and explained he was a Debt Collector.
As my phone number was ex-directory, this alarmed me as to how he had obtained it. He explained I had been difficult to find, but a few underhanded moves had given him my details.
Masood had left many debts behind when he had done a bunk. Personal ones would take time to recover, however a business debt of almost four thousand pounds could be taken from anyone connected to the old business.
As Masood wasn't in the country it was easier to trace me. I explained to the Debt Collector I was only a sleeping

Director. He wasn't interested.
He began to phone most evenings late on, always pleasant at first then turning nasty and threatening.
I now know that many large well known Companies sell their debts on to unscrupulous Debt Collection Agencies. These Agencies are nothing more than bullyboys who trade under the Collection Agencies banner.
As I said earlier I had to begin thinking about where we were going to live. Now that I couldn't work due to my health and with this bullyboy now pestering me I needed to find a solution.
I contacted a new Lawyer in Livingston. I arranged a home appointment and prepared myself to fully explain my situation.
They sat and listened while I talked. I watched their eyes, would they sentence and condemn me as others had willingly done?
I'm glad to say, they did not. They spoke, made statements, their words filled the room and yet I don't think I really heard them.
The situation left me in a permanent tired state. How much more could my shoulders take?!
Moments of fear, and a sense of being lost entered my mind continually. My Phantoms chased me in the night and my blackness returned.

In the next street to me lived our Local Councillor, so I popped a note through her door asking her to call in and see me, which she dutifully did.
I explained the whole situation and she listened intently.
She approached the Local Development Corporation, and explained my situation.
When my house was sold I was to contact them and a house would be allocated to us. The house went on the market; hopefully it wouldn't take too long to sell.

The blackness consumed my nights and my Phantoms haunted my days, yet to everyone outside my front door I smiled.
The girls were in a protective bubble. My main aim as usual was to keep them safe, very safe. So as we began to pack our boxes my usual cheerful mode kicked in.
From all our bedroom windows we could see Dechmont Hill. It was a hill near by, not too big a hill but after what I had been through it appeared like Everest.
I made a promise to the girls that when I was fit I would take them to the top of Dechmont for a picnic.
When they were at school the real work began for me to find us a home. I walked around my area of Livingston noting down all the addresses of houses lying empty.
On my Councillors advice I wrote to the Development

Corporation continually advising them on the empty houses I had viewed from the outside and would be willing to accept.
The house sold and an entry date was set. Now that I had an entry date my fears of being homeless rose to terror stakes. Ronnie offered to store my household goods in her garage and put us up in her home. I was very touched by her gesture.

The day dawned when I knew the picnic time had arrived. My friends mother-in-law who looked after her daughters for her, arranged to come with us for company. In fact she came to make sure I'd be fine. With an adult with us if I took ill the girls wouldn't get frightened, which was very caring and thoughtful. As the girls and their friends jumped up and down at the top of the hill squealing with delight, shouting words of encouragement I puffed and panted, each step heralding my beginning into a new life, a new journey.

All afternoon the sun shone, the girls ran about playing and I stored my strength for our walk downhill and home.
As we walked along the back path towards our cul-de-sac, Ronnie strode towards us. Her face beaming as she said, "I've been up in that bloody car park at the bottom of that bloody hill several times trying to get you."

"Why?" I asked.

"They've offered you a great house, but you have to tell them as soon as possible" she said.

After I dropped off our things we walked to the top of the cul-de-sac, across the road and around the corner.

There stood a large five bed-roomed terraced house. As we looked through the broken window I knew this was it.

A voice said, "Hi, what are you up to?" I turned around to see the Brownies, Tawny Owl standing smiling. Her Mother lived at the entrance to this cul-de-sac, so they were able to give me plenty of advice and gossip about my neighbours.

Next day I picked up the keys and went to view the house. Upstairs four bedrooms plus bathroom. Downstairs a large sitting room with a bedroom that I would make into a dining room.

A large breakfast kitchen, a small downstairs toilet, and lots of cupboard space.

The front garden was small and the back garden wasn't too big with an excellent drying green. I was home.

The move was organised. My Dad, brother and all my Dad's brothers, my uncles, arrived to help move me in. No van, no old man with young lad this time. This time everything I owned was hoisted up onto willing shoulders and moved.

As I bade farewell to each room, my usual ritual was easier this time. I had a wonderful feeling, I could not describe it but I felt it deep within.

Moncrieff Way

Moncrieff Way was situated across from Munro Way. Most of the windows looked on to a small cul de sac. Upstairs there were two large spacious bedrooms plus two single bedrooms. I removed the wall between the single rooms and this spacious room became Louise's bedroom and playroom.

Bedroom number five was situated downstairs leading off the sitting room so I decided to turn this room into our dining room. The kitchen was large and airy with the back door leading to a decent sized garden. The house also had a downstairs toilet and a good-sized bathroom upstairs. I was very pleased with our new house; soon it would be home.

I was still recovering from my bout of ill health so it took me a little longer than usual to get it ship shape. The girls could still play with their friends from Munro Way so they settled in quickly.

Louise had begun horse-riding lessons at the local stables not far from Livingston. From the age of three she had been horse mad. As she attended once per fortnight I found I was able to make her wish come true. Where her interest came

from I'm not sure. When she was two, her and Lyn had been given a rocking horse each so maybe…
She took to horse riding like a duck to water. She had waited a long time for this moment so I was determined she would have her wish. Her smiling face always lifted my heart.

Most of the neighbours were friendly but one in particular gave me hassle. He tried to intimidate me and at times most of his obnoxious family joined in however I was not going to play his game. His wife was down trodden and I always felt sorry for her. I chose to ignore him as often as possible but when I found it difficult to ignore him I would contact the local police. They would visit him, talk to him and he would settle down again. His excuse! I was a snob in his eyes and he wanted to rule over me as he ruled over everyone in the area. I wasn't going to play his game, so now and then tensions flared.
Eventually I had to take serious steps. One evening just after tea he came banging at the back door while I was uplifting a message from Mag's in Munro Way. On my return the girls were terribly upset so I decided to call on him to find out what his problem was. He ranted and raved at me while his family looked on; he then picked up a very large bread knife and threatened me with it. I spoke slowly

to him explaining that I would not allow him to intimidate me and if he chose to carry on I would call into his local pub and tell everyone he was harassing and bullying me. I then turned my back and walked away from his open door and headed up the long path. He came after me and brandished the knife at me while I continued to walk slowly away showing him no fear. Inside I prayed that if he chose to plunge it into my back that it would be quick. At his garden gate he stopped but he still continued shouting and cursing. With the help of the police, the C.I.D. and the local housing authority he was moved.

As I was unable to work I decided to become a Parent Helper at the girls Primary School. The Headmaster was a jovial character who had a firm hand. He always teased me about my visit to the school before I moved to Livingston from Hamilton. He had never had a parent interview him before agreeing to send their children to his school. Although he teased me his respect was evident. I helped with Primary One. One of my tasks was to set up their play area and help supervise playtime for six children at a time. I got to know the teachers and became friends with some of them. Education trips were another of my favourite duties. I was interested in the Education system and I wanted the girls to gain as much as they could from their school days. I was always willing to give up my time whenever the school requested my help. I always found it enjoyable.

With Munro Way now sold the hounding debt collector was once again determined to get his money. A local Lawyer put me in touch with a Glasgow firm of Accountants. I telephoned and they suggested a home visit. Their accountant called Eric and his assistant made three home visits explaining the whole situation and solution to me before I agreed to be voluntary sequestrated, in other words bankrupt. The whole idea at first filled me with dread and a sense of failure. I spent many sleepless nights pondering over all the facts.

Massood had left behind many debts and if one debt collector had found me it wouldn't take long before the others followed.

The merry-go-round of debts and worry had to stop. This was my only solution to this hellish situation. So I phoned Eric and agreed to sign the voluntary sequestration papers as soon as possible.

My hand was shaking so much I found it difficult to hold the pen and with tears blinding me I found it difficult to focus on the dotted line. Over a coffee Eric once again explained why this was the right decision.

My head was bewildered but my heart knew it was right.

With all my rebate application forms completed I now knew how much money I had each week to live off.
We would never have luxuries or extra money to squander but we would have plenty to eat, and a warm and comfortable home, what more did we need?
When you are sequestrated you cannot apply for credit, so whatever we needed I had to save up for. I did have a friend who had a home catalogue and whenever I needed anything she would order it for me and I would pay her.

Colin and Shona had their first born a baby boy. When Shona first became pregnant my mother in law explained they didn't want me to know about it, but as she thought this was awful she begged me not to let me on that she had told me. As we never saw them it would not be a problem.
When their baby boy arrived the same silly scenario came into play. My mother in law told me, but as she had not been told officially to tell me I had to wait before I could send a card. Why we had to be left out and treated in this cruel way always caused me great heartache.
On our first visit to see the baby Colin was out, so the girls, mother in law and I popped in to see the family's new arrival. We were not allowed to hold him. As usual our presence was a hindrance and the atmosphere was unpleasant, however we all persevered.

When Shona was changing the baby's nappy she put the dirty one into a neat little disposable plastic bag. As I thought it was a cute invention I said so.

"Things have changed since you had a baby" Shona sneered.

In my mind I said "Oh yeah, push, pant, pain, no I don't think it's changed." I decided it was time to leave.

The Christening was a gut-wrenching ordeal. At the Church Colin stood beside Shona and took the vows of Parenthood. His brother hadn't taken the vows and my mind wandered to thoughts of Ron.

Back at their house I was allowed to hold the baby for photographs. As baby lay in my arms I said to myself "Come Ron look at your nephew through my eyes. Hold him as he lies here in my arms as though they are yours."

After the usual family photographs were over I found myself sitting beside both sets of parents and other oldies while Colin and Shona's friends sat in the dining area all throwing daggers in my direction.

Have you ever found yourself in a room full of people who don't want you to be there? It is not pleasant, so after a short time I made our excuses and the girls were happy to leave.

I like conversation, but to sit in an awkward silence or trying to make idle stupid chitchat in an alien environment

is not my idea of a pleasant time.
Shona's family and friends bar one always looked at me with disdain. Maybe they weren't aware but I didn't fit their mould, I'm glad I didn't.
My previous experiences had opened my eyes towards others around me. I had come this far and survived, yet at times people's small-minded attitudes could upset me. On these occasions the blackness would consume me for nights and the days could find my senses numbed.
I had asked Colin to take on the responsibility of my girls if I died when I had been in hospital. I'm glad I had lived because now I knew they wouldn't have loved my girls as they deserved to be loved. My girls were most precious to me and they only had me to give them the love they deserved.
My in-laws, Colin, Shona and the baby came to visit me only once in our new home. I had very little but what we did have was clean, albeit all second hand. Shona sat perched on the edge of the sofa frightened it might bite her and refused coffee. They didn't stay long; I was so relieved when they had gone. To date Colin and Shona have never been in my home since that day.

At the local stables Louise was enjoying her lessons and I had begun to chat often to the lady Mrs. Comrie (Liz) who owned the family run business. Outside the Riding School stood a portacabin that was always locked. I asked Liz what it was. She explained it was a Tuck and Tack shop but as she had no one she could trust to run it, it was always closed. I asked if I could look inside. It was messy, dirty and unorganized however it had great potential. Over the next few days I made out a plan on how to organize it. On our next visit I agreed a time to go down to the stables when the girls were at school to discuss my plan to help.

I suggested I could open and run the shop on a Saturday and Sunday in return for Louise's riding lessons. This was agreed and when Lyn gave up her drama class on a Saturday morning she also began taking lessons.

The girls were now having lessons both days and older helpers and yard staff began to teach them how to do stable management. They were so eager to learn, so in no time at all they were competent in and around the yard.

Mr. Comrie (Ian) was a brilliant horseman with a vast wealth of knowledge, experience and competition success. He took to the girls and passed on his experience with kindness, fun and occasionally anger but they soaked up every morsel of knowledge like a sponge. When they rode in his lessons they had no fear. He knew his horses and he recognized that the girls rode well, so any challenge he set them would sometimes make them nervous but only for a few moments.

He brought to the surface a joy of horse jumping. Any height or spread they welcomed. Not all jumps were perfect but that is how one learns.

Soon we were down at the stables on a Friday afternoon after the half-day from school plus the weekends. School holidays followed and Liz and I organized fun lessons, Gymkhanas, mini camps and lots of other fun filled days. Over the next nine years we made lots of new friends and the girls gained a vast knowledge on horses, stable management, in fact any job that needed doing they learnt it.

Their holidays were fun and as we spent only evenings at home this reduced my consumption of gas, electric and phone bills.

Outdoors in all weathers made the girls robust, although as Lyn was hit with bouts of asthma some jobs on the yard she couldn't do. However she always found something else to keep her busy.

I became known as Mrs. Etta and all the children were always respectful towards me. Young children who wanted to stay behind after their lesson to help out looked upon me as a Mother figure. Parents found this comforting to know I was always on hand.

After Ron died I had set up ground rules to help me bring up the girls. I explained to them, as long as they weren't broken life went smoothly.

The rules.

If something happened good or bad they were to tell me when we had our long chats at bedtime and if something needed sorted I promised to do all in my power to sort it. Finally, no lies. Plain and simple and they worked.

I have never felt the need to smack my girls, whenever they overstepped the mark the change of tone in my voice was enough.

I have only smacked them once and I still feel guilty about the incident, although the girls cannot recall. Louise was three and Lyn was five, they had been given china-faced dolls as gifts and they were frightened of them, so the faces got broken and as the girls were blaming each other I had to make a stand.

One smack on the bottom with my worn slipper, stern words about telling lies and asking whoever was to blame to own up at bedtime left me in a state.

Ron had only been dead four months and my nerves weren't holding up too well. However at bedtime the culprit owned up. Lyn was brave and explained why the dolly's bad faces had been smashed. The faces frightened them.

That night the blackness and flashbacks of my own physical

abuse plagued me.

Never again would I raise my hand and to this day I have kept my word.

I was always around my girls during the great times at the stables and we became good friends, I now have a very strong bond with my girls. We didn't have much money but my time was more valuable.

I made friends with people from all walks of life, Lords and Ladies to the humble postmen and to every one I was known as Mrs. Etta. At Christmas, the presents we received from clients and helpers always made me cry. Peoples' kindness at times overwhelmed me.

I began to organise a night out once a month to the local Italian Restaurant for the stable helpers and clients. The first meal was for eight adults and ten helpers a couple of years later it was for twenty-six adults and twenty helpers. Two long tables took over the rear of the restaurant. Adults at one table and helpers at the other and once the meal was over and during coffee everyone would intermix.

My girls had always been good at dining out, and when I socialised I always had them with me so these nights were great fun.

Maureen and Bobby had a young daughter called Emma who had a pony that was stabled at the riding school. Emma was only a couple of years younger than my Louise and they became very close friends. Whenever they were going abroad on holiday they always invited Louise with them as company for Emma. Maureen and I also became good friends and she looked after Louise as she was her own. I will always be totally grateful for their kindness towards us as a family.

Emma and Louise are still close friends and although they don't see each other as much as they would like they always pick up from where they left off.

Lyn's primary school chum Darren was her first boyfriend. His parents had a boat "Sly Day" on Loch Lomond and they spent every spare moment up there.

Lyn was invited to go with them and she had a great time. His parents Josie and Alan became very good friends. They very kindly invited us up to their boat every summer for a few days holiday. Darren and Lyn would spend time learning about how to have fun on an outboard without falling into the Loch, while Louise would have fun with Sarah, Darren's younger sister who was the same age as her. Josie and Alan plus their friends in their boats would meet up with us at Luss on Loch Lomond, then we would all set off for a small island, set up camp and totally unwind. I will always hold these memories and acts of kindness close within my heart.

I also began helping out at the Brownies and soon I became the Brown Owl due to no one else being available. My pack had great fun and I kept as near to the format as possible!
To fund raise we had a Fashion Show and every Brownie and their parents pulled out all the stops. We raised enough to have a full day trip to Millport, a small village on the Isle of Cumbrae near Largs.
We took the coach to Largs, then the Ferry over to Cumbrae, then on to Millport. We had a meal at the local hotel, a small gift for each Brownie and games on the beach. We also took some parents and grandparents' too so it was a fun packed day and everyone slept on the trip home.
I gave up the Brownies when the school where we held our weekly meeting was closed down. The Brownies were all dispersed to other packs.
To this day unexpectedly when I am out shopping a young woman will come up to me and ask how I am. So many children, now young women with happy memories of those fun filled nights
Their kind words fill my heart.

Opposite the stables there was a kennel and cattery

boarding business and as my Louise was mad keen on animals she was desperate to get a wee job there walking the dogs. A couple of older helpers at the stables worked there a couple of shifts per week and this made Louise determined to do so too. She begged me to go over and speak to the owners and plead her case. Enter into Louise's life the owners Fiona and Ken. Fiona agreed to give her a trial and soon she was a competent and reliable employee. Lyn also began dog walking and the money they earned was theirs to spend on whatever they wanted.

By earning their own money it instilled into them a sense of responsibility at handling their earnings. In the years they worked there I am so proud to say they never squandered their money.

My dad suggested a trip to Blackpool with the girls to see the illuminations. My mum was interested in going with us and my dad thought it would be a good idea as it would give us time together and maybe it would help heal the rift between us. Ronnie and Joe my friends from Munro Way very kindly offered me their new car for the trip and I kindly accepted. As my dad waved us off I wasn't altogether at ease but I had to make the effort for the girls. The day trip was a success, however as we set off on our homeward journey a few miles out of Blackpool the car began making a horrendous noise. I had to pullover onto the side of the road and contact the breakdown service who duly arrived and informed me the engine had seized and it was serious. He would have to tow me to the nearest services on the motorway. At the services the full impact of the seriousness unfolded. Ronnie and Joe had been having an ongoing running complaint with the garage since they purchased the car due to an oil light being on continually. The garage maintained it was a faulty bulb, now I knew it wasn't. After many phone calls to Joe who in turn had to make many calls to the garage of purchase, they arranged for a replacement car to be brought to me. Four hours later we resumed our journey with a vehicle that carried the advert of demonstration car on every available part of the bodywork!

South of Lockerbie in the middle of nowhere the brand-new demonstration car broke down! I was now stranded on a quiet stretch of dual carriageway that had road works taking up one lane and as the car was dark coloured it was not easy to see. I moved several traffic cones to make a space then pushed the car through the space to make our position safer. I was now faced with finding help but where? Some distance back we had driven past a new petrol station on the opposite side of the road so as that was my only way of getting help, I set off. The girls and my mum cuddled together in the back seat and I warned them not to get out of the car because as it was so dark they may get hurt by any passing traffic. I opened the boot so that approaching traffics attention would be made aware of a breakdown and slow down.

The walk was a nightmare. Being dressed fully in black and walking along the roadside in the pitch darkness I didn't have time to be scared. The climb over the central reservation and onto the other side of the dual carriageway was a challenge.

The staff were most unhelpful and eventually after I became annoyed they agreed to let me to use their phone. The breakdown services were amazed I had broken down again and with arrangements in place I headed back towards the car. Two hours later I had to make the long walk again. I was informed the breakdown vehicle couldn't find me so once again all the details had to be gone over. A further two hours past and still no one appeared. By now the girls were cold and frightened and my mum's unhelpful comments were grating on my nerves.

Across the road and about half way up a hill a small light of a house caught my attention. The garage had been closing as I left the last time so that was of no help to me but maybe the house was. Once again I set off over the central reservation and dual carriageway. I found the dirt track with

little difficulty and began my hike. The sky was the deepest black and the stars shone brilliantly guiding my way. On approaching the run down house I heard the low booming bark of a dog. I took a deep breath and knocked on the worn and weather-beaten door. It creaked open and a small frail woman said "Come in my dear I have been watching your car for some time, are you in trouble?"
A very large basset hound attached to a very long rope padded over and drooled all over my shoes. I had never seen such a large dog and I was having difficulty keeping myself from running out the door. While making my phone call a large man with a stoop appeared from a back room and made me jump. However his smile made me acknowledge he was lost in his mind in a world of his own and I returned his smile.
The conversation with the emergency services was now becoming tiring. Maybe if I lit a beacon the man who was looking for me might and I mean might just find us! The knock at the front door made me jump and there stood a young man who worked on the roadwork's who had come to look for me. The woman on the phone confirmed they had now found my car and they were awaiting my return.
I thanked the couple warmly, patted the dog and set off on my downward hike with the young man who was laughing and joking at my explanation of the night's events.

With car fixed, girls calmed down and my mum warned to shut up we set off on the remainder of our journey home. An hour from home the worst lightning and thunderstorm I had ever seen descended on us, however we kept singing along with the music tape that was playing and tried our best to ignore the mayhem that was going on in the Heavens above us.

Two days later the young man who had rescued me telephoned and asked me to meet him in Lockerbie for lunch and I agreed with no hesitation. I explained I knew I had to meet this guy and Ronnie offered to look after the girls after school.

He was a delightful David Essex look alike with torn and ripped jeans who smiled a lot. I explained I didn't normally meet strangers and he laughed and put me at my ease.

"I had to meet you again because something about you told me to spend time speaking with you," he said. He also explained he didn't normally meet people he helped during breakdowns. The afternoon passed pleasantly and every subject was explored and discussed. As I was preparing to leave he said, "I will always remember this meeting. I know I won't live forever but our meeting was meant to be."

He leaned through my open car widow and kissed my cheek and said "That house where I found you is derelict, apparently no-one has lived in it for years so maybe your

late husband helped me to track you down that night?"
"I'd like to think so" I replied.
Then I kissed him back.
A few days later through the company I tried to contact the young man to thank him for a wonderful time. His boss retuned my call and informed me the young man whose name was Ned had been killed while working on a very exposed part of the road works the day after he met me.
I hung up the phone without uttering a word. Ned had been my Good Samaritan that night.
He was someone I would never forget.

Colin and Shona had another baby boy and as usual we weren't to be told about the pregnancy until near the birth, but as usual my Mother in-law told me again I was to keep hush until it was confirmed we were to be told.
I do not think for one moment that any of the Pearson family took on board the full hurt this caused my girls.
Once again we attended the Christening and once again the usual treatment was dealt out. As I held this new family addition once again I asked Ron again to look at him through my eyes, and touch him through my arms.
A family friend made a comment to me that made my heart and emotions well up.
"I would have thought it would have been nice to ask you

to be a God parent as your Ron's widow. As Colin only had one brother it would have meant a lot to your children and Ron's memory" he said solemnly. I couldn't find an answer so I kept hush.
Would Colin and Shona's boys ever be told about Ron?
Would these boys know their Uncle's girls?
Would they all come together to share a family bond?
Somehow I didn't think so, Shona wouldn't allow it, I was sure of that.
However maybe one day! Miracles do happen!

I met a woman called Jeanette while she was a guider with the Girl Guides and her husband David worked on the oil rigs. The girls and I were invited to their house often for tea and their older girls used to spend time amusing mine. While David was away on his two week off shore stint he would allow me the use of his car. Having the use of a car two weeks out of four was excellent. It allowed me to do a large shop for bulky household items; gave me the opportunity to visit friends and return to Hamilton to visit my in-laws. I still kept in touch because the girls were a part of Ron's family, although the feeling of belonging was sadly missing. When David was away Jeanette and I would spend time together discussing our past and she renewed my faith in people. The offer and use of the car was kindly accepted by myself and to date I have never forgotten their kindness.

In August 1993 I made a visit to our new G.P. He was a youngish man with a kind face and a nervous smile. As he was new he had taken on the task of reading each patient's medical notes before he met them.

His task was huge when he decided to read mine!

He listened as I explained. Every year leading up to Ron's anniversary of his death I would feel unwell. I could not explain exactly as no words seemed to fit how I felt. As he listened he tried many times to make eye contact with me and eye contact was something I avoided like the plague. Dr. O'Reilly from St. Francis told me not long after Ron was killed, I avoided eye contact because I didn't want anyone to see my pain. Now years on I was an expert at avoiding people's eyes.

The G.P. then began to ask me lots of questions.

What was my first reaction on being told of Ron's death?

My answer:

I entered into a bubble. I hadn't been allowed to identify Ron, and this had left me bewildered, abandoned and lost.

A cocoon of blackness had engulfed me.

The feelings of being lost on a vast open ocean with no sails, wheel, anchor or safe port to head for and an overwhelming fear of not seeing my girls into the safe haven of their lives was the best way of describing my true inner feelings...

The Doctor suggested pills to help me and I said gently "no one ever finds a solution at the bottom of a bottle, drugs or drink, so no thanks."

He then suggested that I see a psychotherapist, I wasn't ill as in physical sense, but I was worn out emotionally.

After two other appointments chatting about his solution I finally agreed to go ahead with his suggestion. An appointment for a home visit every second Friday was arranged.

The first Friday arrived and I sat and awaited my fate. A knock at the front door brought my nervous feeling rising in a rush. There stood a man in his late thirties, medium built with a head of red hair and an infectious smile. He introduced himself as Edward and made himself at home as he sat down in a relaxed manner. I made us coffee then sat looking at him and thought "Well you're here, so?!"

He smiled and asked me to begin anywhere I wanted to tell him about my life since Ron's death. The only way to explain was to go through it methodically so I did.

Occasionally he would ask a question but most of the time he sat with an unexplainable look on his face.

His visits lasted throughout most of his wife's second

pregnancy, the arrival and the sleepless nights of the new baby.

One Friday he arrived as usual and as he sat himself down in his now usual armchair he announced this was to be his last visit, when I asked why he said "You never really needed me, you have taken yourself through an emotional breakdown on your own. You were almost over the last rung of the emotional ladder, I only steadied it."

He continued, "Throughout my career I have met many people whose lives have been ruined by only one incident. I cannot believe what you have come through. A journey of immense turmoil as in emotional, mental and physical upset on your own. You truly are the most sane person I have ever met." I was gob smacked.

"I sincerely mean what I am telling you," he continued.

His words were genuine and I was taken aback by his respect. He agreed my humour had played a large part in keeping my sanity.

As he left he reminded me I had a wealth of experience to share with others. He wished me well as he waved goodbye.

On my next visit to my G.P he discussed Edward's report with me and he agreed with his outcome. I had come along a very difficult path but I had an inner resilience that kept me going and I had to be truly admired.

The yearly symptoms never returned after my time talking to Edward and I moved on in many ways.

I was always an avid reader and now I decided to read more than usual. Books from psychology, emotional well-being to poetry and biographies of anyone I admired.
Reading, helping out at the school and running the Tack and Tuck shop at the stables and visiting friends kept me busy.

A close friend who was a cleaning supervisor in a large bank on the outskirts of Edinburgh offered me night shift work with her while an employee was of sick. I would leave with her at 9.45pm and return at 5.30am. My friends Ronnie and Mags from Munro Way offered to be on hand for the girls and my dad also agreed to be on hand if the girls needed him during the night. I sat down with the girls and discussed it in full, as I had to know within my heart they were happy with the situation.
I'm glad to say it was a success and the extra money was wonderful. It only lasted a few weeks and when I stopped the girls were happier.

When Lyn was at High School I attended a first year Parents night. I was in a conversation with a couple of

teachers when one of them suggested I should become involved with the School Board. The Board was short of parent members so would I think about applying? I said I would think about it.
A few days later an Application Form arrived by post.
I completed it carefully and spent a few days working on my personal statement. My statement included my commitment to my girls' education. Children are our future and each one needs to be educated and nurtured into a well balanced adult.
A few weeks later I received a letter welcoming me on to the Board.

By the time Louise went to High School I was well settled into the Boards role and procedures. I was inquisitive, outspoken and the children's needs were always my priority. The meetings were not always serious from start to finish but as usual my sense of humour kicked in to lighten any occasional tense moment.

I now began to spend every clear night sitting outside relaxed and warmly wrapped up speaking to the stars and watching the bright eye catching objects dance across the blackness. As I sat I asked mind-boggling questions about my life and the awareness of unsaid answers filled my

mind.
The feeling of being at one with a presence unseen but definitely felt. A knowing that I could go beyond but not totally understanding where beyond was. A peace so strong I could and did embrace. My body sat relaxed in my chair and my inner soul was taken on a journey.
Since the beginning of time man has looked out into the blackness and followed the stars.

A bubbly lady called Moira who owned a travel business in Edinburgh promoting and organizing cruises attended the stables with her young daughter. They both spent time on a Sunday enjoying their love of horse riding. Moira was in the middle of going through a marriage split, which meant her moving from the family home into a new one of her own. I gave her my time and support to help her move and settle. Then she took on the task of going it alone in business and once again I gave my time and support willingly. In return she very kindly arranged a family holiday for us at a greatly reduced cost. The girls and I enjoyed a splendid three night mini cruise to the Orkney and Shetland Islands. The weather was fabulous, the food was superb, the accommodation was first class and the nightly Heavenly spectacle was wonderous. I will always hold her act of kindness close.

I also met Lorna and Richard at the Riding Stables and Lorna and I became good friends.
She was pregnant when I first met her and Lorna's son from a previous marriage attended riding lessons. Her husband Richard was in the Royal Navy and was a submariner on nuclear submarines. He went on long patrol duties so he would be away for a couple of months at a time. I really enjoyed their company and Lorna and I had long chats about many subjects.
When her baby son was born I would look after him in the portacabin while Lorna watched Darren during his group-riding lesson. He was a beautiful baby with big crystal clear blue eyes. I felt a special bond with him and I knew within my heart he was a special gift.
Richard's work moved him from Rosyth to Faslane and they moved to live in Helensburgh. As Lorna did not know many people there we began to drive through as often as possible to stay overnight.
Their new house was a large split level detached house so it wasn't a problem to stay over.
The back garden had a small duck pond situated through a small gate which in turn led to a small river, which ran through rocky terrain. Lorna, Darren, the girls and I spent many summer nights exploring this river's nooks and

crannies, while Richard was always left to baby-sit. Once the kids were all tucked up in bed, us adults would talk long into the night.
Richard usually gave in and went to bed.
Lorna shared my interest in the Universe, dimensions of time, where as a race we were going and history's mistakes? On those marathon nights we could have changed the world for the better.
One visit to their home would bring about a change like no other.
I awoke with a start in the middle of the night to find myself sitting on the edge of the sofa bed, in the upstairs lounge where I slept with the girls. I was frozen. I didn't know if I was getting in or out of bed, but I was almost blue with the cold. The girls were deeply asleep and warm to my touch. I got into bed and fell into a deep sleep.
The household had already had breakfast, gone out to buy some shopping and everyone was doing his or her own thing when I finally awoke and I was amazed to discover it was late morning.
Lorna asked if I was all right, I nodded, she then said I looked awful. I went to have a bath and I was taken aback at my reflection from the mirror. I looked grossly dehydrated, my skin was grey and my eyes appeared cloudy. I also ached from top to toe. I ran a bath and as I

eased myself into the water I noticed several small bruises. By the time I was dressed and sitting in the kitchen drinking a welcome cup of coffee, in the far recess of my mind something I couldn't see but could feel made me uneasy. Something had happened last night but what?

A noise was echoing round and round in my head, but I couldn't explain or identify what the noise was. I asked Richard if they had mice, his face was a picture at my question, but he said he would check. The kitchen was situated on the upper floor, and Richard pulled out every appliance and checked. While he carried out his task I continually drummed my fingers on every surface and object I could find to duplicate the sound.

We would normally leave after teatime but now I had an uncontrollable urge to get home. Under the circumstances Lorna agreed it was best that I drove home in the day-light. The drive home was awful; I was convinced someone or something was following our car. On our return home I felt I had to make the house into a fortress.

I double locked the front and back doors, made sure all the windows were locked with the curtains drawn and all the lights were on. Before the girls went to bed I checked all the upstairs cupboards and under their beds. I felt scared but I did not know why.

After a full week the problem had not subsided in fact it

had increased. I kept up with my usual daily routine but I was always drumming my fingers on everything I came into contact with.

Where I usually spent nights star gazing I was now scared to do so. For what reason, I couldn't explain. Over the next few weeks I lifted all the bedroom carpets and sanded down the floors and varnished them. I emptied and reorganized all our cupboards, all the possessions we did not need or want I gave away.

Our home had the minimalist look long before it was in Vogue!

I also spent many nights talking to Lorna on the phone and I explained I was scared, as I could not remember what had happened the last night we had stayed.

I needed to know what had happened, it was imperative I found the answer. By finding the answer maybe the noise like a tapping, no ticking, no like a scratching or whatever the hell it was, would go away.

Over the next six months the electrics in our home were checked several times due to bulbs blowing, the television changing channels, the microwave having a mind of its own and sockets blowing. The lights continually flickered and if the Hi-fi was on the sound would go quiet then loud without anyone being near it.

I also became aware of being taken somewhere during the

nights when I was asleep.
I would wake up in the morning with dirty feet and the bed sheets sometimes marked by earth, tiny stones and twigs. I also became aware of having a vast knowledge on subjects I couldn't even pronounce.
I was in an Edinburgh bookshop when a book cover loomed towards my eyes. The subject: Alien Abduction. I bought it and had devoured all the pages within two days. I could understand people's paranoia but more so I could understand their sense of being in a timeless zone. On one hand I gave it serious consideration that maybe this is what I had experienced but on the other hand I dismissed that theory.
Then an article in a daily newspaper about two men who believed they had been abducted by aliens not too far away from where we lived caught my eye.
I sought out one of the guys and phoned him. His name was Gary. He was most helpful, he listened to my story then gave me various phone numbers and names of people who could help me.
With numerous books on alien abduction from the Library and bookshops I was fast becoming an expert on the subject but in the far recess of my mind I knew I was on the wrong track. However I was willing to go down this road in search of the answer I knew awaited me somewhere.

The first couple of phone calls I made to various people who could help, proved fruitless. The next put me in touch with an organisation that sought out answers for strange and unexplainable phenomenon. I invited them to my home and a suitable date and time was agreed.

The girls had maintained a humorous outlook on all that had been happening and I had made it fun, so as not to frighten them.

Gary arrived before the others and laid out all his newspaper cuttings on his encounter plus other articles he had collected on U.F.O.'s and aliens. The material was interesting but again something vital to me was missing.

The others arrived and I was introduced by Gary to Helen and Donald. We sat around the dining room table and after I insured the girls were settled in their rooms I began to relate my story.

Helen insisted it be taped so a tape recorder was set up. Then her interrogation and I truly mean interrogation began. She was savage in her questioning.

I reminded her I had invited them into my home to help me and I did not merit this aggression. Donald apologised and explained some people claimed to be abducted because they sought the limelight, so I wasn't to take it personally.

Helen complained about being cold so I turned up the heating. Soon she was wearing her own coat, Donald's jacket and scarf and she still complained.

Next she spat out the words "Why did you not tell me and warn me you were a channeler?"

I was taken aback "What is a channeler?" I asked.

She insisted on leaving immediately and she wouldn't speak to me directly or shake my hand as she hurried out the door while Donald and Garry tried to apologise as they also rushed out.

The tapes lasted three hours, and I was still no further forward at finding my answer.

Next day I telephoned Helen to enquire how she was. She was still spooked and explained she did not want to speak to me about the previous nights events and gave me the name and telephone number of a man who would be able to help me. She also agreed to pass on the tapes to the man and send me copies.

After a few days dissecting the facts of that night I telephoned the man Helen had told me about.

His name was Reg Hall from a University in Central Scotland.

Before we agreed to meet he had listened to the tapes a couple of times. When he met me at my home I was intrigued wondering why such an unassuming middle aged man was so interested in the subject of strange phenomenon.

I didn't disappoint him, every time we met or spoke on the telephone he was always taken aback at the information on subjects I gave him that once he had checked always-proved right.
How did I know all this? He would continually ask me, the answer was always the same. I had no idea.
He asked me to do relaxation exercises as he wanted to try regression.
I found relaxing very easy. Enjoying many nights sitting out under the stars had taught me that. A few weeks later we arranged an evening at my home and we began.

He suggested I took myself back to that night in Lorna and Richard's in Helensburgh and retrace my steps.
With a warm atmosphere, comfy armchair and dimmed lights I began to relax. As I concentrated on my breathing I visualised myself back sitting on the edge of the bed. Reg said, "What do you see?"
"A dim light shining through the glass door into our room from the kitchen" I said.
"Talk me through what you do next" Reg continued.
I get out of bed and walk towards the door. I am now standing next to the breakfast bar with one hand upon the worktop, I explained.
He asked me what I saw.

With tears running down my face I recalled what sight had stood before me. As then it was happening again and the feeling of being at one with an amazing, awesome and unexplainable presence filtered into every fibre of my being.

"Tell me what you see, find the words to explain" Reg blurted out with excitement.

"She" I said.

"What she, how do you know it's a she?" He questioned.

"I feel it's a she," I said.

"Although to say it, is disrespectful. I will not say it" I went on.

"She is beautiful; the feeling she is giving to me is wonderful," I explained.

"What's happening now?" he went on.

She has raised her hand and laid it upon my left shoulder, she has spoken to me without saying a word. Everything is going to be all right, I'm going to be fine, she is telling me that.

"Describe her to me" he said. "She is about five foot tall, very slim, long limbs and is made of a pure white light. Although white isn't exactly doing her justice, she is pure, totally pure. Her touch is light but awesome in its receiving. The noise is a shadow memory that will go when I am ready to take on board what has been given to me and when

I am ready to accept her touch?" I concluded.

Reg sat looking at me with total disbelief at what he had witnessed. In his opinion this was alien contact at its most awesome.
He was excited but I still wasn't sure about his explanation.

My mind was now similar to a large office with multiple filing cabinets bursting at the seams with mind-boggling data.
I began going to the Library to read every newspaper from one end to the other. I read worldwide events and on a score rating out of ten the events I had foretold or had been shown that were correct always made a nine or ten.
This began to frighten me but 'she' would always appear in my minds eye and remind me, everything would be all right.
I also began reading all the material on alien abduction or contact that I could find. Although the material made fascinating reading somewhere in a far recess of my mind I knew the facts didn't ring true. However I was willing to take on board any suggestions that might bring me nearer the truth of the events of that night.
I was invited to meetings and seminars on the subject and I did meet some lovely people who were like me, searching

for an answer, and others who were total space cadets who were sure “Beam me up Scottie” was only a whisper away. Unexplainable events can have a chaotic effect on one’s mind.

Reg had an abundance of people who were only too eager to allow him to prod their stories, take down notes and extract every small detail about their experience. However he was never forthcoming about his own opinion on the subject and when challenged he would always remain silent. He was a highly intelligent man with no sense of direction or common sense. He never used two words when only one would do.

Time and time again events written down by myself would come to pass. Some nights became journeys into the unknown. Whenever I awoke the feeling of being home overwhelmed me, and with new data filling my mind I felt I had to use it, or tell someone, but who would believe me? The question was always why me? I had no influence on the world stage of events, so why me? always echoed around in my head. I suggested that there were more people like me and if we were all brought together and we all aired our experiences the total mass of information would be awesome.

However Reg dismissed it by saying “no Government or Country would allow such a meeting, nor would they

believe anything that was said." His words startled him, he had said too much. I knew this by the look on his face.
Life continued as normal as possible, daily commitments helped me to focus.

My Father in-law had been diagnosed with Parkinson's disease and although the relationship between us had improved it was never the same. Parkinson's is a terrible wasting disease; the person's facial expression is morose and a vacant look gives the impression that their mind has gone, however the person's mind is still able to work as it has always done. The body carries out functions that the mind cannot control and it causes great distress.
The girls and I visited my in-laws as often as we could. The girls were upset by Papa's shaking but they were always gentle towards him.
During our visits he would occasionally mention Ron. He would tell the girls some wee story about their Dad when he was young. Since Ron's death till now he had never uttered his name. Now for the very first time I realised Ron's death had devastated this man. His emotions had been buried deep within him and he would never be able to unburden the grief that had taken its toll on him.
The time had come for me to forgive him for his verbal attack on me that had been the reason for me leaving

Hamilton. His deteriorating condition meant he had to have respite care in the local hospital. I went to visit him alone twice and we chatted about trivial things. Because of his facial expression I couldn't be sure if my words reached his mind.

The ward sister explained that written words were easier for sufferers to absorb. With this information I sat down and wrote him a letter. I explained the situation surrounding Ron's death had taken its toll on all of us, and I forgave him for his harsh words.

One day he would know the whole truth for himself, however he would only know when the time came for him to be in Heaven with Ron.

I visited him soon after he received my letter and he patted my hand and tried his best to smile, but it was the look in his eyes that gave me the knowledge my words had touched his heart.

As I left I kissed his forehead, it would be the last time I would see him.

A few weeks later he died. He was returning to his bed from a call of nature when the ward sister approached him and enquired if he was all right. He said he felt unwell, collapsed and was dead before he hit the floor.

I'm glad his passing was quick; he had suffered untold

emotional turmoil, now he was at peace.

I was running the Tuck Shop at the stables when the phone call came. Colin said "Hello Pal, I am phoning to tell you my Dad has died." I told him I would be through as soon as I could. His words sounded so unemotional and cold although I knew the loss of his dad would have a terrible effect on him.

A dull pain and a heavy sensation gripped my chest and my breathing became very laboured. As I was in the shop surrounded by clients and young children I was finding it difficult to cope so I took myself off to the house on the yard to regain my composure. I felt I had been winded and the pain wasn't subsiding quickly.

The girls were busy so I decided to wait until we were going home before I broke the news. I telephoned my parents and broke the news to them. I asked my Dad to drive me through to Hamilton after tea. My Parents picked us up from the stables and as we sat in the back seat of my Dad's car on the way home I broke the news to them about Papa.

Louise whispered "He's beside Dad now, so he won't be alone anymore."

Lyn sat silent gripping my arm at first and then the questions flowed. Lyn's school exams were due to begin the following day so I eased her upset by answering as truthfully as I could.

Lyn was almost sixteen and Louise was fourteen, this was the first family death since Ron was killed and I found my mind going back to that morning when I told them of their Dad's death.

After tea my Dad and myself set off for Hamilton. When we arrived at my mother-in-law's house Colin looked relieved to see me. My Mother in-law continually said "I knew you'd come, I said you'd be here as soon as you could." She was in shock, I knew that look so well and I also knew how she felt.

My Dad felt uncomfortable so he decided to make himself scarce. I knew he was going off to have a drink in the pub he used when he had lived in Hamilton. I asked what had happened and Colin explained. I felt numb, this family hated me and yet they both sat with a look that they were pleased to see me.

I explained due to Lyn's exams and Louise's schoolwork they wouldn't be attending the funeral. I did not want the girls around any family members who may be unpleasant towards us so my decision was final.

My Dad agreed to attend the funeral with me. I had been invited to sit in the family car for the funeral so he would follow on in his own car. The night before the funeral my

Dad called off attending with me because he felt unwell. Whenever my Dad didn't want to go anywhere he always used the excuse he had eaten a dodgy pie! So I went alone.

I spent some time at the cemetery before going on to my Mother in-laws house. My nerves were shot to hell. I was totally alone. The Pearson family disliked me so this would be a day I wanted to pass as quickly as possible. As I busied myself making tea for family from Joe's side of the family my stomach was doing somersaults.

A cousin of a cousin asked if I was Colin's wife. "No, I'm Ron's widow," I said.

As I walked into the kitchen I felt a rush of nausea sweep over me. Shona arrived with the words "Oh, your Colin's wife." An air of confidence replaced her disapproving look and she became chatty and amicable for the rest of the day. To date I have never been in her company.

Once back at the house Shona made her excuses to get back to her boys.

At the Hotel I wrote a quick note to Colin offering if he wanted to chat about his Dad or his grief he was to give me a call. As he left his Mum's house I gave it to him. He chose to ignore it, however I know the offer was made with pure intentions.

Before I drove home in the early evening I paid another

visit to the cemetery. I sat on my usual bench; I related the day's events to Ron.
A few weeks later my feelings were dashed to hell again. Joe had been cremated so I asked and offered that his ashes were interred beside Ron.

After my mother in law and Colin had discussed my suggestion, it was decided to reject our offer. Joe's ashes were to be scattered in the Remembrance Garden without any fuss. "It was over and done with," were her final words on the subject.
My kind gesture was thrown back at me and once again my non-status was evident.
The girls were upset by their rejection of our offer. Dad would have to remain alone in the cemetery, as they did not want Papa beside him.
I contacted the school to explain our recent upset, as I was concerned it may have caused upset to Lyn's exams. I requested a copy of a death certificate to send to the school who in turn included it with Lyn's exam papers.
The death certificate was sent but I am so proud to say that it wasn't needed, Lyn's results were excellent. Soon life resumed its normal routine.
Sometime after Joe's death I was informed that two Halifax Gold Accounts had been opened for the girls. They had to

be kept in my Mother in-laws name as joint account holder and under her address, and once a year the girls would have to sign a document pertaining to tax.
Whatever money was in the accounts was to help the girls go to University or some form of Further Education. As it was explained in a half hearted manner I thanked her kindly but somehow I don't believe the girls will ever have the accounts financial security.

I had changed so much. I was intelligent, knowledgeable and I felt at one with something or someone I couldn't see but I had an inner sense of knowing.
Life had become tolerable in a wonderful sense. I was now working through the data stored within my minds filing cabinets.

The School Board was moving into a more challenging role and I was elected as the new Chairperson.
Reg Hall was invited to appear on several television programmes to talk about U.F.O.'s and alien abduction and other strange phenomenon. I had been invited onto a couple but I declined the offer. After watching the programmes I was so glad I had declined. Everyone in authority will always dismiss the possibility of anything superior.
Man has come a long way in his development however his

ego refuses his mind to accept anything that has no concept of what he has been programmed to believe.

I took on a job on a short-term contact at a local factory working within the department packaging gammon joints. I began at 6am and finished at 2pm. The girls were now at an age to put themselves out to school however I phoned them every morning while they had their breakfasts to hear their voices and to reassure them and myself. The money was to boost our cash box for goodies so I kept my head down and clenched my teeth and got on with it.

The job was soul destroying, the other workers were unpleasant, very often rude and the management could not understand why I had been so desperate for the job.

Out of fourteen people who worked in the department only one was pleasant and he was a man who was near retrial age who was responsible for cutting up and preparing the joints. On my first day he invited me to have my breaks with him and I must admit he was a saviour. On the day I left he gave me a box of chocolates and thanked me for all the interesting conversations we had shared. As I walked through the factory gates for the last time I didn't look back.

The experience of working in such an awful place with obnoxious people taught me a great deal about myself.

My Dad began to drop in two mornings a week about seven thirty. He would arrive after he took my Mum to work. He would have breakfast with the girls, take them to school then return to have a second cuppa with me. It was during those visits that he began to ask many questions about the events surrounding Ron's death. I decided it was time to explain and I didn't omit a single incident.
The full facts upset him dreadfully but he said knowing made him understand my behaviour and actions. It also made him look at me as I truly was and his respect for me was evident.
After a few months our relationship had improved so much it had almost recovered to how it had been before Ron's death.
He was shocked and upset by all my explanations and details however he was determined to help me as much as he could. I explained I didn't need his help I only wanted his understanding. I am pleased to say he gave it unconditionally and with warmth.

The girls excelled at school and we all settled down to a very relaxed way of life.

I spent time examining all the data that was still pouring

into my mind while very learned men listened and involved themselves with trying to explain and understand.
Numerous newspapers carried stories on the subject and Reg wrote two books that very briefly highlighted my involvement. However as time progressed myself and others began to admit my gift was in no way connected to alien abduction.
My dad maintained it was "Venus doing her job." Although he would never tell me exactly who Venus! was. I knew it wasn't the planet he was referring to and he would only say, "When the time is right you'll know."
The long nights sitting out under my stars were enjoyable and a deep inner peace and purpose began to settle comfortably on my shoulders.

My dad's health began to cause concern and I found myself spending more and more time with him. I now had the full use of his car so this made life easier. He decided to come home with me one night and as we drove along the dark country road an unusual sight in the sky made me pull up and get out and view it. I drew my dad's attention to it and he also got out to look. With no hesitation he said, "It's Hale Bop the comet and when it's gone so shall I."
"Dad don't say that" I replied.
"It's only Venus doing her job pet" he answered. He never

mentioned it again.
A few weeks later his health was fading fast and his family doctor suggested that a brain scan at the hospital was needed. My dad's reply was "I'll tell you when I'm ready," and Dr. Lang agreed.
Late one night he phoned to ask me where the moon was. He couldn't find it or see it and he was most distressed. I went outside and there it was as bright and beautiful as usual. I told him I could see it and he said "Good you've found it, now it can lead you."
"Lead me where dad?" I asked.
"To where you're going silly. It's lighting your way" he replied.
A few nights later I met Dr Lang at my parents' house after I had telephoned him to tell him my dad had said it was time. My dad thanked the doctor for looking after him so well over the years and was tearful when he left. At the front door the doctor said "prepare yourself, I think your father has a brain tumour. I'm so sorry."
I didn't want him to be taken by ambulance so I carried him down the two flights of stairs on my back and settled him into the car. I wasn't exactly sure on the easiest route through Edinburgh to the hospital but his hand signals and few words sufficed.
We drove along three long tree lined roads bedecked with

vibrant pink apple blossom trees that were beautiful to the eye. On arrival at the hospital I told him to remain seated until I got the hospital staff that were expecting him. When I returned to him he was standing leaning on the car looking skywards.

He was admitted to a surgical ward as the neurology wards didn't have a bed and soon he was tucked up and settled. As I left him that night I wondered if his precious Venus would call on him. I prayed she did.

The ward's surgical team had to have instructions passed onto them from the top Professor of Neuro Surgery as to what was required for my dad. The brain scan was done and soon the Professor himself made the results known to me. He was a small man similar to Danny D'vito and he spoke with a beautiful Irish lilt. His calmness and professionalism held me together. He explained the tumour was most unusual in its formation and that it was a rare type that unfortunately not a lot was known of. One fact that was certain, it grew quickly and aggressively. No treatment was available unless I wanted them to try to remove it with surgery however with my dad's medical history he would most certainly die on the operating table.

As his words echoed and spun around the room and my head he held my hands and said it was a very difficult decision and if I needed time he would understand.

With a large intake of breath the answer came to me.
"No surgery. My dad is petrified of dying. How long do I have to prepare him before I must say good bye?" I asked.
He explained with the help of drugs he might last three maybe four months.
Before he left he agreed I had made the right decision. "If it had been my Father I would have chosen your path" he said.
I had always been named as my dad's next of kin since I had married. My mum knew but as it was my dad's wish she never complained to us although she did to others. My mum had suffered a seizure after a horrendous temper outburst and it had caused her to become slightly disabled. The nerves at the nape of the brain stem had been damaged and this affected her balance, which meant she had to be supported to enable her to walk about unaided. Her disability was not as extreme as she made out and she put my dad through hell as he looked after her. This was her payback time for the marriage she had trapped herself into. Now with the prospect of my dad dying the onus was going to come in my direction. I knew that my brother wouldn't offer too much help, as he couldn't bear to be about her too much.
The night before I was going to inform and explain to my dad that he was dying I lay out under the stars and asked for

Venus to help him prepare and guide us through the emotional minefield the whole family was going to have to journey.

The following day as I entered his small room he was sitting near the window looking out towards Edinburgh Castle admiring the view.

"I've lived in Edinburgh all my life and I have never failed to be moved by the Castle's beauty. I feel so proud of it, it's as though I built it myself" he said.

I sat at his feet and slowly and quietly spoke the words I dreaded. He asked me to help him into bed and said, "I've never been a bad man. I don't deserve this. I'm sleepy now I'll see you later."

I tucked him up and kissed his forehead and said "Oh dad I so want to wrap you up in cotton wool and make this all better."

"You will pet. You'll help, I know who you are and you'll lead me gently and at my own pace" he replied.

A young junior doctor on the medical team took me for a coffee when I left my dad to sleep. He offered me great comfort and support and I will always be grateful to him.

My next-door neighbour Maria insisted on speaking to me the next day before I left for the hospital. The doctor had been into see her and had insisted on her going to hospital.

She had refused. Maria was a very beautiful lady who was 32 stone and very rarely left her home. She explained an incident that had happened to her when the doctor had left. Out of the corner of her right eye she had sharp pain and light like lightening. She went onto to tell me in detail about her funeral arrangements that were in place. All paid in full plus where all the documents that would be needed should anything happen to her. I listened and didn't humour her because she had a seriousness about her that didn't merit it.

Very late that same night her daughter awoke me hammering on the front door screaming hysterically. Maria was sitting on the downstairs toilet, dead.

She had complained about feeling faint as she sat on the toilet and had she sent her partner to get a chair to allow her to lean on the back to give her support and to save her from falling. Before he returned with the chair she was dead.

Her four children aged 9 to 21 tried to take in the tragedy and her partner was numb. I spoke to the paramedics whom I knew and they informed me she was already dead when they arrived. Nothing could be done.

While several policemen and two undertakers pushed, pulled and heaved her massive bulk out of the toilet; dragged her into the kitchen and puffed and panted as they moved her onto a low wheeled stretcher I stood alone. As they pulled and pushed the body along the back garden and lifted it into the hearse I stood alone.

Maria was lady with a heart as big as herself. I was going to miss her terribly. I stood alone to pay my respects and to say a silent farewell.

I organized with the Professor a special visit last thing at night to settle my dad; share with him a small nip of whisky and to be alone with my dad. During the day with the constant stream of family and visitors I was never able to be on my own with him. These night time moments allowed him to plan his funeral, share his inner fears and tell me the memories of his life that he was taking with him.

He had decided many years earlier that he would not die a vegetable with no dignity left because he would be unable to function with a conscious mind. I was only married a few months when he asked me to promise him I would help him to die if he ever was in that situation. I had given my promise willingly because he was my dad and I loved him. Now the request was looming before me.

The nurses gave him pills and tablets to take and he spat them into a tissue and hoarded them until I took them away at night.

He didn't want his family to watch him wither away, he was going when he still looked as he did and not some ghoulish forlorn figure lying wasting away. He informed

the medical team of his request and after many long laborious chats it was agreed that when he was past the point of no return he would be administered the needed drugs to allow him to drift away. One condition was imperative to him; I had to be there each step of the way and everyone agreed.
A couple of weeks into his decline he insisted on seeing each of his grandchildren to say goodbye and take with him in his mind's eye their beauty. My girls looked upon him more than a granddad. He was a father figure to them so I knew this was going to be especially difficult for them. Lyn's asthma could cause a problem so with the help of my dad's medical team I went to visit the sister of the emergency department and informed them when my girls would be visiting and arrangements were put in place. The visit went well and my dad's speech remained with very few hiccups. As my brother's two boys' left he told them not to forget him. To my girls' he didn't say too much because they didn't need his words. They had the imprint of his love tattooed onto every part of their beings and memories forever deep within their hearts.
A brother of my dad arrived so we all decided to go for a cup to tea and allow them a few moments together. As we sat in the café Lyn began making a funny breathing noise and I knew I had to move fast. I dashed along to the

emergency department and told them to expect us in a few moments. Her condition was deteriorating so fast. I hoisted up her slumped figure over my back and shoulder and moved as fast as I could.

Mayhem broke out with wires, tubes and monitors bleeping loudly. Her facial pallor draining and her frightened stare fixed firmly on me as I massaged her toes. I knew this was serious and I had to remain calm and focused for her sake. The room was full of nurses of all grades and the young junior doctor was injecting all sorts without any questions of her medical history and was noticeably unable to cope. I was about to raise an objection when the door behind Lyn's head opened and a small slight built young man walked in. Within a few seconds he said in a controlled tone "Silence the monitors, now, we don't need the noise."

He checked monitors and medical charts then approached and asked to speak to me outside. Before he did he spoke in a hushed tone to the duty sister who then ordered everyone out except two nurses. The young doctor was told to go and wait in his office. Outside he asked several questions about her health and commented on my calmness. "My daughter needs to know she is safe. I can only do that by remaining calm" I said.

He went on to say "Your daughter's heart is beating at an alarming rate and it is imperative we slow it down, however this procedure carries a high risk in that she may arrest and die. I am so sorry to have to be so blunt but I need you to reassure her she will be fine. It will be touch and go for several hours and as soon as I can see an improvement I will admit her to a ward."

"I won't allow her to die," I said.

Lyn slowly responded and between going from her ward in the old part of the hospital and my dad's in the new wing I was shattered. On her release two days later she insisted on going to say a final goodbye to her granddad and she coped brilliantly.

The Consultant of the surgical ward went to see my dad with his team and I arrived a short time after they had been chatting to him. The Consultant explained he was going to prescribe anti-depressant tablets for him, as this would lift his spirits and no doubt a year from now he'd look back on this episode and smile!

When he left my mum growled and spat out her usual hatred and I calmed my dad before going after the Consultant and his team.

"Excuse me but who the hell do you think you are to say those awful uncaring words to him," I roared.

"I am sorry but its usual practice to lift the patients mood," he explained.

"Oh I'm so sorry my DYING father is not singing and

dancing up and down your bloody ward," I continued.

A nurse ushered me into a small private relatives room and spoke kindly while I paced like a raging lion. I growled and roared as the whole situation reached the part I had buried. Buried until I had the time to deal with it. Buried until after my dad's death. Now I couldn't bury it and the thoughts of saying goodbye to a wonderful man who was my father, my friend, my guide who showed me the stars and the only man who believed in me as I was. I couldn't let him go, I wasn't ready. He repeatedly said one day the world would listen to me and he truly believed so in his heart, so he had to stay.

The consultant entered the small room and I growled at him. In return he said, "I am so sorry about your father I wish there was something we could do. I am also very concerned for you because I know the whole family expects you to carry this burden for all of them and I can see it's taking its toll. Would you allow me to make you an appointment with the ward psychologist who will offer support to help you to face the terrible road that lies before you?"

"Go to hell" I exploded.

Next day the young junior doctor Paul talked me into accepting the offer of speaking to the psychologist and so I began to see twice a week a lovely middle-aged woman who was to become a friend.

My dad was moved into a ward that contained six beds, this was an uplifting time for my dad as two older gents there made friends with him. They were tickled pink when I made my late night visits. They were both bachelors'. One was in his late eighties and the other was in his seventies. They asked me if I would be kind and tuck them up in bed too and I agreed with a bundle of humour thrown in for their amusement.
My dad was coping well and my stories of his unknown journey he was about to go on made him smile and laugh and I knew he was slowly becoming prepared.
His speech was almost gone but if he gave me one word I'd make the sentence and he'd tap my hand to tell me if I was right. The staff on the ward thought our closeness was wondrous to witness. The neurology department still didn't have any spare beds so the Professor called a meeting with the staff of my dad's ward and asked them if they thought they would be able to provide the care my dad would need as he deteriorated. Each and every one agreed. One nurse summed up all their feelings by saying "Tom is a true gent, it will be an honour to see him through to his end."
Each and every one of them did and their kindness and words to uplift my flagging heart kept me going.

An early morning phone call alerted me to an accident my dad had suffered. He had fallen out of bed and sustained shocking head injuries. The nurse appointed to care for him was very upset because she had no idea how it had happened. A short conversation alone with my dad provided the answer. He threw himself over the edge of his bed and his head came into contact with the sharp edge of the cabinet and the floor. The whole right hand side of his face was black with bruising and his eye was totally closed and so swollen and infected it was oozing puss.

I told him off for upsetting the nurse and pointed out it was the wrong side he had bashed. His thinking was to bash the bad side and instantly die from the trauma to the tumour. Due to him being a horrific sight my mum insisted on no visitors and as he had said all his final goodbyes he agreed. He couldn't bear for people to witness his injuries but I lifted his mood by calling him several awful names and he always smiled with his eyes.

During his working life he had been a Lothian Transport bus driver and as word went around of his illness old work colleagues began to call to see him so an arrangement was set up. Any visitors who called when I wasn't present left their details on a list. The list would enable me to contact them after my dad had passed over.

Sue, a lady I knew from the riding stables was also

attending her mother in law who was a patient in the same ward. She always made a point of speaking to me and in her own way she gave me emotional support without being in my face about it. Whenever I am in emotional pain I don't allow anyone to get close to me as my defence barriers come into play to protect myself from letting others know how I truly feel. Sue was one lady who refused to acknowledge my defence barriers and her acts of kindness came from her heart. Her few chosen words at the right time always uplifted my spirits.

Old Arnold who was in his eighties said to me two nights before he died "Your dad told me to tell you he is extremely proud of you now and always."
Old Arnold was a lovely gentle gentleman, I am so glad I took the time to tuck him into bed those nights.
Five weeks after my Dad was admitted he signalled to me he was ready. The special medical team was informed and the pump device was inserted without too much fuss. As he slowly crept into a deeper state of unconsciousness I continually spoke about all the things close to his heart and mine.
The first night after the pump was installed I arrived home exhausted at 12.30am. The phone rung at 12.50am. The night sister who I knew from the riding stables was calling

to tell me my dad's breathing had changed. "I'm on my way" I replied.

I gently wakened the girls and told them I was going to the hospital.

Lorna and Richard were wonderful during my dad's stay in hospital. They fed the girls and checked on them constantly. I will always be very grateful to them.

On my drive to the hospital every light was at green and I walked into the ward at 1.10am. The night sister was taken aback when she saw me. "I've just phoned you."

I spent the night listening to his laboured breathing and began taking on board every breath was taking him away.

The next night was the same and my brother joined me albeit he was terrified. My brother left to have a break outside to smoke a cigarette when I became aware something was happening. My dad's breathing was now very shallow with only a noisy breath once in a while and his face took on a serene look like a mask. The room that was lit with only a very dim light began to brighten with a golden sheen. I felt slightly alarmed but I couldn't move, I was rooted into my chair. The whole room now began to fill with a multitude of tiny bright star shapes. I wanted to move and get someone but again I couldn't move. As the tiny silvery bright stars multiplied I was drawn to my dad's bedside and I placed my hand upon his chest. The room was now alive with the golden sheen and the multitude of stars was continually growing. So beautiful I find words difficult to truly explain the sight. I kissed his forehead and told him to go with his "Venus." If this is what I was witnessing and experiencing then "Venus" was doing her job well. His facial mask changed and I knew his inner soul had gone. His breath was now very shallow and I knew it was only his body that was holding on.

His body gave up soon after. My first act was to remove from his overhead light the small Indian dream catcher I had hung there at the beginning of his illness. Take it outside and blow any dreams from it that he hadn't taken with him.

The medical staff were excellent and it was arranged for me to come to the hospital the following day to sign the papers for the post mortem.

My dad had spent his whole life helping others and now in death he could continue. His brain tumour was so rare that the post mortem would allow medical knowledge to be gained and hopefully help others.

I went to view him one last time. As he lay before me he was unrecognisable and he looked like a withered and horrific ghoul. This was not my dad. It was the empty shell of what used to be my dad. I fled the viewing parlour and drove back to my mum's house along the tree lined roads I had driven him weeks earlier.

During the last week of his life he kept on repeating trees to me over and over again and I was upset at not being able to understand him. Maybe one day I would.

However the memory of the golden night when "Venus" called will always remain deep within my heart.

His funeral was beautiful, albeit my mum tried to ruin it by becoming attention seeking, however the multitude of family, friends and old work colleagues who turned up took my breath away.

At the meal after the funeral a well-known villain who had attended school with my dad and always had a pint with him whenever he dropped into my dad's local approached me and said, "Thanks for inviting me. I don't think your mum's too pleased I'm here."

"I invited you and I'd like to buy you a drink for being such a good friend to my dad over the years" I said.

"No allow me. Your dad was someone I truly admired and his love for you will always out shine any star. I still remember meeting your dad the morning you were born. He wasn't happy with your mum but your birth made him glow and that glow never left him. It only dulled when you fell out after your husband died but I'm glad to say it was glowing bright on my last visit at the hospital" he replied.

His words and words of many others that day filled my

heart with great pride. My dad was born 29/8/29 he died 28/5/95. His time was short but his impact on my life will go on,

Two nights after my dad passed I was driving home very late from my mum's house with Lyn when my attention was drawn to a house, on the outskirts of the road that led to our home, that was on fire. Without any hesitation I made my way to the street where the house stood. I told Lyn to remain in the car and headed towards the house that was now an inferno. An older gent who was most distressed was trying to re-enter the house so I manhandled him bodily and remained wrestling with him until all the emergency services arrived. The police asked me to remain with all the family in the ambulance until a full search of the house was complete and I agreed to do so as long as Lyn was escorted home. The body of an old lady was found and I was asked to remain while they were informed. The four adults who were sitting huddled with only the clothes they now possessed clung to me and I spoke with kindness and knowledge of their grief. I remained until they were taken to an older daughter's house nearby. On my return Lyn told me she had not been brought home by anyone. She had driven my car home herself and she was most distressed because she had witnessed the old lady at the

widow during her final moments. I attended the funeral of the old lady I never knew and at no time did I ever take on board what I had done. The family very kindly suggested I should be honoured in some way and the police agreed however I declined their offer.
I see members of the family from time to time and I am glad they are rebuilding their lives.

I was now visiting my mum three times per week and the stress was taking its toll.
I was still attending the hospital psychologist once a month and the visits always gave me the strength to carry on.

The night before Lyn's eighteenth birthday party my brother, who was working on a building site in the middle of nowhere near Loch Rannoch, was in an accident involving a motorbike which belonged to a friend who was working on the same site. Lorna and Richard very kindly took over the organizing of the hall and the buffet for the party while I had to drive up to Perth Royal Infirmary to discuss with the surgeon his injuries. His wife sat quietly while my mum drove us all nuts with her constant moaning and complaining. As the full details of the accident emerged I decided a stern talking to was required towards my brother and his pal who had been driving. He needed major surgery to save his left arm and I suggested brain surgery to stop him from being so bloody stupid with his life.

I arrived home with an hour to spare and Lyn's birthday party was a huge success.
My mother in law, Colin and Shona attended to which I was most grateful for Lyn's sake.
My brother's accident meant daily trips to Perth Infirmary to visit him and this became a strain. However I kept my spirits up by not falling into the 'why me' mould.

Seven months later when most of the strain had alleviated a message on my answering machine brought me sheer terror. The message was from the police in Edinburgh trying to contact Mr or Mrs Pearson in connection with their daughter who had been involved in an accident. I contacted the number that had been left and during my return call a shaking deep within me overtook my senses. With very few details Louise and I drove into Edinburgh to the hospital. On our arrival my heart was pounding and the screaming within was unbearable. We were ushered into a small family room and as my memories of losing Ron came flooding back I paced. The Consultant arrived and before he could introduce himself I said "Please, tell me she's

alive. Oh God please, tell me she's alive."
"Yes she's alive but she is one very lucky young lady because she shouldn't be. I have transferred her to a ward so I will take you to see her" he said.
As Louise and I accompanied him he detailed all her injuries and I knew I would have to tap into any emotional reserves I had. Keith her boyfriend was sitting by her bedside and as I approached he stood back to let me near. I enquired how she was and her growling reply startled me. Lyn had offered to give Keith a lift home that morning before visiting her Gran however at a roundabout a large 4x4 shogun jeep ploughed into them and pushed her small Ford Fiesta into the central reservation where the car became embedded and she found herself trapped unable to escape. Keith had managed to force open the passenger door and escape however on realizing Lyn was trapped he re-entered the car to reassure her. The smell of petrol convinced Lyn the car was about to explode or catch fire and Keith calmly told her if that was the case then it would do so with them both together. They had only been seeing each other for a couple of months and these loving words bonded them.
My mum felt guilty because she had bought Lyn the car as an 18th birthday present.
I informed my mother in law but no words of comfort or

interest came our way.

Lyn's injuries meant she was bed bound and unable to walk. Her moods were foul and I took on board very quickly that the loving, funny and thoughtful daughter I had loved and cherished for 18 years was missing, lost somewhere in a physiological prison. Keith took time off work and we took it in shifts to sit with her, as she was frightened of being alone. I also made arrangements for as many visitors as possible to pop in.
I am sorry to say that not once did any of Ron's family visit or take any interest in her progress. I continued to phone my mum in law but I did so only out of duty. Their lack of interest and no visits made Lyn's attitude towards them change and I must state not for the better.
Our doctor informed me that there was no physical reason for Lyn not walking and he stated that the only person who could get her on her feet and make her walk was myself. So the challenge began. I dragged and bullied her every step of the way while my heart was being torn apart. She did walk and I have the grey hairs to prove it. I also bullied her into driving again and my mum very kindly bought her another car so she could regain her independence. University had to be put on hold because the psychiatrist she was attending didn't think she would cope with the strain, however she

eventually gained a good position in a large company and life slowly progressed but did not resume from where it had left off that terrible day.

Lyn's mind was encased in the terrible and frightening scenes of her being trapped. Her dad had been killed in a horrific car accident and she thought she was going to die the same way. No one will ever be able to feel or understand her fear. She was also attending the hospital and a physiotherapist to help with the injuries to her back and pelvis. Her mood swings and harsh words tore into the hearts of Louise, Keith and I yet we remained loyal and true to who she used to be and with our love and support would be again her true self.

I found myself many a time sitting in some lonely spot crying to the moon and asking my stars to give me the strength.

For the next three years I wrote many letters; helped the lawyers to fight Lyn's case and never stopped in my quest to have justice done.

A Professor who was to become Lyn's beacon was sure she would disengage from the mental torture of being trapped once the settlement had been agreed and received. Ron's family let her down when she needed them and I know this upsets her. I have never said one bad word against Ron's family to my girls however I don't have to as their own

actions have condemned them.
My darling daughter did disengage however a small part of her is still lost but deep within my heart I know it can and will be found.

As the first anniversary of my dad's death approached my psychologist friend I was still seeing once a month informed me she wasn't seeing me again. I had come a long hard road but I had always been in control and coping. She had only kept my path in view.
My dad had spent time saying his good byes to everyone however I felt he hadn't said one to me. He had however. He left me a good bye that would echo within my heart forever, however it took me a little time to acknowledge the fact.
Remember he had said the words trees repeatedly to me before he died?
My dad had been a gardener all his days and on the evening we travelled to the hospital he guided me along tree-lined roads. Those trees were pink apple blossom. They began to bloom on his admittance into the hospital and their last blooms fell on the day he passed. Every spring, apple blossom trees fill my heart with loving memories of a wonderful man.

The Awakening, Healing & Rising

I resigned from the school board as chairperson as I couldn't commit the time it needed and as I had removed as much stress and strain as possible from my daily life I was now ready to find a new challenge.

I began working part time in a local toyshop and after a short time an older woman called Martha came to work beside me. I instantly felt a connection towards her and we became good friends. She asked me if I had ever attended a spiritualist church and I said only once with Aggie shortly after Ron had been killed but as I wasn't in the right frame of mind I never went back. She invited me to attend the local one with her and I agreed.

I was late in meeting Martha outside the spiritualist church so I walked in on my own. I acknowledged her and squeezed in between two women sitting next to her. The room was full of people of mixed ages and it felt welcoming. I settled myself and slipped off my shoes and relaxed into what was happening. The medium was a tall slim gent who was a dead ringer for Larry Grayson. His manner was gentle and he commanded himself as he stood and spoke. He came towards me and said, "Can I come to you please?" I nodded in reply.

"You have always thought he meant to hit the brick wall but I can tell you it was truly an accident. It was sudden and very quick but he has never left you. He walks with you and will always do so," he said to me. I was startled by his remarks and he continued to tell me things that only Ron and I knew and had experienced. Tears began to stream down my cheeks and the words he spoke became Ron's. I was listening to words that were being said by Ron in his usual manner that I knew so well. Martha passed along a tissue to help me wipe away my free flowing tears. I felt cocooned by loving arms and I knew this was real. Nobody present knew me and I didn't feel embarrassed as my tears continued. I felt safe, reassured and loved. I had come to a place that was going to show me something as yet unseen by myself. I thanked him and he moved on to speak to someone else as I wrapped myself into this lovely warm feeling. After the service I approached the medium and thanked him for his words. He replied, "I didn't do anything, you did. The love and your link you had was allowing me to be your channel." I thanked him and joined Martha who was gob smacked at the message I had just received.

I began to go most Sundays and I usually received a message that was in no doubt from family and friends who had died. Their words explaining a memory pertaining to the one who had passed over and myself was always accurate and I began to listen to the guidance being offered. I met a lovely lady called Liz who attended with her mum Betty. Liz was a working medium and we got on like a house on fire. She had a wicked sense of humour that I liked and something about her made me decide to encourage our friendship. Martha decided to stop going to the church, however I decided I could attend on my own because others who attended spoke to me and made me feel comfortable. After several months in which Lyn had attended a few times and Louise was too scared to, Liz asked me to join her developing circle. My acceptance was out before I had digested her offer.

I was entering territory I had never contemplated before. The university boffins, who I will write about in my next book, had used me as a guinea pig in the past and I had survived so maybe this would be as interesting or enlightening. After the service the room was cleared and a circle of chairs was set out in the middle and everyone took a seat. I felt so at home. This circular setting felt so familiar that I relaxed quickly.

Liz instructed and guided everyone present into a calm and

relaxed mood and soon I was being taken to a place that was very familiar to me. I focused and the feeling of being home grew so much that my emotions were soaring as high as a cloud. The moment was overwhelming and I felt an awakening deep within my being.

For the next two Sundays I joined the circle and I was immediately overcome with the same feeling I had received from the encounter I had experienced at Lorna's and many times since. Liz asked us to let go of our minds and open our hearts. I was instantly engulfed in an aura of light and a wide-open vista came into view in my minds eye.

I was home.

All my life since that first encounter with the bright light when I was 10 years old I knew I had been waiting for something and now here it was.

My mind was desperately trying to make sense of what was being shown to me but the words someone or something unseen kept saying to me.

"Walk with your heart."

Over the following week the filing cabinets stored within my mind began to open and I began going on incredible journeys within my heart.

My clairvoyant senses were slowly but surely awakened.

I chatted to Liz several times on the phone however I didn't reveal I had an ability. I wanted her to help me and not be her guinea pig. I had been drawn to her for a reason and this was my chance to find my truth.

The following Sunday as I sat in my heart space within the circle Liz asked me to ask my Spirit Guide to come forward.

I was terrified, overwhelmed and now completely whole.

Completely whole as the one who had walked with me throughout my life now came forward.

My search was over.

I was now so overcome with love.

Love like I had never known.

Love that was so pure I could feel it like a cloak encircling me.

This was love that no words could ever explain.

Love that was so awesome in its receiving I was now ready to listen, to be guided, to be enlightened and shown my true path.

Two nights later I had become used to the voice that now spoke to me.

A voice that had spoken to me all my life but I had been unable to really hear.

Now my senses were listening and it felt so right.

Over the next few weeks I learned the difference between listening and listen.
I was now so relaxed and a happiness that I had never experienced in my whole life came to rest.

The girls took on board my new found happiness and our home became even more homely and welcoming. All our friends took on board and welcomed this awakening and each one became closer because they truly believed I had found what I had been searching for all my life.
The search was over.
I was now ready.

The developing circle within the spiritualist church was stopped due to a couple of small minded people getting jealous of what Liz was achieving however I knew I didn't need it any more. Although Liz was always on hand to offer support and guidance.
A few weeks later I wanted to know my guide's name so I phoned Liz and asked her. "Don't ask me ask your guide" she replied. "How do I do that?" I asked. "Just ask," she said.

Years earlier, a month after my dad had died, I was out walking and I found a very small sapling of a tree lying on the path. I picked it up, brought it home and planted it. The girls' thought I was mad because it was half dead but I explained I felt I had to plant it as it was like a sign for me. I had always been a keen gardener like my dad although I had stopped very abruptly when Ron died. Now I began nurturing this tiny sapling and in turn I began to find and be given other plants and soon my gardening hobby had returned.

I now sat snugly wrapped up staring up at my stars and admiring my fine large tree that now took pride of place in the far away corner of my garden. Liz had said, "Just ask." So I relaxed and as the wonderful feeling of being truly loved overwhelmed me I said out loud.
"You have been with me all my life waiting patiently for me to awaken to your presence and now I have. I listen and you enlighten me. You know me by my name, please, tell me yours."
"I have always whispered your name on the breeze.
I now stand before you and I shall blow my name through the leaves of our special tree that stands guard over you now and always."
I listened and as the trees branches began to sway the gentle

sound of his name filled my whole being and washed over me.
Our union was now complete.
I was home.
Home, deep within my being with a love that had walked with me through many lifetimes.
I was truly at one with my spiritual guide who had waited so long. Now his waiting was over and we both knew I was ready for my journey.

Over the next several months I walked with my heart and truly listened to the words my guide spoke.
I became awakened and truly at one with my guide as we both journeyed along my life's path and relived all my situations.
I accepted into my heart the lessons each encounter had brought forth and I welcomed them.
With each situation thanked for the experience my heart healed and my inner spirit soared.

At work I began to listen and read with my guide everyone who walked into the toy shop and by mid afternoon I would be exhausted. People were being drawn towards me.
Very soon I could determine who was going to pass over, albeit unknown to them. I always took time to spend a few

moments offering kind words and brushing my hand across their cheek's or patting their arm.

A great abundance of pregnant women also began to call into the shop and again I spent time speaking to them and offering unspoken acknowledgement to their babies cocooned within. I gave each unborn baby an Angel's Blessing.

I was now speaking in a language that was beautiful to the ear. A language that I felt so comfortable with you would have thought I had been using it all my life.

I never once questioned my words or actions.

I was walking with my heart.

Martha and I spent many days at work doing our usual chores selling and doing displays of the latest toys. However each day was so different due to my encounters and meetings with whoever came towards me. I was bringing forth comfort, guidance and spiritual upliftment with true unconditional love.

I was home.

Truly home. Home within my heart to a place I had always been but had never understood. Now my understanding was growing with each new day and I welcomed it gladly.

I began to give spiritual addresses to congregations and very soon people were seeking me out and asking for

guidance from my guide.
Crystals began coming into my life more. Ron had bought me a couple whenever we were on holiday and Liz told me of a shop in Musselburgh that sold them in abundance at very good prices.
Sue the lady from the hospital and riding stables was then and is now a very close personal friend. On our visits to the crystal shop and various other places our bond was to become so strong that I knew she was someone special to me.
Alan sold the crystals and Elspeth offered Reiki healing sessions so after a few visits I decided a Reiki treatment was in order.
Reiki teaches one about Universal Law, which brings forth Universal Energy that brings forth Universal Balance to those who wish to enhance their spiritual growth. Reiki is a very ancient and simple healing tool, it enables oneself to take charge and be responsible for one's own healing throughout all levels of one's own body and spirit.
On writing this I have met people who claim to be Reiki Master's and I am upset by their pettiness and hostility towards others whose gift may take a different course from their own.
We may all be sailing in different boats, but we are all heading in the same direction towards the same destination.

Just because someone's boat is not the same size or model as others, it does not mean that their spiritual journey is any more or less arduous.
Some so called Reiki Master's will never be able to stand in their own power because they spend too much time wallowing in petty jealousy. I am out spoken on this because as I have said I have met a few who leave a lot to be desired, however I have had the joy of meeting many who are a pure delight and joy to mankind.
During my Reiki sessions my guide connected very strongly and my acceptance and learning knew no bounds. I decided to enrol and embrace the teachings of the Reiki Fist Degree course taken by Elspeth. Held over two days and along with another three people I went in with an open heart and a very strong feeling that I was about to embrace another gift.
Heather, one of the women I had met at the spiritual church, was now a close friend and she decided to join me to enhance her gift of healing. I found the two days fabulous and the inner knowledge still untapped within my memory filing cabinets was unleashing itself at a rapid rate. I felt alive, as in at one with the whole universe.
Elspeth took us through the whole grounding procedure to connect with the Universe and bring forth inner balance but I felt elated as I had the inner knowledge that this was

normal for me, albeit I couldn't explain why.
When we were embraced in the Universal Attunement I became so in tune with everything and everyone within my whole universal being that I was being guided to my true awakening.
During those two days I found I had the ability to allow spiritual beings to come forth through me.

A young woman who was sharing our experience had recently lost her husband which I knew nothing about. As I was holding her hand I became aware of a young man who was in Spirit running towards me from behind. I was truly taken aback and frightened but my faith and trust in my Guide never faltered.
He had walked with me all my life and I had now at long last, embraced and acknowledged him so I was truly protected and loved in return. He told me to breathe and remain calm. This young woman needed this. I was unaware of what was taking place but I could see her reaction to my words. Afterwards everyone present was speechless.
Her husband came forward and took her hands and spoke loving words then kissed her. He had been killed in a motorbike crash and he wanted her to know he would always love her and keep her safe.

Afterwards, the upliftment and the comfort she had received was so special to her she glowed.
This would be the first of many similar experiences to come.

After my fist Attunement I was emotional because I had been shown by my guide who and what I was.
The enormity was so huge my mind got in the way and I needed time to take the vision on board.

With each further Reiki session I was being taken back by my guide to acknowledge my many past lives and embrace the teachings from those lives, which would in turn enable me to walk my true path.

Sue became my main sounding board for all the data that I needed to express. I was now a powerful channel. She also gave me messages at times when I had to be told via another. Sue became used to this procedure and she embraced it without any hesitation.
Elspeth was aware of something unusual about me but she wasn't prepared to fully take on board the full facts within her heart, however she knew something was definitely different.
I had an overwhelming urge to complete the Reiki Second

Degree and I did so very quickly. During the Attunement as my guide stood proud and tall by my side he instructed me with kind words and overwhelming love to accept who I truly was.
As the universal energy cascaded over me I recognized the Phoenix arising through the souls of my feet and I felt the huge surge of deep knowing lift me up and allow me to see myself soar as I had done in my ancient past.
Now I was truly one.

For the next nine months I walked the walk as my ancient ancestors had done and with each step I became stronger and the knowledge of who and what I truly was came to rest within my heart. My guide enlightened me at my own pace and a deep knowing filled every part of my day.
My girls also embraced Reiki and they both awakened an inner knowledge that one-day they will both fulfil. They have watched me blossom and within their hearts my words of truth to them are being stored for a time in their future.
Sue and Louise completed the Reiki First Degree together in which Sue insisted on paying. They both had fun and it was an interesting journey for them.

When our body, which is the shelter for our inner spiritual soul, passes over we go home.

Home to the higher side of life, to spiritually heal from our lives on the earth plane.
To balance and audit our life's account book and to spiritually grow from our experiences.
With each return to the earth plane we enhance the enlightenment of our true spiritual Soul.
Layers of many dimensions form the higher side of life.
Each dimension providing a deeper knowledge of true enlightenment and unconditional love. Similar to a multi storey building, with each floor marking one's spiritual growth.
We are all on the same journey to achieve pure enlightenment.
The True Higher Spirit is the one responsible for all. You may wish to call the Higher Being various names i.e. God, Allah, the Man upstairs and so on however there is only One True Higher Spirit. On the earth plane we choose to take on board the teachings of structured religions however we get so lost in the religious package that we lose sight of the true message. Religion is based on control and fear. I can understand that many people are drawn towards it. This is only my personal opinion.
Jesus was someone who came to teach us and show us true unconditional love in its purest form and because the so called religious men of their time looked upon him as a

trouble maker they crucified him. He spoke with truth from his heart as spoken to him by The Higher Spirit whom he called Father.

I have a dream that one day we shall all take one small step in the form of acknowledgement of our inner spiritual being to begin a global awakening.

I was now working with my guide taking on board the vibrations of others and channelling pure spiritual energy. My whole way of life was changing before me. My sessions embracing spiritual energy helped to enhance my gift that I had had since I was a child, albeit I was naïve to the gift at that time.

I knew deep within I had to complete my Reiki teachings and embrace all it had to offer me. The Reiki Master course was several hundreds of pounds and I was short of that kind of money. My close and dearest friend Sue gifted me the money and a date was set. Her kindness knows no bounds. By her kindness she was acknowledging a deep awareness of who I was and her actions were those of true unconditional love in its purest form.

A date was set for Elspeth to take me on a retreat to a cottage in a remote part of the west of Scotland. We would leave on the Monday evening and return Thursday evening.

A few weeks before we set off I told several people including the girls and friends that something truly awesome was going to take place. However I felt Elspeth would not be prepared to take on board the enormity of the Master Attunement I would receive.

By now my special tree was enormous and whenever friends came to visit they were always over awed at his size and beauty. On the run up to me leaving to do my Reiki Third Degree & Master's journey I spent time sitting under him, standing hugging him and being truly at one with him. During my time spent in relaxation near him I recalled an event that made me laugh and contemplate what Ron's part in my life was.

Before we were married he came to pick me up from work one summer evening and as he stood leaning up against his car my workmates called to me to come and see what he was wearing. He had on moccasin soft slip-on shoes, his jeans, a colourful vest and a band of material wound around his head in a Native American Indian style. Everyone was laughing at him and I was black affronted. As I approached him through fits of giggles I asked him what he was playing at being dressed up in such a rig out. He replied very straight-faced. "I am like your Indian and you are my Phoenix as you are his."

"Are you alright or are your suffering sun stroke?" I asked.

"You choose not to listen and you choose not to see so don't blame me. So get in the car squaw and let's get something to eat," he replied.

While he drove I looked at him and his attire and profile gave me a feeling of de-ja- vu however it didn't last. Throughout the eleven years we were together we told that story several times not knowing why but it always brought forth laughter!

When Elspeth came to pick me up she was late and I felt she wasn't quite in the mood for going. I introduced her to my special tree, she was taken aback at his size and she took on board his wonderful vibrations. On the drive through Glasgow I noted she was beginning to relax and I listened while she off loaded her past few days turmoil. As we waited for the ferry to take us over to Dunoon we were now chatting together in an animated way, which was relaxing. The drive up and over the hills once we reached Dunoon was interesting. It was now dark and a thick mist had fallen and most of the road was single track. Now and then the car's headlights would fall on sheep sitting or meandering on the road and my heart was in my mouth as Elspeth's driving was reminiscent to Cruella de Ville from 101 Dalmatians. Since Ron's accident I hated being a passenger in a car, any car and I always like to be the one in

the driving seat so with sweaty palms and a racing pulse we continued our drive upwards and onwards.
Sometime later we stopped at a house near a staggered crossroads in the middle of nowhere to pick up the keys for the cottage. As Elspeth approached the house she suggested I might like to get out of the car and look at the sky. She knew of my kinship with the Heavenly stars. The heavy mist had suddenly disappeared and as I leant on the car and looked skywards the awesome view of the Milky Way and beyond was so powerful I wanted to cry. Tears didn't flow because my eyes were drawn to a huge moving shape similar to a flat pyramid. The shape was slowly moving in a triangle flow and the brilliantly lit edges made it appear like a jewel. Elspeth was walking back to the car when I went to draw her attention to the jewel star when my Guide whispered to me "Hush this is only for you little one." I remained silent but the feeling of love washed over me.
Another short drive followed before we turned off onto a rough track which was only used for logging lorries. The single track was very rough with trenches or each side and with the mist still thick the journey uphill was scary.
Elspeth told me to look and I would see the gable end of the cottage coming into view. I laughed through nerves and told her I couldn't see the end of the car never mind some gable end!

She then turned sharply into a small opening and bumped over the grass and explained she couldn't get the car any nearer so we would have to carry all our belonging up to the cottage. With the headlights on full beam the scene was barely lit up however we struggled with our gear and Elspeth led the way. At the small porch door as she struggled with the keys she announced she was frightened of the dark! My first thought was well if she's scared and she comes here regular then there must be something to be scared of, so very quickly all the hairs on the back of my neck stood up and my sweaty palms and racing pulse returned. As we fell in the door she told me to walk straight ahead and she would go and switch on the electric. I fumbled with the door latch and just as it opened the light went on and before me stood an old couple who said, "Welcome to our home."

I called to Elspeth and informed her an elderly couple were welcoming me but I didn't hear her reply. By now my gift allowed me to see, hear and feel my connection with the Higher side of Life and I was never scared by the encounters. I was blessed to be in a position to do so and I always felt humbled.

Elspeth gave me a tour of the cottage. The family room consisted of a table, chairs, an old three piece suite which was the original one the family had brought in 1938, a

dresser, a standing cupboard and a sink with two units, an electric cooker and fridge. The fireplace was the original black leaded ingle and hearth. The feeling of peace and tranquility in such a very basic setting was wonderful.
The bedroom had a lovely small fireplace, a bed recess that housed a very large double bed, a large couch which folded out to a double bed, a small set of beautiful wooded drawers and two old comfy armchairs. On the wall hung family photographs and I instantly recognised the old couple that had welcomed me.
The couple were Mr and Mrs Simpson and they had owned the cottage since the early 1900's. Some of their family had been born in the cottage and it was used to raise a wonderful family whose loving vibrations and family love bounced from every wall.
The toilet was adequate with a large old-fashioned wash hand basin where one could have a complete wash down without having to immerse oneself into a bath.
A ladder led to the loft which had been converted to hold four ¾ beds and two old wooded chests that held blankets galore. A large chest held old family photographs taken at the cottage and from each photo the love and happiness shone out.

After lighting the two open fires and eating a quickly made

yet delicious meal we wrapped up in our woollies and went out to sit outside on the old worn bench and delight in the Heavenly spectacle of stars. We retired to bed sleepy yet contented at 3.30 am.

Next morning we awoke about 10.30 and the sunshine beckoned me to come outside. The view was overwhelming. The cottage stood at the top of a small glen half way up a hillside. On either side of the glen huge trees of many shades of green offered a cocoon like protection. A huge ampi-theatre. Down the glen the view took in the far away shore and the island beyond. The sky was clear electric blue; the grass and trees in so many shades of green that it was a delight to the senses and the brilliant reflection of the white washed cottage in the sunshine made the whole scene appear magical. I sat on the bench and allowed my whole being and all my senses to be drenched in this glorious setting as Elspeth made our breakfast. We ate heartily and the day was spent talking over my many life's issues, my solutions, my journey and my gift that I was blessed with. I talked and talked. I explained and detailed all my channelled philosophy.

I had an audience that was unseen but every word I spoke out loud was being taken up into the Heavens and I was being heard.

With each passing word from my lips a slow acceptance of what I was and what I was capable of bringing forth to others filled my heart.

The philosophy that I spoke I did so from my heart with a confidence that was not out of big headedness or ego but out of true unconditional love.

I was slowly accepting that my spoken words were truth. I knew so because my heart was telling me and my head wasn't anywhere in the equation.

That night we once again sat outside counting the shooting stars and taking in the Heavenly spectacle that was beauty in its simplest form until 3.30am. I slept like a baby and snuggled in the recess bed as I was cocooned like a butterfly awaiting the morning to alight afresh.

Elspeth had warned me that she was a terrible snorer however during our three nights stay she didn't snore once. She also admitted that in all her visits to the cottage with others this was turning out to be very different but most enjoyable and rewarding. I was touched by her words and I felt within that we had only begun to scratch the surface of what this visit was going to bring forth.

I had decided that my first Attunement would take place outside on the green lawn in front of the worn wooden bench and in full view of our now nightly Heavenly spectacle. After a lovely meal we wrapped up warmly and with the relaxing music of my choice echoing around the glen I sat myself on a small chair in the middle of the lawn. The blackness of the sky was so dense, the brightness of the stars awesome and the trees standing like impressive giants set the scene.

As I sat and waited for Elspeth to prepare herself I was suddenly overcome with a great fear, an awesome fear that was tingling over and throughout my whole being. I was so scared I wanted to run somewhere anywhere to feel safe and yet I was rooted to the spot. The sight of a multitude of sparkling tiny lights like eyes lit up the tall trees like Christmas trees and still I felt frightened.

As Elspeth approached me my Guide whispered,

"Do not be afraid. Many have chosen to come forward and share this moment with you. You have been loved all your life and also in previous lifetimes. Come with love and receive what is rightly yours. Your heart is open, allow the power of the Universe to fall upon your shoulders and wear the plumage that is yours."

As the last word drifted away I instantly relaxed and I acknowledged all those present. The moments passed as Elspeth went through her rituals and once again I was transported to a place I knew so well and I accepted the teachings I was being given. Given to pass on to those who would choose to listen. To those who would chose to come towards me and receive words that would hopefully awaken their hearts and enlighten them to achieve all they are capable of.

Sometime later I awakened and rejoined Elspeth who was sitting on the bench relaxed. She admitted that the Attunement had been powerful and awesome and that she felt brilliant. For the rest of our two hour stay outside I walked around spouting forth the words I had been given, recalled funny stories of my life and went into details about a few of my past incarnations shown to me during the Attunement. I also answered the many questions Elspeth asked without any thought regarding the answers but somehow my replies were in depth and acceptable.

Next day Elspeth suggested I listened to several spoken tapes by an American woman who explains her theory on the meaning of our journey on the earth plane. I agreed with a few of her theories and dismissed many others. I was fast becoming exhausted as my energy was being used up at an alarming rate so Elspeth decided we went down the glen to the nearby village for an ice cream and a stroll along the shore to give me a break. She had also arranged for us to pop into visit one of the Simpson family who lived nearby. They were a delightful couple and their oldest son who popped in was very friendly. I was introduced to everyone when the son said “Oh dad she’s got that look in her eye,

the cottage has found its way into her heart, she'll be back."
I agreed I was totally in love with the place and I knew deep within I would return. The visit was lovely and Tom didn't need encouraging to look out the family photograph albums for me to browse through. I asked many questions and he appeared delighted at my interest and his answers on the history of the cottage were amazing. When sitting outside the cottage during the day I was constantly being shown a scene of a celebration. Many family members dancing and others smiling and mingling while the whole setting was in brilliant sunshine. I was certain it was a celebration of a wedding. No sooner had I asked Tom he went off in search of an album that may help. No wedding had ever taken place at the cottage during their ownership but a family member who had been married in Greenock came to celebrate afterwards with all the family who were at the cottage. As he handed the photograph to me I became excited because every detail I had explained was contained within it. An uncle had brought his new wife and the celebrations went on well into the night.
Elspeth and I gave two spiritual healings. The first to Tom's wife Irene and the other to their son. My vibration and spiritual link was now noticeably stronger and when we had finished on the son I conveyed to him the details about him my guide had told me. The look on his face was a picture as

he said “You’re bloody good. You can do that anytime because it was great.”

The visit was most enjoyable and I knew I would be in their home again. The drive back was once again a sweaty palm job and I was so relieved when the car was parked and we stumbled in the dark towards the cottage. While Elspeth waited on the vegetables to cook for our deliciously awaited meal I asked her to look out all her crystal points she had with her. She was adamant she had brought none with her however I was just as adamant that she had the number I needed for my next Attunement that would be later that night. She searched through her numerous bags and similar to a magician she brought out the requested crystal points. As she handed me each one the look of disbelief on her face was funny and I could offer no explanation. Soon I was holding fourteen and I was a happy bunny as I set off to lay them out as I was being instructed to do so by my Guide. During our meal I tried to explain in an easy manner that whatever scene was being set I had no control over.

Earlier while sitting beside the shore Elspeth explained that many clairvoyants work in toilet water, some work in eau de cologne and rarely some work in perfume. I was the bottle, she said. This wasn’t news to my ears as I had been given that message on a couple of occasions. She also commented that she was aware her Spirit Guide was not around. I replied quite innocently "He is standing back as a mark of respect." She visibly bristled at my words and for a split second I detected anger and hostility however her usual easy manner returned and I didn't say anything else on the subject.

After our meal she asked me if I wanted to do the Attunement outside and I replied no. While Elspeth washed up I moved the armchairs back to make an open space in the centre of the sitting room. With the fire well stoked and a multitude of candles lit the scene was one of beauty.
I then laid each crystal point on the floor to represent a circle of twelve.
The remaining two were laid in the middle of the circle with the pointed ended facing each other. Between the two points I laid a large rose quartz crystal and then placed a wooden chair in the middle so I was sitting over the central crystals. Elspeth's facial expression asked many questions and I offered a simple explanation. "I don't understand why, I only know this is the work of my Guide. I have been told many times this would be awesome in its receiving so I await whatever."
"I have never done anything like this and I don't know what to expect so I guess we'll just go with it girl." She replied.
With the sound of the soothing music, the gentle glow from

the candles and the fire's glow softly caressing the room I took my seat and relaxed. Elspeth looked as though she was about to enter new territory and I smiled at her to encourage her to go with it.

Waves so awesome I still don't have the words to explain began to cascade over me continually and very soon I was acknowledging those of the Higher Realms. Elders and Guardians who sat within my crystal circle and I willingly allowed my heart to soar. I gave my full respect to the Higher Spirit who had blessed me and bestowed on me my gift to allow me to help enlighten and awaken those who chose to hear my Truth of Voice.

I stood tall and strong and accepted the vision of my true path. I had walked the earth plane many times and I had arisen like a Phoenix only a few times. Now I was respectfully acknowledging and with pure unconditional love accepting my birth contract.

I was now soaring like a bird with plumage glowing bright like fire embers.

I was soaring far beyond where the cottage stood in the darkness of the night. I was soaring towards a pure light that was my source.

All those people I had met during this lifetime who had offered me words that I had stored would become the beacons that would light my path when I recalled their

spoken jewels.
With a deep heart felt respect I accepted the Symbol of who I truly was.
A Phoenix.
When I awakened back in the room the candles had burnt down and the fire was in urgent need of attention to stop it from going out. Elspeth was out cold, sound asleep without a snore to be heard. I stood up and stretched, lifted the chair and placed it at the table, put the kettle on and brought in coal and stoked the fire. I replaced the candles and sat and waited for the kettle to boil. I felt so serene, calm and renewed in a way I still cannot find the words to fully explain. I made a cup of tea and put a cup out for Elspeth, as I was so sure she would wake up any moment. Exactly one hour after I had awakened Elspeth was still out cold so I asked my Guide to bring her back. I had no sooner finished saying the word "back" when she sprung into the present.
Her appearance was dishevelled, disorientated and she asked me what had happened. While she sipped her tea I went over the events and she admitted she had never experienced at any time anything like what had just happened to her albeit she couldn't recall any details. We sat in calm silence and allowed the presence of an unseen but truly heart felt energy surround us. A short time later

we retired outside to our usual worn bench where we talked far into the night, counted our shooting stars and listened to the animals of the night calling to each other.
A glorious feeling of being at one with something or someone was now accepted fully with the greatest respect. I was a Phoenix and although it had taken me a long time to reach this knowing, I now knew the messages being channelled to me as I journeyed along my path on the earth plane knew no bounds.
I would stand tall within my own energy and light and speak with Truth of Voice.

After a fitful and deep night's sleep I awoke to the sunshine once again beckoning me outside. Breakfast was so tasty and as I stood next to the sink washing up I looked at my reflection for the first time since I had arrived. I was astonished at my appearance. I had a lovely pink glowing complexion, my eyes were sparkling and I positively radiated.
I asked Elspeth if she noticed anything different about me and she spoke about all the things I had noted into myself. I had a positive spring in my step and I felt so happy and alive I could have burst.
Elspeth then explained I had to practice doing Attunements on my own so after I received instructions I set forth.

When I finished connecting spiritually with my wonderful Guide I asked to do the Attunements outside in the sunshine and Elspeth agreed. By doing so this would give her time to tidy up before we were due to leave.

Outside I placed the wooden chair in the middle of the small lawn and began.

My dad, all my grandparents, all family and friends lined up to come towards me and be spiritually at one with me. Tears fell continually from my eyes and once again I was over taken with an unexplainable yet powerful and awesome feeling.

My Guide stepped forward and asked me to sit with Him on the grass, I did so without a moment's hesitation.

I have always found wearing shoes a tiresome chore and at every opportunity I kick them off and go barefoot. I now sat cross legged and with the palms of my hands laid against the blades of grass surrounding me.

I was told to feel, truly feel the beat that was pulsing through my whole being.

The brilliant and sharp colours of everything around me startled me. Colours now so awesome and my senses so alive I felt I was in a very large living painting.

Words known to us on the earth plane do not allow me to do full justice to the experience.

The glen fell silent as I continued to sit on the grass and all my family and friends from the Higher side of life joined me.

I heard their words, I saw their smiles and I felt their unconditional love bathe over me.

My Guide asked me to look down the glen, which I did.

The vision I was seeing made me blink several times and I asked my Guide to reassure me that what I was seeing was true.

He smiled and nodded and as I returned to look down the glen the full spectacle came forth before me.

A tall Highlander (McPherson) led the masses that walked behind him up through the glen towards where I sat.

Masses of Spiritual beings from my many lifetimes all nodded in acknowledgement as they came to rest all around.

Their warm smiles filled my heart and their chatter embraced my ears.

My tears still fell but as they were tears of pure joy and love I did nothing to wipe them away.

Elspeth came out of the cottage to ask if I was o.k. and to offer me lunch. As she approached I told her not to touch me and she admitted she wasn't going to. She sat down on the grass and asked what I was experiencing. I tried to explain but she said it didn't matter because she could tell by my expressions that it was awesome. She also said "I can pick up from your vibrations the wonder but I do wish I could see and hear Spirit like you. I'll have to do with this but I shall never forget this moment."

My dad had always told me to walk with my heart, now I truly did and I always would. Everyone melted away and with Ron and my Dad standing before me truly connecting they bid me farewell, not good-bye. They turned and waved as they melted into the tall trees and I realized I was now fully whole in mind, body and spirit.

I now also acknowledged the inner screaming had stopped.

I was at one with God.

With the cottage packed up I took many photographs of the inside of this wonderful cottage sanctuary and as I continued taking snaps outside I ran out of film.

As Elspeth made her way to the car I faced the cottage, bowed respectfully, and bade it farewell, not good-bye but a very fond farewell.

All the way down the rough track tears blinded me and I felt I had left a small part of me there. In the nearby village I bought another film and Elspeth took me back to the cottage to finish taking photographs of the glen and the surrounding trees. We didn't go back into the cottage and I was relieved at this because I didn't think I could cope with the overwhelming emotions, but I knew on my return visit I would welcome what awaited me.

Back home I unloaded my belongings from Elspeth's car while she admired my special tree that I now affectionately called "my big man." She stated that since we had left on Monday it appeared to have grown upwards and outwards. In fact it stood most stately and splendid and she appeared truly in awe of it. I waved her off and went to sit below his branches and reflect on the past few days' events. With each word he appeared to sway as if he was in agreement with the events.

I was now ready to acknowledge and welcome into my heart the other Guides my Guide brought forward to me.
I also walked the walk within my heart again with my Guide by my side receiving the teachings from the Higher side of Life.

The first night my Guardian Angel came forward during a meditation I nearly passed out.
After I had done the one eyed blinking routine several times I became calm and felt so stupid at being scared and startled. He was twelve foot tall with a huge wingspan, with

the emphasis on his huge wingspan most important.
He is awesome in stature yet loving and gentle. Simple and uncomplicated I address him as Jed.
No fancy and unpronounceable title, plain Jed is what he prefers to be called. I love him dearly and I thank him every night for looking after me and I call good morning to him when I rise.
Everyone is given a Guardian Angel from the moment they take their first breath however a great number are never called upon or acknowledged. No Guardian Angel will step forward until they are needed. They offer unconditional love, support and guidance. That is their contract yet so many are never given the opportunity to step forward.
During my lifetime I have had help when I most needed it from Angels, on numerous occasions that have taken on human form and I have spent many hours calling them forward and thanking them from my heart.
When life brings you situations that you find difficult. Take time to find a quiet place to sit interrupted and ask from your heart for help. I can assure you, you will feel a peace descend upon you. The sense of peace will allow you to think everything through and will lead you to a solution.

To Colin I ask him to find the time and place to sit at one with my girls and say a simple word of apology to help heal

their hearts and his. All he has to do is remove his mind from the situation and forgive from his heart.
Maybe one day he will come to call.
To his boys, my nephews I pray that one-day they shall know my family because I feel they have lost out on so much by being kept back from us.

Liz Hislop my friend from the Spiritual church said the following to me recently.
"Many mediums and clairvoyants work in toilet water, some in eau de cologne and now and then in perfume. As someone who recognizes you as my mother did before she died you are the bottle."
I can feel the warmth of her words spoken with unconditional love.
I have been told by people at various times in my life and I can recall to mind those who have said to me "if you could put the essence of you and make it into perfume it would be a best seller."
Liz is also the lady who kindly donated to me an amount of money to enable me to support myself while I wrote this book. Why? You ask.
I have always been sent a pure spiritual soul to guide and support me whenever it is deemed necessary although many times I have been unaware at the time. Liz is one of those

spiritual souls and I give her my deep respect and heartfelt thanks for believing in me.

Sue is a treasure, my Angel of Time. She was sent to me and I am blessed. She knows and gives unconditional love as it is truly meant to be given. She is my sounding board, my channel when I need to hear via another voice and she truly believes and sees me as I am. She also 'adopted' my daughters and is a source of kindness, guidance and support to them at any time. With her continual acts of love and kindness her spiritual growth blossoms.

Time has moved on and I now welcome private and group readings. I have met many who travel from all over the world to Edinburgh to see me. I also travel all over Scotland and I am always truly uplifted by the wonderful people I meet.

During a spiritual reading my guides embrace your heart with unconditional love to enable you to find the ability to bring forth well being to achieve all you can.

My readings bring comfort and up-liftment. Reassurance and guidance. Hope and confidence to continue with your life's journey.

I enjoy giving lectures on Spiritual Awakening of the Inner Self. My lectures are always filled with laughter and I do

not use fancy words but I speak truth of voice so that all present will embrace the message my Guides bring forth. I am always blessed that many who attend are touched and feel they can understand my words and go onwards on their own life's journey with a spring in their step and deep knowledge within their hearts. I love those times.
Each new day brings forth to me a true sense of joy and happiness and a willingness to share my truth of voice with anyone who comes towards me.
I have spoken to many groups but I would love to take my truth of voice into the prisons to those who can't come to me due to the bars that encase them.
Into the schools to the pupils in their final year to offer encouragement and spiritual guidance and many more places.
I wish to help others focus and find wellbeing to enable them to attain their true ability to find their true capability to achieve what is rightly theirs.

I keep being shown a painting that I shall own one day that depicts my coat of arms.
I stand in the middle. A White Bengal Tiger sits on one side of me; on the other there stands a glorious stag; at my feet there lies a wolf and above my head is the words Truth of Voice. Whenever my Guides bring me forth the

visualisation of the painting I weep, as it is truly beautiful. The painter of it I have yet to meet but I know I shall.
My two beautiful daughters are both intelligent, very caring, funny and a great joy to me. I am not only Mum I am also their best friend and I love them so much. Not a day passes when I do not thank the Higher Spirit for bringing them back into my life. Once again!
They fill me with emotional love so powerful words cannot describe.
I am truly blessed.

Throughout the time I have spent writing this book I have laughed, I have cried but I have had time to reflect on my situations and my solutions.
The inner feeling of being at one within the realms of the Higher Spirit gives me the strength within my heart to walk my true path.

"To everyone, good bad & indifferent, who has walked into my life, I thank them all for the experience as it has made me into who I have become"

"Should one person be able to take something from this book that will give them hope to deal with what is going on in their life, then what I've experienced and survived will have been worth it"

Printed in Great Britain
by Amazon

54302228R00253